THANK YOU
FOR YOUR
SERVITUDE

ALSO BY MARK LEIBOVICH

Big Game

Citizens of the Green Room

This Town

The New Imperialists

THANK YOU
FOR YOUR
SERVITUDE

Donald Trump's Washington
and the Price of Submission

Mark Leibovich

PENGUIN PRESS ◆ NEW YORK ◆ 2022

PENGUIN PRESS
An imprint of Penguin Random House LLC
penguinrandomhouse.com

Copyright © 2022 by Mark Leibovich
ISBN 9780593296318 (hardcover)
ISBN 9780593296325 (ebook)

Printed in the United States of America
1st Printing

Book design by Daniel Lagin

To Meri, Nell, Lizey, Franny, Eloise, and Iris

CONTENTS

THANK YOU
FOR YOUR
SERVITUDE

LAST CALL AT
THE TRUMP HOTEL

———

December 2020

The view from the Trump International Hotel was bleak by the end. It had been a steady fall from its peak, when the atrium lounge had become the social center of Washington, at least Donald Trump's Sodom and Gomorrah version of it. I was sitting alone at the lobby bar on a Friday night, finishing a shrimp cocktail. My reporter colleagues and I had been dropping by semi-regularly for four years, starting when the property opened in 2016. Sometimes I would meet friends here, or sometimes I would come in alone and observe what our radiant laboratory of self-government had become under the current ownership.

The venue made for a nice addition to downtown, situated in the Old Post Office Building, on what had been a dead stretch of Pennsylvania Avenue between the White House and the Capitol. It gave every impression of being a tight and well-managed operation, unlike the proprietor's side hustle down the street. But the scent of abandonment had been creeping in since Election Day. First, the coronavirus ruined the business, and then the hotelier himself finished the job by doing something unforgivably off brand—losing.

We were a week or so into December, and the hotel's chandeliered concourse was empty except for some bored bartenders. A few North Carolinians in "Make America Great Again" caps had just departed, and a bunch of Proud Boys were posing for a team selfie next to the Trump sign out front. They appeared to be in town for a "Stop the Steal" rally scheduled for the weekend, one of the preliminaries to the Big One. I could hear a faint "Four more years" chant petering out over a distant megaphone. Roger Stone, the felonious Nixon-era menace and longtime Trump acolyte, greeted a group of supporters near the entrance.

For the most part, though, the scene felt pretty well played out. Trump's usual collection of pet rocks had stopped showing up at the hotel weeks before. There was no sign of any Rudys, Bannons, or Lewandowskis; no Secretary of the Treasury Steven Mnuchin or his wife, Louise Linton, or the tiny dog she kept in her tiny purse (an actual, breathing lapdog); no trace of the Trump leg-humpers from the House; and no hint of the Sean Spicers, Kellyanne Conways, or any of the other Washington C-listers who were bumped temporarily up to B-list status by their proximity to Donald J. Trump.

The grand mezzanine offered them a relatively safe space in an otherwise hostile city. "There is a comfort level at the hotel," said Rudy Giuliani, who practically lived here, usually at the BLT Prime steak house, which at busy hours became a petting zoo for Trump's "guys." He had his own table, delineated by the "Rudolph W. Giuliani, Private Office" nameplate.

I would see Rudy rushing off to smoke a cigar outside, pressed for time but always grinning for photos and resting his hand a bit low on the skirts of his lady friends. Here, Giuliani was restored to being America's Mayor again, and the Trump Hotel was his new Ground Zero. No one would hassle him over his legal troubles or blame him for getting the president impeached (a time or two) or suggest that maybe he should switch to club soda, before it got too late. It was definitely getting late.

In its time, the Trump Hotel was full of people racing the clock—the grandkids dashing around the concourse, playing tag with Uncle Barron. You could pick out the Made Men in the lobby, Trump's "adult" children strutting around as if they owned the place. Don Jr. and Eric would be nursing drinks, with those stiff Trump smiles and simultaneously bloated and angular cheeks. At close range, they flashed scared and darting Trump eyes, as if bracing for a light fixture to fall. You could tell the boys really wanted to be recognized, especially by Dad.

The likes of Senator Lindsey Graham would look so powerful in here and feel so appreciated. Over four years, he had made himself a top deputy in service to the Alpha. He never looked more enthralled than when he was skipping from table to table at the Trump Hotel getting thanked for all of the wonderful things he had done for *our great president*. There might be some Turkish businessman chasing after him, trying to get a meeting with the boss down the street, or some Oath Keeper wanting an autograph. Lindsey always said he tried to be helpful.

No one would pester him at the hotel with those tiresome "What happened to Lindsey Graham?" questions that so many of his judgy old Washington friends were asking. They were lucid enough to remember the dead-eyed, chubby-cheeked South Carolinian when he served as John McCain's proud sidekick, bathing in all of McCain's reflected glory and honor and moral authority. This was before McCain died and Graham would, in his mind, trade up to become one of Trump's favorite golf amigos. Maybe it brought him some grief, but also big cachet at the palace, and free drinks.

I once asked Graham a version of the "What happened to you?" question: how he could swing from being one of Trump's most merciless critics in 2016 to such a sycophant thereafter. I didn't use those exact words, but Graham got the idea.

"Well, okay, from my point of view, if you know anything about me, it'd be odd not to do this," he said, a bit defensively. I asked what "this" was. "'This,'" Graham said, "is to try to be relevant." Being hooked on Trump made him "relevant." It was a hell of a drug, and he had to keep his dealer happy. Nearly all elected Republicans in Washington needed Trump's blessing, and voters, to remain here. "If you don't want to be reelected, you're in the wrong business," Graham told me. "I have never been called this much by a president in my life." He admitted that it would be hard to give that up.

They all said as much. "I could get Trump on the phone faster than any staff person who worked for him could get him on the phone," Kevin McCarthy, the House Republican leader would brag, flush with relevance.

What would you do for your relevance? That's always been a definitional question for D.C.'s prime movers, especially the super-thirsty likes of Lindsey and Kevin. But never did it render itself in such Technicolor as during the Donald Trump years. How badly did you want into the clubhouse, no matter how wretched it became inside? Was it enough to turn the Republican Party into an authoritarian griftocracy or yourself into an accomplice to a national trauma? Could you live with that?

Relevance always comes with a price and a shelf life. Either you're in power or you're out, well positioned or not. Traditionally, the local biorhythm is cyclical, a revolving membership of bodies orbiting in and out of the sun, depending on which party controlled the sun. But the sense of borrowed time was acute at the Trump Hotel. Everyone was always rushing around the lobby, trying to maximize their haul before the sun set.

At least there was some expectation that after Election Day, or whenever Trump finally gave up the ghost, things might finally calm down a little bit.

OKAY, ELECTION DAY MIGHT HAVE BEEN OPTIMISTIC.

I returned to the Trump Hotel a few days before Christmas. The state Electoral College delegations had all met on December 14 to affirm Joe Biden's victory. Soon, theoretically, it would be safe for the forty-sixth president and his "total pros" to inherit the whirlwind and restore order, for Tom Friedman to be welcome again back at the White House, for Democrats to get on with their lefty overreaches, and for the donors to start bitching about how Biden was not properly glad-handing them.

Then, the inevitable backlash: the polls tanking and the Carter comparisons replacing the LBJ comparisons and the "concerns about Biden's age" kicking in. And the dump Kamala rumors and all the new variants. I hate to be jaded here, but—oh, what the hell—these things do tend to run in patterns.

But what if the old patterns no longer applied? What if Trump had pounded all the familiar assumptions into oblivion and Republicans into submission? He was, after all, not conceding defeat yet and still going on like a maniac about disappearing ballots and corrupted voting machines and CRIMES OF THE CENTURY! Everyone kept wondering how long this postelection meltdown would last. Some of the GOP's self-appointed "grown-ups" were becoming alarmed. Trump was "on the verge of looking like a sore loser," Karl Rove cautioned on Fox News. (Karl always had a sixth sense about these things.)

I was sitting in the hotel watching the bar TVs. The cadaverous faces of Senators Graham and Mitch McConnell filled the screens. The muted Newt Gingrich popped up for his "hit." Was that Bill Bennett taking his turn? Yes, Bill Bennett, the Reagan-era secretary of education whose best-selling morality tome, *The Book of Virtues*, lent him a lifetime gravitas as America's conservative conscience—and who had since refashioned himself as a reliable evangelist for the most immoral and unvirtuous figure ever to occupy the White House. "I believe this election was fixed," he parroted a few days earlier. It was always such an honor for President Trump to have Mr. Bennett's support.

Other Serious People kept describing Trump's gambit to remain in office as a "last-gasp attempt." This was another Big Lie. There was always another gasp with Trump. Before it was over, there would be dozens of courtroom clown shows, 147 Senate and congressional Republicans voting to not certify Biden's victory, a mob spearing and pummeling a police officer with an American flagpole (Old Glory still attached), seven dead (two Capitol cops by suicide in the days following), ghastly videos, hundreds injured and arrested, and another impeachment. We were a nation choking in gasps.

I kept staring up at the TV. Giuliani was now gulping up more air on Fox. He flailed his arms and was doing his best to go down fighting, or go through the motions thereof. Trump loved to see people fighting for him on TV. It was like a pixelated therapy for him. He felt *seen*. Rudy had become the president's favorite therapy dog.

At this point, though, the situation had gone well beyond just another episode of *All the President's Feelings and Moods*. No one expected Trump to depart with any particular grace or statesmanship or loser things like that. But this was getting scary. Trump was now talking about some massive protest rally that he envisioned for D.C. on January 6. His words and his crowds were becoming more desperate and belligerent. It felt as though things were building toward something "not very nice," as Trump might say.

By year's end, General Mark Milley, the chair of the Joint Chiefs of Staff, was telling people he believed the president was in "serious mental decline." Trump kept retweeting some account called @catturd2. As presidents do.

The caseworkers continued to preach patience. "Give it time," Lindsey kept telling everyone. He knew Trump had lost, quite obviously. He was just giving Trump the "space" he needed to come to grips with it. Likewise, McCarthy explained to squeamish colleagues that by echoing the president's stolen election claims on TV, he was merely trying to "manage" Trump until the defeated president could accept reality— always a shaky proposition with him.

"What is the downside for humoring him for this little bit of time?" a senior Republican official was quoted as saying in *The Washington Post*. The blind quote, oft repeated, became an instant classic in the genre of "takes that did not age well." It was held up as a dark marker of where things stood for a party that stood idly by while Trump solicited foreign campaign help and mocked war heroes and disabled reporters and entire ethnic minorities and it only got worse. "Humoring him" had essentially become the GOP platform.

But "humoring" was also too passive a descriptor for what Republicans had been doing long before Trump arrived. They had for years pushed and weakened the barriers that Trump would later obliterate. Newt Gingrich never hesitated to destroy opposition to his Republican Revolution, no matter what norms or whose reputation he had to torch; nor would he hesitate, a quarter century later, to suggest possible jail time for the January 6 investigators. Gingrich's House GOP descendants became eager saboteurs of Bill Clinton and Barack Obama, willing to shut down the government or play brinksmanship with the debt ceiling or (on the Senate side) blockade a Democratic president's Supreme Court nomination. They mostly ignored Trump's ugly questioning of his predecessor's citizenship, and accommodated a growing white nationalist element in their ranks.

Still, certain lines and traditions were sacred, we were told. Trump would certainly abide by the word of the courts and the sanctity of elections. The conservative radio host Hugh Hewitt—one of those "thoughtful" Trump defenders who was still allowed on *Meet the Press*—tried to reassure. He went on Megyn Kelly's podcast and told everyone to relax, there would most certainly be a peaceful transfer of power because that's how we roll here in America, *greatest country on earth.* "I would just say to everybody: It will be fine," Hewitt said, another "take" that did not age well. The podcast aired on the morning of January 6.

Okay, just make it to January 20; *then* everything will be fine. That would become the next benchmark. Just land the damn plane. Surely the situation would quiet down as soon as Trump took his final ride on Air Force One down to Palm Beach, with TVs set to Fox News. He would savor one last favorite in-flight breakfast of grilled sirloin on a bed of cheesy grits with two over-easy eggs oozed over a buttermilk biscuit. Maybe he would fire off a late last-minute pardon of Judge Jeanine's ex for relaxation, after Bible reading.

Trump would leave behind a city stunned and locked down: a razor-wire fence encircling the Capitol, plywood covering downtown, and twenty-five thousand National Guard troops protecting the government from the president's own supporters—not a great look for a healthy democracy. But Trump always saw himself as a disrupter, with a mandate to "shake things up." That's what "his people" demanded. And he would never let them down, as he always said. Promises made, promises kept.

I WAS ALWAYS MOST FASCINATED DURING THESE YEARS BY THE VIEW from the Trump Hotel—much more so than by Trump himself. Like most people, I doubted Trump would ever get here. I never thought his campaign would amount to much beyond a whoopee cushion detonated in our polite Kabuki theater. And like most people, I was extremely wrong.

But I still never found Trump to be that captivating as a stand-alone character. As my *Times* colleague David Brooks wrote: "We've got this perverse situation in which the vast analytic powers of the entire world are being spent trying to understand a guy whose thoughts are often just six fireflies beeping randomly in a jar."

Trump had been around forever, and his political act was largely derivative. His promise to "drain the swamp" was treated as some genius coinage, though in fact the platitude had been worn out for decades by both parties. Nancy Pelosi promised to "drain the swamp" as far back as 2006, just as the Reagan-Bush campaign of 1980 had vowed to "Make America Great Again."

Far more compelling to me were the slavishly devoted Republicans whom Trump drew to his side, who got the free desserts at BLT. These were the careerists who capitulated to Trumpism to preserve their livelihoods. They did what they had to do to keep dining out here. If nothing else, they talked a tough game.

"I know how to deal with bullies," Chris Christie used to boast back when he was still a self-respecting New Jersey governor and presidential candidate. "You can either sidle up to the bully, or you can punch them in the face. I like to punch them in the face." No one pushed around a tough-guy governor from Jersey—except, apparently, a whining, spray-tanned drama queen with dyed orange hair from Queens.

Christie promptly ended his campaign in 2016, sidled up to Trump, and won a good seat at the table for the better part of four years. He was always strangely in awe. They all were, the Lindseys and Rudys and Lyin' Teds and Liddle Marcos. They all had their reasons and their weaknesses.

Trump served as a big mirror to the political world he was surrounding in full. He imposed his own character study, and the results were endlessly depressing. The Republican Party became like a political version of that Stanley Milgram experiment on obedience from the 1960s. Milgram, a Yale behavioral psychologist who had studied collaborators of the Holocaust, assigned his subjects the role of "teachers" and instructed them to administer electric shocks upon innocent neighbors ostensibly in the next room. The force of the shocks was apparently becoming more and more painful as the victims screamed and begged them to stop. Yet most of the teachers (65 percent) kept following instructions to continue.

"The essence of obedience consists in the fact that a person comes to view himself as the instrument for carrying out another person's wishes," Milgram concluded. "He therefore no longer regards himself as responsible for his actions."

Republicans demonstrated much of the same fealty during the Trump years. They became deft at believing they were guilty of no dereliction. (If asked, Milgram's subjects would claim that their actions were not as harmful as they appeared.) They forged ahead and convinced themselves it was fine, maybe even brave. They were doing the work needed to help *their president* stand athwart the woke tide.

"The cliché says that power always corrupts," wrote the biographer/

historian Robert Caro. "What is seldom said," Caro continued, "is that power always *reveals*." Power reveals the most about those who enable its abuse. Republicans became the party that made Trump possible and that refused to stop him even after the U.S. Capitol fell under the control of some madman in a Viking hat.

It was always rationalization followed by capitulation and then full surrender. The routine was always numbingly the same, and so was the sad truth at the heart of it: they all knew better.

"I was always amazed at how Trump completely ate the Republicans' lunch, and how they just allowed it to happen," said Representative Adam Schiff, Democrat of California. But they also knew that if they stayed on the right side of Trump, the "good Republicans" could always do business here. There was no better anchor tenant for these times than the Trump Hotel.

THIS BOOK IS ABOUT THE VIEW FROM THE TRUMP HOTEL. IF NOT always physically, it is set against the unholy backdrop and sensibility that the owner fostered during his Washington residency. It is about the dirt that Trump tracked in, the people he broke, and the swamp he did not drain.

You will almost certainly recall many of the episodes described in the chapters ahead. In all likelihood, you'd rather not relive many of them. I sympathize. There have been, and will be, exhaustive accounts written about what occurred at the White House and in the country during these years. My goal here is not to outdo anyone in terms of revealing Oval Office intrigue, Palm Beach dipshittery, or (Lord help us) Trumpian psychoanalysis.

The idea is to tell the story of this ordeal through the supplicant fanboys who permitted Donald Trump's depravity to be inflicted on the rest of us. I wanted to catalog their descents into servitude as they made their deals and swallowed their pride, such as it was. I wanted to debrief them as they learned to survive, get what they could out of the deal, and with any luck keep their jobs, as well as their Gold Card statuses at the owner's various casinos, including his flagship payola palace at 1100 Pennsylvania Avenue.

In its time, the Trump Hotel served as a one-stop destination for all the busy parasitic suck-ups who made the Trump-era swamp work for them. This was a tidy operation in an untidy time. The age-old D.C. sport of self-dealing, social climbing, and self-promotion had never enjoyed such a garishly centralized arena.

Trump himself came in for dinner sometimes. His visits were never discreet, as when the Obamas might sneak out for "date nights" to some trendy D.C. bistro, always trying to slip in and out with minimal fuss.

But Trump would never eat at any place that didn't bear his brass-lettered name. Nor would he think to order anything beyond the usual comfort foods: French fries, shrimp cocktail, and a well-done forty-ounce tomahawk steak; chocolate cake or apple pie for dessert; and chilled bottles of Diet Coke. He required a big, applauded appearance—that was essential.

I always figured that a decent portion of the clientele was just hoping to get lucky and catch the president in his abundant flesh as he peacocked his way to Table 72, his regular round booth in the middle of the mezzanine. They were like those obsessed bird-watchers who showed up at some remote location in India on the very small chance they'd catch a glimpse of the white-bellied heron (an actual rare bird in India!).

It was like catching the pope in St. Peter's Square or, maybe better,

Hefner at the Playboy Mansion. Even for non-Trump fans, these episodes could prove rewarding.

"I saw Trump coming down from dinner once," said Michael Steele, a former chairman of the Republican National Committee who despised the president and was more than happy to say so a million different ways on MSNBC, which itself became a lucrative pundit gig for scores of so-called Never Trump Republicans. He liked hanging out at the Trump Hotel nonetheless. "It was fucking crazy," Steele said. "Trump made this slow walk down the staircase overlooking the lobby. People were cheering and chanting and standing on the tables, and he would be waving like a tin-pot dictator. It was a total fucking trip in there."

People who recognized Steele at the Hotel of Homage did double takes but were mostly nice to him. He once ran into Don Jr., who greeted him as "Mike" and could not have been more welcoming. Because, you know, good people on both sides.

If you were Trump certified, you could do a lot of important business in "America's Living Room," as the Trump Hotel liked to bill itself. You could curry favor with the president while partaking of his class and elegance. Stephen Miller, the president's droopy-eyed deportation zealot, and his fiancée, Mike Pence's press secretary, Katie Waldman, held their wedding reception at the hotel, as did at least half a dozen other Trump staffers or appointees.

The criminal likes of Roger Stone, Michael Flynn, and Dinesh D'Souza became royalty in the gilded sanctum, before and after their commutations and pardons. Trump's favorite felons could lobby for federal clemency via four-figure bar tabs. You want a selfie with Manafort, Sarah Huckabee Sanders, or that MyPillow guy? Dinner hour was your best shot. Or slightly later, if you wanted to catch one of those pillowy-haired, Trump-loving congressmen, after their Fox hits.

Leader McCarthy was always a big-ticket regular, solidifying his status as "a key ally of President Trump." McCarthy often described Trump to colleagues as "a massive headache" and a "major pain in my ass." But McCarthy also knew that alienating Trump would blow up any chance he had of becoming Speaker of the House after the 2022 election. So he was always a diamond-level ass-kisser when it counted.

McCarthy was once flying with Trump on Air Force One and noticed that the president ate only the cherry- and strawberry-flavored Starbursts. In a move that made him a legend in the annals of Washington supplication, McCarthy arranged for a special gift jar of Starbursts to be sent over to the White House—with the oranges and yellows removed. The president was said to be touched by the gesture.

This was just the kind of attention to detail that made McCarthy another purebred in Donald Trump's kennel of acolytes. "My Kevin" is how Trump referred to his favorite GOP ally, a term of ownership as much as affection. The Never Trump conservative Bill Kristol called McCarthy "the piano player in the House Republican brothel."

Trump's presidency produced a mishmash of such characters. Representative Matt Gaetz, the high-haired Republican from Florida, was another elite brownnoser whose name rated first-person possessive treatment from the president. "My Matt" had the perfect look of a lawyer on a billboard. He loved performing for Trump on TV. He carried his own makeup bag.

So many details of Gaetz's bio reeked of "too good to check," yet were in fact true. He grew up in Seaside, Florida, in a house that was used in *The Truman Show*, a film about a man (played by Jim Carrey) whose life takes place on TV. Trump would call Gaetz at all hours, which the congressman was always quick to broadcast. He called when Gaetz was "on the throne," in nightclubs, and in flagrante. ("And yes, I answered," Gaetz wrote in his memoir—and yes, he has a memoir.) He was arrested for DUI after a night of drinking at an Okaloosa Island, Florida, nightclub—called the Swamp.

Nicknames and marketing slogans flourished at the Trump Hotel: I heard "the Mother Ship," "America's Living Room," and simply "Headquarters." In a cover treatment, *Time* magazine christened this the "Swamp Hotel."

The obvious joke was that Trump kept vowing to "drain the swamp," the "swamp" being Washington's insular and permanent culture whose nobility moved easily between government, K Street, Wall Street, and the consultant class. The "drain the swamp" mantra worked, at least as a campaign message.

As for the culture the swamp referred to, it thrived undisturbed, waiting for the next self-styled disrupter to come along and promise to drain it. The only thing Trump drained was patience. If anything, he merely perfected the notion of "the swamp" and refashioned it in his own unscrupulous image. He turned the swamp into his own gold-plated Jacuzzi.

Was Trump the by-product of a degenerate system in which American democracy had become a gold rush of cheap fame, wealth creation, and narcissistic branding madness? Or had he merely wielded the tools of this transformation—his money, celebrity, and dominance of the media—against the forces that had engendered this disgust to begin with?

Trump's invasion of our politics had that very chicken-egg dilemma at its center: Was he an antidote to our politics, or the most broken manifestation? Whatever he was, his opponents were no match for it. If Trump had one well-developed intuition, it was his ability to sniff weakness in people. He also had a nose for it in major American political parties.

CHAPTER 1

THE PROBLEM

———

August 2015–March 2016

Everyone had a theory about why it was their turn.

Chris Christie kept pushing the idea that voters tend to favor presidential candidates who represent the biggest departure from the incumbent. He was their departure. "That is the argument people make to me about why I should run," Christie told me, just before he started his prolonged public campaign of "looking at it." "They say, 'No one could be more the opposite of Barack Obama from a personality standpoint than you. Therefore, you're perfect.'"

Governor Perfect had built-in assets. New York–D.C. media and GOP donor types loved him. He was great on WFAN and a superstar banterer in the TV greenrooms. He was a merciless but familiar brute, like the New Jersey Turnpike. He would stay within certain lanes, unlike Trump. But if you were sick of the same old robots, clowns, Clintons, or Bushes, Christie was your viable off-ramp.

I ran into him in Cleveland before the first Republican debate of the 2016 campaign, or "cycle," as the pros call it. It was a Fox News production, billed on the chyrons as "The Rumble in the Rust Belt." Christie arrived at Quicken Loans Arena a few hours before the cattle call. He tossed out towel-snapping insults at reporters, comparing us to jackals, snakes, maggots, and other beloved creatures.

As he entered his backstage holding area in Cleveland, Christie compared himself to a penned-in bull, eager to make America his china shop. I wished him luck.

Likewise, Rand Paul, who was entering the arena at an adjacent loading dock. He had heard that libertarians were, at long last, "having a moment" in America. Why not him? He was younger, slicker, and less of a crank than his patriarch dad, Ron Paul, the libertarian congressman from Texas and a three-time presidential candidate. Rand had even gone straight enough to get elected to the Senate, from Kentucky. He was an odd duck, no question, but was he any worse than Ted Cruz? John Mc-Cain once referred to them both as "wacko birds."

Cruz was at the debate, too, convinced this was *his* moment. He was elected to the Senate in 2012 and in short order proved he had zero interest in achieving the kinds of things senators had traditionally prided themselves on, like passing laws, getting committee assignments, and earning the respect of colleagues. These were never distinctions that would impress the Fox News bookers, or the blood-lusting "base," so he never saw the point. Becoming a maximum nuisance was far more productive for his purposes.

He would do things like promise to shut down the government unless Obamacare was killed. This was never going to happen, for many reasons, two being that the president was still named "Obama" and the Constitution still granted him veto power. Cruz's colleagues knew this was a wasteful and self-destructive effort that would succeed only in "stirring up the crazies" (another McCain term).

"If you killed Ted Cruz on the floor of the Senate, and the trial was in the Senate, nobody would convict you," Lindsey Graham once said. No one exactly rushed to Cruz's defense, either, unless you counted this "defense" from Senator Al Franken, who maintained that he *did* like Cruz, or more than most of his colleagues did. "And I *hate* Ted Cruz," Franken said—important caveat.

Still, Cruz's unpopularity in Washington was a defining asset, to his mind, in that it lent him credibility as an irritant. It offered proof that he was not concerned about fitting in with these grimy swamp creatures. He was happy to play the turd in the Republican punch bowl. His problem was that Trump proved to be an even bigger turd, glowing orange and impossible to miss.

At the risk of pushing this metaphor WAY too far, Jeb Bush was the innocuous lemon slice in this punch bowl. Trump dismissed Bush, the former Florida governor, as "low energy," a brutally effective descriptor for a candidate whose logo included an exclamation point—"Jeb!"—in a desperate attempt to inject vitality.

Bush had been anointed the early "establishment favorite" by those who anointed such things. He was accustomed, by birthright, to such deference from professional Republicans. Trump never bothered with deference, at least when it came to Bush, as opposed to, say, Putin.

Neither did Marco Rubio. The former Speaker of the Florida House had been a protégé of Governor Jeb's years before, which compelled a few media Freuds to trot out the trusty oedipal cliché about son overtaking Dad. Others preferred the Rubio-as-Judah construction. Who did Marco think he was, anyway, *not waiting his turn?*

What the media geniuses all agreed on was that Trump's turn was about to end. His noisy parade float would assuredly run aground in

Cleveland, because there was no chance that he could share a stage with a supposedly elite field of Republicans without having his basic ignorance exposed.

Plus, the serious anchor people had arrived and would make certain of it: in particular, Fox News' Megyn Kelly, one of the three moderators, had fashioned a formidable reputation for herself as a "real journalist," armed with *tough but fair* questions. She also met the minimum Fox requirement of being attractive and blond, the Roger Ailes equivalent of spelling your name right on the SAT.

"You've called women you don't like 'fat pigs,' 'dogs,' 'slobs,' and 'disgusting animals,'" Kelly said, asking Trump to kick things off.

And we were off.

Again, you might recall some of this. Sorry to rehash. These episodes can feel as old as time and as endless. They're worth going over here, though, if only in brief and as a reminder of the low point where Trump began, to counter the dumb trope from his apologists that somehow Trump devolved as the campaign wore on. "To see what is in front of one's nose needs a constant struggle," George Orwell wrote. This was always right in front of the Republican Party's nose.

Trump would suggest the next day that Kelly's "nasty" demeanor toward him at the debate was because she was getting her period. Not classy!

This alone would make him irredeemably toxic to women voters, right? No less an authority than the former First Lady Barbara Bush would weigh in to say as much, and wasn't Babs a Grande Dame/Sacred Cow Republican at some point?

What's more, an even greater authority, Twitter, agreed, so this had to be true: The clown was dead!

—

LONG LIVE THE CLOWN!

The power of Twitter to codify misguided groupthink had become much greater in 2016 than it had been the last go-round, in 2012. This gap between wise-guy Twitter and Trump World reality was all too evident when I attended my first rally that summer. The pageant featured a packed crowd of seventeen thousand at the American Airlines Center in Dallas. Thousands more snaked around several city blocks and fed into an overflow mosh pit.

FUCK POLITICAL CORRECTNESS! screamed the big banner held by a guy in front of me in the metal detector line. I tried to interview him but got nowhere.

"Fuck the media," the man told me. (I recognized the sentence structure.) "And fuck Megyn Kelly." I tried to tell him that I was not Megyn Kelly, but he was not impressed.

His friend was slightly more reflective. "We're just sick of being told what to do," said the friend, a contractor named Michael Lopez. "Especially by y'all in the media."

"America is being pushed into a corner," echoed Matt Yelland, a sixty-year-old electrical engineer, just before Trump took the stage. That was a common sentiment among Trump supporters, who loved his disregard for Republican manners and sacred cows. "Trump didn't get into politics to play by somebody else's rules," Yelland said. He could care less that Trump would not commit to supporting the GOP's eventual nominee, the kind of thing that "party leaders" considered sacrilege but that many real voters believed was proof of Trump's unwillingness to be bullied. He didn't care, either, about what aspersions Karl Rove was casting upon their hero on Fox News—well, Trump himself cared, but that was just Trump (being Trump).

"Karl Rove is a totally incompetent jerk," Trump railed from his Dallas stage. The crowd went nuts at the put-down, which was itself remarkable: the "architect" of George W. Bush's political rise being abused at a Republican campaign event in Bush's home state of Texas.

WHERE WERE THE GOP'S DESIGNATED ADULTS AND *INFLUENCERS* to restore order? Erick Erickson, editor of *RedState*, a leading conservative publication, tried. He disinvited Trump to the annual RedState Gathering of presidential candidates in Atlanta that weekend. Take that, Donald.

"If your standard-bearer has to resort to that," Erickson said, referring to the Megyn Kelly/period unpleasantness, "we need a new standard-bearer." Alas, Trump was undeterred.

It kept going. Reince Priebus, the Republican National Committee chairman, was beside himself, but trying to be comforting in public, for the sake of the children and, more important, the donors. This robust debate was healthy and natural and *part of the process*, he kept saying. Privately, he tried to reassure everyone: this would not last; Trump would implode soon enough.

The other candidates figured the same. "I don't think a lot of the people on that stage were convinced that Trump would stay," Christie recalled to me later. "What we were all trying to do strategically was stay alive so that we'd be viable if one of two things happened: either Trump gets out, or he does something disqualifying. Everyone up there had the same theory of the case."

Bad theory. Nothing changed, except Trump started winning primaries. Where was Jeb? Wasn't he supposed to be the front-runner? His heart was never in this. The exclamation point was always more of a question mark.

Bush was gone soon after the voting started. Same with Christie, but not before he obliterated Rubio in a debate in New Hampshire, taunting him for his cyborg adherence to "memorized thirty-second speeches." It was classic Christie, beating up the smaller, less threatening target (Rubio) while winning favor with the real bully (Trump).

Trump sought out Christie after the debate, threw his arm around him, and praised the governor for "destroying" Rubio.

Trump won New Hampshire in a rout; Christie finished sixth and quit the race with zero delegates. Trump called him on the night of the primary and told him he loved him. This was obviously meaningful to Christie, who recounted the exchange fulsomely in his memoir. He then turned around and planted a big wet kiss of an endorsement on Trump's powdered forehead.

This was a much bigger deal than Christie's paltry vote total would suggest, because it offered Trump a seal of approval from a big-name Republican. Christie kept talking up his long friendship with Trump, how they had so much "history" together and how loyalty was always very important to him. "Where I come from, friendship is important," Christie said. "Loyalty is everything." (Yep, friendship and loyalty, totally unique to New Jersey.)

The whole "we go WAY back" thing is always a red flag from would-be tough guys. And there was always a sense with Christie that no matter how hard he sucked up to Trump, he was destined to wind up like one of those peripheral hangers-on from *The Sopranos*, whose limp corpse wound up getting tossed into an icy swamp.

Still, Christie had a seemingly limitless appetite for, among other things, being humiliated by Trump. This was true of a lot of people, but Christie was special in this regard. Trump mocked him for his weight ("No more Oreos"), ordered him around, and basically treated the former Garden State governor like Mr. French, the portly and exasperated butler from the old show *Family Affair*.

Not everyone was moved by Christie's claim of loyalty to his dear old friend Donald. "An astonishing display of political opportunism" was how Christie's own campaign co-chair Meg Whitman described his heel turn.

Christie's support "gave a stamp of credibility to a thoroughly uncredible candidate," wrote Tim Miller, Bush's former communications director. "Like every other pathetic, podgy, scared, insecure bully who has ever disgraced a schoolyard, Chris Christie talks a big game."

Christie was a bit stunned by this blowback, but that was the price he paid for the rebound relevance Trump offered him. "This is politics," he said. "You make certain judgments."

TRUMP IS "NOT WHO WE ARE," RUBIO DECLARED, DEPLOYING A ROYAL "we" that apparently did not include the Republicans who kept voting for Trump by massive margins. Things were getting desperate enough for Graham to say he'd even support Cruz before he'd support Trump.

Cruz called Trump "utterly amoral" and a "pathological liar" (basically true) after Trump described him as a sleazy asshole whom everyone in the Senate hated (also true). For good measure, Trump suggested Cruz's wife was ugly and his father was somehow caught up in the John F. Kennedy assassination.

The party elders were now rallying to Rubio as their preferred Trump alternative. I met up with the Florida senator in Nevada, a few days before that state's Republican caucuses in February. We were sitting aboard his campaign plane—on a short flight from Reno to Las Vegas—and I was detecting a slight whiff of Marco-mentum in the recirculated air. "This was a great day for us," Rubio kept telling me. His undertaking was as urgent as ever, he said, because he knew the GOP elders were counting on him to stop Trump. He had their endorsements to prove it. He vowed to be worthy of everyone's trust.

We were surrounded on the plane by a retinue of Rubio-backing Nevada dignitaries: the state's lieutenant governor and a former governor, a congressman, and a senator. It seemed as if every hour brought a new endorsement of Rubio from another vintage piece of the Grand Old Furniture: Lamar Alexander, Bob Dole, a senator from Indiana, the governor of Arkansas. Together, this cavalry of grown-ups would lock arms around Rubio and save the GOP from its bender with the casino owner. This had all gone on for far too long.

The night before at a rally in North Las Vegas, Rubio strode onto a stage crowded with a bunch of new brand-name validators: seventeen in all. They included a buffet of Nevada pols, someone from a reality TV show called *Pawn Stars*, and Donnie Wahlberg: once a New Kid on the Block, now all in for Marky Marco.

This brief Pyrrhic hot streak for Rubio in Nevada epitomized the insane fantasy that an all-powerful Republican "establishment" could swoop in and impose its will. They would anoint their choice and unleash their onslaught of elder gravitas, and Trump would never know what hit him.

"You can sort of feel it coalescing," Rubio said as he waved his hand around the campaign plane, showing off his growing entourage.

Personally, the only thing I could feel coalescing was nausea. The plane had hit a patch of rough air. It started bouncing and shaking, as if we were flying through a blender. Rubio was unfazed and kept delivering his lines:

"I'm best positioned to bring this party together."

"I honestly believe the American dream is in trouble."

"I offer a new generation of leadership for the twenty-first century."

"This is getting a little hairy," I said to Rubio, of the worsening turbulence. "Just think," I went on, "I might be the last human being to ever have to listen to these talking points." This might have been disrespectful on my part, but I seemed not to care and neither did Rubio. The end might have been at hand, anyway.

Finally, the plane landed, and Rubio received word that he himself had landed a bunch more "key endorsements." He'd earned the support of—drumroll—the former New York governor George Pataki. Senator Jeff Flake of Arizona also lent his name to Marco's juggernaut, as did Senator Orrin Hatch of Utah. "Marco has a unique ability to effectively communicate detailed conservative plans," Hatch affirmed.

Marco also had a unique ability to effectively communicate that Donald Trump had a small penis.

He proved this at a rally a few days later. "He's always calling me Little Marco," Rubio told a bunch of college students in Virginia. "And I'll admit the guy is taller than me, he's like six-two, which is why I don't understand why his hands are the size of a guy who's five-two. And you know what they say about men with small hands."

A dick joke! The college kids loved it.

Trump responded at the next debate with a robust defense of his manhood. Because of course he did.

"It's not a problem, believe me," Trump said. The press declared this to be another "new low," at least for this week. Everyone was "deeply saddened" and "deeply troubled." We were supposedly better than this.

And once again, you might recall all of it.

Rubio seemed to be emboldened for a time. He enjoyed this Miami street-fighter version of himself: Marco from the block, the fine young choirboy who could bust chops with the best of the big boys. But mostly, he wanted me to know, he was a man of *conviction*.

"I'm as conservative as anyone in this race," Rubio told me. "But I am the conservative that can unify the Republican Party and also beat Trump." He kept collecting new endorsements like snow globes.

"We got Pat Toomey," Rubio boasted the night before the caucuses, after the Republican senator from Pennsylvania had jumped aboard. Yet for some reason, the voters of Nevada were not following Pat Toomey's lead, either. Trump won by twenty-two percentage points. Rubio edged out Cruz for second.

Rubio managed to win in Minnesota and Puerto Rico—two more snow globes. And the District of Columbia. Who knew there were Republicans in D.C.? (I live here, I didn't, but they both like Rubio, apparently.) Maybe this could be something to build on for next time.

But what if the "bright future" Rubio had been promised in the Republican Party never existed, neither the future nor the party? After the ordeal of his campaign subsided, Rubio tried to reclaim a bit of retroactive stature. "This man turned the most important election in a generation into a freak show," Rubio told me. "I allowed myself to get pulled into a portion of that." He sounded, at this moment, tired and sheepish, less a man in a hurry than a pol out of time.

He expressed regret that he had stooped to Trump's level. "It's not who I am," he said. It never is.

Over the next few months, Rubio traveled the path to full capitulation. He reaffirmed his continued unease with Trump in the most self-aggrandizing ways possible. He deployed the humblebrag maneuver of preemptively ruling himself out to be Trump's running mate. "I have never sought, will not seek and do not want to be considered for Vice President," Rubio said in a Facebook post. I suspected Rubio did this in part to annoy Trump, which it did, of course.

Later that spring, Rubio finally took the trouble to say that he would in fact support the inevitable Republican nominee. He simply had no choice, Rubio said, given the alternative, "now that it's apparent that Hillary Clinton is going to be the Democratic nominee." As if that prospect came out of nowhere.

Rubio now held the astonishing position of saying he would vote for someone he previously declared unfit to hold the American nuclear codes. I envisioned him under a mushroom cloud, telling his kids that at least Dad didn't vote for the ghastly Hillary.

You knew this was where it would wind up. Not just for Rubio, but also for the other would-be Trump stoppers, no matter how tough and appalled they claimed to be.

There was one sad and telling episode in March, at the end of a debate in Detroit. It had been a night of sky-high dudgeon over Trump, with plenty of scorched-earth rhetoric from his Republican rivals. Rubio, Cruz, and John Kasich discharged frantic warnings about how Trump was a cruel/know-nothing/calamitous con man. Cruz had just called Trump a "pathological liar" and "a narcissist at a level I don't think this country's ever seen."

But in the end, the debate came down to the one question for the non-Trumps: Would they still commit to supporting the Republican nominee, even if that was this lying, narcissistic madman with zero impulse control sharing the stage with them? If Trump was really such pure evil, shouldn't that override whatever musty notions of party loyalty they still clung to? I'm assuming you remember how this turned out, also.

CHAPTER 2

THE JOKE

———

Coming to terms with Donald Trump as the Republican nominee is like being told you have Stage 1 or Stage 2 cancer. You
know you'll probably survive, but one way or the other, there's
going to be a lot of throwing up.

—Christopher Buckley, *The Spectator*

June 2016

By now, the various paths to capitulation were all too familiar.
When defeated rivals would get around to admitting that yes,
they'd be voting for Trump, they always strained to convey their unhap-
piness over the situation. "Not with any great joy," was Rubio's default
caveat. "It gets harder every day."

But there are always considerations. Rubio became just another
dispiriting casualty of Trump's moral slaughter of the Republican Party.

He was another in the parade of leaders willing to discard every principle they once held for the purpose of staying in office.

One after another, Trump's victims performed their rationalized devotion to their abuser. The GOP's submissive community was expanding by the day. It was a diminishing spectacle, to say the least.

Again, we'll try to move through this fast.

Nikki Haley, the alleged rising star Republican governor of South Carolina, had endorsed Rubio and trashed Trump up and down her state. "Donald Trump is everything we . . . teach our kids not to do in kindergarten," Haley said. This set off the predictable back-and-forth: Trump tweeted that "the people of South Carolina are embarrassed by Nikki Haley." Haley called Trump "scary."

But not as scary as seeing her ambition thwarted. Haley wound up endorsing Trump, who made her his ambassador to the United Nations.

Texas's former governor Rick Perry called Trump "a barking carnival act," a "toxic mix of demagoguery, mean-spiritedness and nonsense." Which did nothing to stop Perry from eventually endorsing Trump, and Trump from naming Perry his secretary of energy.

Trump compared another of his primary opponents, the neurosurgeon Ben Carson, to a child molester, which did not stop Carson from later endorsing Trump. "You're going to see Trump pivoting," promised Carson. This wasn't brain surgery. Upon receiving Carson's endorsement, Trump described his former rival as "a special, special person." He later named him HUD secretary.

Cruz, meanwhile, had called Trump an "amoral bully" and "a sniveling coward." This was shortly after his father, Rafael Cruz, said that electing "the alternative" to his son would signal "the destruction of America."

Yet Cruz still insisted he would support Trump if he became the Republican nominee. He said he was not happy about this, either, but again, you learn to adapt. Hopefully, Trump could, too: "pivot," as the pros say.

The "pivot" stipulated that at some point a leading presidential candidate would evolve into a more suitable version of a mature nominee. He or she would "pivot" his or her attention away from hard-core party supporters in favor of the broader general electorate. In Trump's case, ideally, that meant scaling back his racist-uncle, insult-mongering open-mic act.

Trump and his various conspirators would periodically offer hints that some "pivot" would be in the offing. In an April briefing with the RNC, Trump's then–senior adviser and future campaign manager, Paul Manafort, acknowledged that the flamboyant candidate had been playing a "part" during the campaign. "He gets it," Manafort told RNC members. "The part that he's been playing is now evolving into the part that you've been expecting."

I spent enough time around Trump to know that he was fully aware of playing different "parts" from minute to minute. "I'll pivot when I need to, sure," Trump told me that spring when I asked him when he'd start acting ("with all due respect, Mr. Trump") like a more serious and solemn standard-bearer. "That's what politicians do. They just change, and no one says anything about it, like it's just expected. They just pivot. I've never seen anything like it. So, I'll just pivot, too, when I need to. People seem to want that."

The notion of a Trump pivot was of course preposterous. While he was certainly capable of altering his views with stunning speed, it would maybe be more difficult to pivot away from saying Mexicans were rapists. (Would Trump negotiate "great deals" with Mexico's more moderate "problem solver" rapists?) If your campaign is a cult of personality, can you really modulate that personality and still retain the cult?

Trump made some early gestures of trying, though. He started talking about being "a unifier" and pretending to care about whether GOP lawmakers got reelected.

He briefly ceased his derision of "weak" party leaders and "stupid" lawmakers and "useless" political hacks. In return, many of them became cautiously hopeful that their Rottweiler could become trained to stop having accidents all over their tidy house of democracy. Or at least make a show of it, so they could say they tried.

"As I get closer and closer to the goal, it's gonna get different," Trump told Fox News' Greta Van Susteren. "I will be changing very rapidly. I'm very capable of changing to anything I want to change to." Part of the perverse beauty of Trump was that he could be weirdly forthcoming about how full of shit he was.

TRUMP DROPPED INTO WASHINGTON IN MARCH, OSTENSIBLY TO PAY a courtesy call to ambivalent Republicans. There were quite a few of those. Many of them, though, attempted to sound open-minded about trying to tolerate Trump, if not embrace him. But Trump needed to give them something to work with. The table manners of "paying respect" still counted a great deal.

Trump took meetings on Capitol Hill and said all the proper things about how he "looked forward to working" with everyone. He visited with the *Washington Post* editorial board, also much appreciated. Trump was adept at this game. He was, at heart, a hospitality guy whose default mode tended toward the solicitous shtick of a manager or maître d'.

You need anything? Having a good time? It's an honor to have you here.

Trump just wanted people to like him; was that asking too much?

Please, just be nice to him. Whenever Trump offered a scouting report about someone, it was based almost entirely on whether that person had been "nice" to him, or "liked" him. His vocabulary could be so basic and childlike.

"If you say nice things about Trump, he will like you," Graham said, in his capacity of Trump explainer, one of the many ways Lindsey tried to be "helpful." In other words, Graham would explain, Trump was not a racist, just so long as people of different races were nice to him. "You could be dark as charcoal and lily white, it doesn't matter," Graham said.

Also, it would be unfair to conclude that Trump admired dictators. "His approach to Putin, Erdoğan, Kim Jong-un, Xi, or whoever was always the same," Christie said. "He felt like, if I'm nice to these people, they'll be nice to me. I don't think it's any more complicated than that."

Is Trump really that shallow? I asked Christie straight up.

Christie just shrugged. Maybe, he said. "I just think he cares that much about being liked."

Now Trump wanted to be the host for the entire country. And maybe it could have worked out, too—Maître d' in Chief. If only there wasn't so much resistance, and frankly rudeness, from so many customers. The bitch about politics was that people get carried away with that checks-and-balances idea, their customer Bill of Rights and the Constitution and all those cumbersome limits that the founders imposed. It can make it difficult to do business.

The scheme ran much smoother in Trump's core industry—as a hospitality guy.

Washington has always been one of those quasi-old-world-power playgrounds that fetishized the power of the "host." Those were the feared and beloved little dictators who determined who got the good tables and who really got "taken care of."

33

———

TRUMP'S CAPITAL SWING WAS DOMINATED BY HIS MAIN STOP ON the visit: a chaotic, rambling tour of his soon-to-be-opened Trump International Hotel. "Trump's new Washington monument," as the *Post* called the $212 million Xanadu of gold-encrusted bathrooms and $1,000-a-night rooms. "It is a luxury hotel his blue-collar supporters can't afford."

But circuses are free, and this would become a priceless spectacle for Trump. Sure, certain bad optics and contradictions needed to be called out. "While Trump was shouting across middle America that Mexicans were drug-smuggling rapists," the *Post* noted, "Hispanic men were building his luxury hotel for him on one of the national capital's ritziest blocks." Hmm, this could be seen as *hypocritical*.

And yet, whatever, *whatever*.

I'm guessing Trump would have been welcomed and maybe appreciated in Washington, if only he had stayed in his hospitality lane. The city has a long tradition of taking in national imprints. Amazon's founder, Jeff Bezos, bought in when he purchased *The Washington Post* in 2013 and grabbed a mansion in Kalorama. A bunch of celebrity chefs opened restaurants. Michael Jordan played a couple seasons with the Wizards.

Celebrities from other realms would occasionally cross over into politics. Steve Largent, the Hall of Fame wide receiver for the Seattle Seahawks, was in Congress for a while, as was the guy who played Gopher on *The Love Boat* (Fred Grandy). The comedian and *SNL* veteran Al Franken was elected to the Senate in 2008. And he was unquestionably the only person ever to both serve on the Senate Judiciary Committee and play a member of the Senate Judiciary Committee (Paul Simon of Illinois) in an *SNL* skit.

"One thing I've learned," Franken told me once when he was still in the Senate, "is that celebrity trumps ideology. I have spent a lot of time over the years heaping scorn and ridicule upon Republicans. But then you meet them, and a lot of people are like, 'Hey, Al, love that satellite mobile-uplink guy'"—one of his signature *SNL* characters.

Trump of course loved being a celebrity, and he could have taken his bit quite far as an occasional visitor. People would run up to him during his visits, saying they were big fans of *The Apprentice* or once played some Trump golf course.

But Trump couldn't just be Shake Shack landing in Dupont Circle or Tom Arnold parachuting in for the White House Correspondents' Association Dinner. He had to be Godzilla dropping into Tokyo.

"There he is! Let's roll," shouted a cameraman as Trump was fast engulfed in a media swarm, the likes of which would not subside for ninety minutes, or five years.

"We're going to change Washington like it's never been changed before," Trump said. "First we're going to make it so beautiful." Concrete dust swirled in the air while a din of power tools echoed between unfinished walls.

"We've gone to a very much higher degree of finishes and marbles, and fixtures and bathroom fixtures and windows, etc.," Trump said. "It's a great thing for the country. It's a great thing for Washington. I think when it's completed it will truly be one of the great hotels of the world." The hotelier/candidate handed out bottles of Trump-branded water.

It was all part of the same hustle. If all went as planned, the whole operation could be run out of their next headquarters building at 1600 Pennsylvania. The future First Lady could hire the hotel's director of rooms (Timothy Harleth) as the White House's chief usher. The future president could hire his former caddy (Dan Scavino) as a top presidential aide and his longtime bodyguard (Keith Schiller) as his future director of Oval Office operations.

As he led the tour, Trump kept saying that he would be destined for Pennsylvania Avenue, "one way or the other."

AROUND THIS TIME, I STARTED PAYING REGULAR VISITS TO REINCE Priebus, the Republican National Committee chairman and the person principally in charge of trying to midwife the shell-shocked former Party of Lincoln into the Party of Trump. We fell into a familiar routine. I would enter his office, usually chaperoned by Sean Spicer, the RNC's chief spokesman, who would later go on to greater fame/infamy in the Trump White House, and indignities beyond. But at this point Spicer was still a mostly amicable cast member of the D.C. hack ensemble who'd been a longtime voice on the phone and face in the buffet line.

The RNC had seen better morale days. Longtime staffers and committee members were spending considerable time complaining about "this fucking Trump nightmare," as one state chairman described it to me. "As a practical matter, they're jumping out windows over there," he added, referring to the RNC headquarters. (As a practical matter, the building is only a few stories high, so the act might not have been suicidal, if that was the goal—*as a practical matter.*)

Apparently, spirits were so low at the RNC that staff had to be told that if they could not bring themselves to support Trump, "they should leave by the end of the week."

In turn, the Trump campaign had zero use for the RNC and took its opposition as a given inside their operation. "We can no longer trust anyone at the RNC," the campaign spokesman Jason Miller said in a speech to his team. "At this point most of them would rather Hillary win than the boss."

Priebus and Spicer had healthy appreciations for gallows humor, which was not a terrible quality for top RNC officials at this point. "I haven't started pouring Baileys in my cereal yet," Priebus kept saying, often enough that it had become a signature line. I would break the ice with Reince by saying something sarcastic, maybe asking him how his party's Hispanic outreach program was coming along after the RNC's head of Hispanic outreach quit rather than work another day trying to get Donald Trump elected.

"The scent of party unity is in the air," I said, by way of cheerfully taunting my new and tortured friend.

"No, that's incense," Priebus said. That's what I was smelling. He pointed out that he had been burning some behind his desk. He owned perhaps the toughest political job in America at that moment. He was the proprietor of the china shop in the Year of the Bull. He would inhale whatever vapors of Zen he could find.

Priebus did his best to stay serenely distracted. He played jazz piano at home late at night and gazed into a twenty-nine-gallon saltwater fish tank that he kept next to his office desk. "You see that big eel?" Priebus asked me one day, pointing out a black slithery creature on the bottom. He noted other fish: "That's a yellow tang, hippo tang, a spotted puffer. There's an anemone. An urchin. An orange clown fish."

He took a hunk of shrimp from a refrigerator and dangled it with a set of tongs into the water. A race to the bottom ensued as bits fell away and the fish vied for pieces of flesh. It was difficult to look away from the feeding frenzy. Front and center was the thrashing Big Orange Clown Fish.

Cheap metaphor alert!

I asked Priebus if Mr. Big Orange Clown Fish reminded him of anyone. Yes, I was being a wiseass. And Reince, with a goofy grin, showed signs of playing along. Until he wasn't.

"That's not funny," he snapped.

No matter how much Trump had roiled the Republican water, it remained Priebus's job to carry it. The presumed Republican nominee appeared on many days to be at open war with the institution preparing to nominate him. The entire campaign had been a proxy battle for the proverbial "soul of the party" that had been escalating between the grass roots (captured by Trump) and the professional Republicans (embodied by Priebus).

Priebus relished being a "party guy," an identity that consumed him from an early age. He spent his youth in Kenosha, Wisconsin, organizing pizza parties for Republican volunteers, putting up yard signs, and listening to Newt Gingrich speeches on cassettes in his car. Party-guy things.

It was Priebus who commissioned and endorsed the findings of the GOP "autopsy" after Mitt Romney's defeat in 2012. The report warned that the GOP was "increasingly marginalizing itself" to a point where it would be "increasingly difficult for Republicans to win another presidential election in the near future." That is, the report concluded, unless the party expanded its aging white base to include more immigrants, ethnic minorities, and women—precisely the groups that Trump was now reliably offending pretty much every day.

"Hey, what am I supposed to do?" Priebus pleaded to me at one point. "It's not like I can snap my fingers and change his behavior, right?" Priebus went on to credit Trump for raising topics that "no one else was willing to talk about." This was undoubtedly true: on this same day, Trump—at a rally in Anaheim—observed that "Mitt Romney walks like a penguin."

AFTER A WHILE, MY MEETINGS WITH PRIEBUS TOOK ON THE FEEL of therapy sessions. He played the role of the betrayed spouse who kept trying to convince his therapist that his tormentor really could change. Trump would soon be "pivoting," Priebus was the latest to promise me. He himself pivoted away from saying that Trump would become "presidential" and began to focus more on Trump's supposed "authenticity." That was a better word—more latitude.

"He's carved out this idea that he's this earthquake in a box," Priebus said.

For a while, it seemed possible that Priebus could contain the earthquake. The "normalization" of Donald Trump became a media watchword. Priebus kept working the phones, trying to coax the vocal anti-Trump elements of his GOP back to the party line and persuade—beg—Trump to lay off the elected Republicans he kept dumping on.

"I have encouraged him to constantly offer grace to people that he doesn't think are deserving of grace," Priebus said.

LIKE MANY WASHINGTON INSIDER-OPERATIVE TYPES, PRIEBUS WAS always saying he "gets the joke." This was his way of reassuring me that he understood what was really happening beyond his surface niceties about unity, tolerance, grace, or the idea that Trump could ever "pivot." In other words, take the bullshit I'm spewing on the record with a grain of salt. Because he "got the joke" and he knew that I did, too.

It would be risky, obviously, for a Republican member of Congress to declare, explicitly, that "Donald Trump is a complete ignoramus," even though that's what they really believed. But none of this had to be spoken because the truth of this scam, or "joke," was fully evident inside the club. We're all friends here. Everyone knew the secret handshake, spoke the native language, and got the joke.

In 2016, the D.C. chapter of the GOP had arrived at a bizarre point where the singular, inescapable "joke" of the party was about to become its nominee.

CHAPTER 3

UNITY—OR ELSE!

———

Let's just get this unity shit over with.

—Senator John McCain

June–July 2016

Even while elected Republicans were saying they would support Trump, many were quite open about his shortcomings—thus laying out "the joke" of the situation quite plainly.

Raúl Labrador, a staunchly conservative House member from Idaho, said that yes, he would probably end up voting for Trump in November, but also went on to diminish him as "not knowing much about the Constitution or politics."

Representative Peter King of Long Island, a GOP House fixture, also pledged support for Trump, despite labeling him "a guy with no knowledge of what's going on."

Priebus's entire job at this point had become managing "the joke" that the GOP was helplessly playing on itself, long before voters delivered their own punch line in November. Consensus in D.C. remained that Trump would eventually flame out, which had a leavening effect on his antics. The act would expire soon enough and could still be safely confined to the Entertainment section (as *The Huffington Post* did, for a while), rather than the Threat to Democracy section.

People spoke of the campaign as a tumultuous bender that would be forgotten like a regrettable weekend in Vegas. "I'm just trying to get through this," Spicer kept telling me that summer and fall, a familiar mantra among many Bubble World Republicans. "We're just trying to limit the damage."

Okay, so maybe Trump would lose, D.C. Republicans conceded. Maybe they deserved it. They knew *they* would certainly survive. Republicans had lost presidential elections before. They'd become quite good at it. And still they always kept their tables at the Capitol Hill Club and their private humidors at Shelly's Back Room, that cigar bar by the White House. It's not as if Hillary Clinton were going to shut down K Street or kill those PAC junkets to Jackson Hole and donor "retreats" at Sanibel. Please!

"Hey, I made a whole lot of money when Bill Clinton was president in the 1990s," Woody Johnson, the owner of the New York Jets and long-time GOP fundraiser, told me that spring. He had previously been the national finance chair for Jeb Bush's ill-fated presidential campaign and was in the process of jumping over to Trump. But regardless, he seemed to be saying, even if Hillary did win, he would still be a billionaire, maybe a few more times over. So we shouldn't worry about Woody; he would be fine—big relief there.

But first, Republicans had to ride out the earthquake and "limit the damage." Spicer told colleagues that when Trump lost, hopefully it would be by enough that he could never come back and run for anything again. At the same time, he hoped that Trump would not get demolished so badly that Republicans also lost the House and Senate.

Participation in the joke took many forms. The most common—especially among Republican elected officials—was avoidance. Early that summer, I called around to a bunch of them seeking comment for a story I was working on that attempted to assess their level of tolerance for Trump, and whether they were any closer to accepting him as their guy. To a comical extent, the elected Republicans all demurred. The Fellowship of the Suddenly Unavailable included some of the most typically quotable Republicans in the game: I tried former presidential challengers like Lindsey Graham ("He's sorta had his fill talking about Trump," a spokesman emailed), Rick Perry ("Thanks for thinking of him"), and Ted Cruz ("Not great timing on our end"). I reached out to previous nominees like Romney ("You are kind to think of me," he wrote in an email) and McCain ("Nah"); early converts such as Chris Christie ("We are going to take a pass this time") and Trump-ambivalent governors like Charlie Baker of Massachusetts ("The governor won't be available").

There was an innocence to these days, a level of security in assuming that Trump had zero shot. This was a bipartisan smugness. "Don't worry, Malcolm," President Obama told his Australian counterpart, Malcolm Turnbull, when the latter expressed concern to him about Trump's early GOP primary successes. "The American people will never elect a lunatic to sit in this office."

Like most Democrats, Obama had the luxury of distance. He could tell himself Trump was someone else's problem. Not so much for Republicans in D.C., who still required a coping strategy.

Their prevailing MO was to keep a low profile, their heads down, and pretend to be "focusing on issues important to my constituents." Trump, too, would pass, like a kidney stone.

Looking back, this was an early-stage version of the denial that would metastasize into many iterations of cowardice over four years. The "head down" approach of July 2016 reached its full maturity with "What is the downside for humoring him" just before the Capitol was ransacked.

"Let's just get this unity shit over with," Senator McCain told me that summer when I ran into him at the Capitol. "The RNC has gotten pretty good at autopsies, I guess." After Trump, a full cremation might be in order.

In retrospect, the joke was a luxury: if he really had zero chance, Trump could still be safely laughed at. His imbecilic authoritarianism felt much more like dark comedy than real possibility.

"Donald Trump has been saying he will run for president as a Republican," the comedian Seth Meyers had said at the White House Correspondents' Association Dinner in 2011. "Which is surprising since I just assumed he was running as a joke."

ON A JUNE MORNING, PAUL RYAN AND SEVEN HOUSE COLLEAGUES visited a residential addiction-treatment facility in the mostly Black D.C. neighborhood of Anacostia. The representatives then took turns giving testimonials about why Republican policies—lower taxes, entitlement reform, less regulation—better addressed the intractable problems associated with urban poverty. This was Ryan at his most earnest. He considered himself one of those "idea and policy" conservatives, a serious and cerebral creature.

After completing the tour of the treatment facility, Ryan stood at a lectern and invited questions from the press. Did Ryan have any regrets about endorsing Trump? "I told you," Ryan said, smiling, turning to one of his hosts. The next five questions were also about Trump until one reporter took pity and slipped in one about the antipoverty programs.

Ryan tried strenuously to avoid discussing the soon-to-be nominee. He took precautions to Trump-proof himself before consenting to take part in even the most banal media treatments. He agreed, for instance, to be interviewed for a Father's Day feature in *People*, but only on the condition that he be asked no Trump questions.

When we spoke, Ryan was much less eager to discuss Trump than Priebus, his old friend and fellow Wisconsinite. "Reince is basically being the adult in calming the situation," Ryan said. "He is protecting that grassroots process. Reince is protecting that from being disfigured or hijacked."

At this point, it did seem fairly evident that the hijacking had already taken place, and the likes of Ryan and Priebus were left on the tarmac.

AS TRUMP'S LOOMING NOMINATION APPROACHED, THE MORE desperate and unhinged everything appeared.

"Just please be quiet, don't talk," Trump said, trying to stem the drumbeat of his intra-party vilifiers. This was a few weeks before the Republican National Convention was set to begin in Cleveland. Horrified GOP establishment figures had taken to begging "party leaders" to figure out a way to deny Trump in Cleveland, a prospect the candidate brushed off with his usual sense of calm and proportion. "I think you'd have riots," Trump said.

"I assume he's speaking figuratively," Spicer said, trying to project confidence.

The conservative radio host Hugh Hewitt warned that Republicans' accepting Trump as their nominee was "like ignoring Stage IV cancer." Hewitt would of course go on to become one of Trump's most devout supporters—just as Perry would go on to become secretary of energy despite previously calling Trump "a cancer on conservatism." It was inspiring how many principled conservatives were learning to live so bravely with cancer.

Romney hosted his annual "ideas" retreat in Utah for GOP office-holders, donors, and business leaders. In a normal election year, this would serve as a unity confab before the convention. But this year's edition resembled more of an AA meeting for Republicans on the edge, albeit one hosted by a Mormon.

Romney set the tone when he told Wolf Blitzer on CNN that Trump in the White House could "change the character of the generations of Americans that are following" and might result in "trickle-down racism," "trickle-down misogyny," and "trickle-down bigotry." By weekend's end, a full trickle-down freak-out in the GOP was at hand.

In a question-and-answer session with Speaker Ryan, the Hewlett-Packard chief executive, Meg Whitman, who was the Republican nominee for governor of California in 2010, questioned how Ryan could endorse such an appalling figure as Trump.

Whitman then went on to place Trump in the company of Hitler and Mussolini. This sounded dark. Romney appeared to tear up at one point. "Seeing this just breaks your heart," he said.

Priebus became exasperated and kept telling everyone to calm down. "Let's stop this and unify," he tweeted, sounding more and more like a substitute teacher being pelted with erasers.

Still, the normalizing instinct remained formidable. Mitch McConnell vowed to *Politico* that Trump was "not going to change the basic philosophy of the party." This turned out to be 100 percent true, except for Trump's "basic philosophy" on foreign policy, free trade, rule of law, deficits, tolerance for dictators, government activism, family values, government restraint, privacy, optimistic temperament, and every virtuous quality the Republican Party ever aspired to in its best, pre-Trump days.

As Tom Nichols would write in *The Atlantic*, "Republicans have gone from being a party that touted virtue to being the most squalid and grubby expression of institutionalized self-interest in the modern history of the American republic."

I kept trying to be open, though, to the idea that someone like Trump was what change had to look like in American politics today given the perverse state it found itself in. Perhaps it took one joke to expose the other, long-marinating joke, the one that both parties in Washington had been perpetrating on America for decades. Surely the anger at Washington that propelled the likes of Trump was justified.

But you don't get to create your perfect change agents in a lab. They don't always resemble the inspirational specimens, like Obama, Reagan, or Mr. Smith. "I'm feeling good about things," Priebus told me. His voice was flat and deliberate, hostage-video mode. He said he was trying to be upbeat.

"I have Hillary Clinton on the other side," he kept saying, clinging to her as a lifeline.

CHAPTER 4

THE INEVITABLE

―――――

Where does the barley come from?

—Hillary Clinton to a
New Hampshire brewery owner

October 2016

There was something off about this campaign from the start. In retrospect, it all felt deeply out of whack, and not just the Trump part of it—all the rules he was breaking and paying no price for breaking, as if really (LOL!) nothing mattered.

Bubble World's adherence to the Clinton inevitability factor should have been its own flashing signal. The mindset felt predictably lazy, given the chaos Trump was sowing and thriving under. Really, everyone was so sure it was her turn now? So certain that they understood the country, just as they were so certain that Trump would never actually run or, if he did, never make it to Iowa?

The Clintons benefited from an outdated mystique that they were bulletproof. This was especially true of Hillary, who outlasted so much adversity for so long and still always managed to get an even bigger job and book deal. Bill humiliated her in the White House, and she landed in the Senate. Obama beat her in 2008, and she wound up at State. She waited out the "vast right-wing conspiracy," faced down hours of Benghazi inquisitions, Bernie brigades, and her own "damn emails." What could This Clown—Trump—possibly do to the Almighty?

Quite a bit, it turned out. Trump's survival instinct went far beyond Clinton's, to a pathological point. What he possessed would easily transcend her admirable human qualities like toughness and resilience. Unlike Clinton, Trump was a desperately untamed figure with no regard for rules, traditions, or ethics. His non-capacity for humiliation or embarrassment created an asymmetric contest. He was willing to say or do or lie about anything. While Hillary had drawn her own suspicions and distrust over the years, she respected certain lines. With Trump, there were no lines.

He committed offenses that would have ended any other candidate's career, and certainly campaigns. He had done this dozens of times over. He was always being caught in lies, getting exposed as a hypocrite and an idiot in new and breathtaking ways. He never apologized or showed even the slightest capacity for shame or remorse. He just kept going and surviving and, somehow, winning.

Yet everyone seemed to think the normal laws of gravity still applied. Why? Because, once again, it was Hillary's turn: all of the right residents of Bubble World had determined so, notwithstanding how dubiously that proposition had fared in 2008. Here we were, eight years later, sixteen years removed from the White House, and two decades since people first started using the term "Clinton fatigue." The Hillary Industrial Complex reconvened to take another whack at humanizing the polarizer, trying (again) to make her seem authentic, relatable, real.

I FOLLOWED CLINTON AROUND FOR A FEW EARLY WEEKS IN 2015, when she was first starting the process of re-re-re-re-introducing herself to the American people. Like early-stage Jeb Bush, her heart never felt in the project. She told a rally crowd in North Carolina that her years in politics had taken a toll on her. "I've built up some defenses," she said, in a line that was, for her, self-revelatory. "When it comes to public service," she said, "I'm better at the service part than the public part."

Clinton told me at one point that she felt more and more alienated from the political and media ecosystem she was now forced to operate in. "My husband and I laugh sometimes about the *Antiques Roadshow*," Clinton said, referring to the PBS show about antiques appraisers that she said she and Bill watched all the time. "Sometimes we feel like we are the antiques on a road show when it comes to politics." If only this production were as quiet and unobtrusive as a PBS show enjoyed by old people.

She wore a look of particular dread when she was out campaigning. Once again, here she was being inspected like livestock and harassed by the hair-sprayed hecklers of the hostile media. The routine was hardly new to Clinton, but her aura of dismay seemed to take hold at an early stage.

"Secretary Clinton, over here," Ed Henry of Fox News yelled at her during one campaign event I attended at a New Hampshire brewery. Henry was a cheerful, toothy-grinned character, ever ready with his dramatic "tough questions" and killer pocket squares. He clearly relished his role as Fox's embedded bomb tosser behind enemy lines.

"DO YOU HAVE A PERCEPTION PROBLEM?" Henry shouted after

getting Clinton's attention. (Henry would himself have a "perception problem" in subsequent years; google "Ed Henry" and you'll get the gist.) This was not the kind of icebreaker you'd wish for when making reintroductions.

"I'm going to let the Americans decide that," Clinton responded to Henry on her way out. She then resumed her attempt to appear interested in what the brewery owner was telling her. "Where does the barley come from?" she asked him.

The Clinton campaign was a bit of a nervous wreck and prone to control freakishness. Before one visit I made to headquarters in Brooklyn, a campaign press babysitter, Jesse Ferguson, asked me in an email if I would please keep "the office itself off the record." I was confused about exactly what it meant to keep a forty-thousand-square-foot office space "off the record," as if the copying machine might blurt out something proprietary.

Clinton's speeches followed the grind-it-out cadence of a State of the Union address written by committee. It was always as if she were rehearsing for the big job rather than running for it. She would clinically mention "the historic nature of my candidacy," as if electing a woman president were simply the next "first" on the progressive to-do list, now that a Black president, national health care, and same-sex marriage had been checked off.

The campaign emphasized data, analytics, targeting. Hillary won all the debates, avoided big mistakes, and appeared to luck into a freak-show opponent who kept setting fire to himself in creative ways every week. She did what she had to do. She put out position papers and spoke regularly to the people she put in charge of her transition.

Still, it felt out of whack. The Trump crowds and energy were insane, for those who cared to notice. Residents of Bubble World did not notice, for the most part, at least beyond covering his events like monster truck rallies. Or they underestimated what the throngs meant or focused disproportionately on the latest chaos and disarray from inside the Trump campaign, which was endless.

You could traipse through newsrooms, greenrooms, or faculty lounges, get off at any Acela stop between Washington and Boston, and not meet a single Trump voter. Yet it was also impossible to come away from any Trump campaign event, or random encounter in nonurban Texas, Pennsylvania, or Florida, and not wonder if the standard models might not apply—the usual polls, pundit predictions, and precedents.

"He's going to win" was something I kept hearing from people inhabiting the Trump bubble. This included people—in many cases reporters—who did not want him to win, who knew what other campaigns were like. These gatherings were just different.

I knew what they meant. The Trump rallies were unlike anything else. People kept coming and coming in big waves, materializing from all directions, winding down sidewalks. Where did they all come from? Were they all being counted?

The internal ethos of the swamp—the usual self-assurance—was another sign maybe something was amiss about the usual models. In a sense, Washington always wins in that its villagers keep making more money and winding up with better titles. But Washington is almost always wrong, and spectacularly so when it comes to "reading" the rest of America.

Groupthink coalesces around flawed assumptions—about things like Saddam Hussein having weapons of mass destruction. Or Donald Trump definitely not surviving that "Mexican rapists" kickoff speech.

Okay, scratch that, no way Donald Trump will ever win the Republican nomination.

Okay, scratch that, Trump will lose to Clinton in a landslide and Republicans will immediately pretend he never existed.

It's Hillary's turn.

I interviewed Madam Secretary that October after an event at a renovated train station in Toledo. The northwest Ohio city was among the country's most economically distressed and home to scores of the white working-class voters who were most passionately devoted to Trump. I drove through town, passing block after block checkered with Trump signs, listening to screed after screed on the radio about the malevolence of Obama and Clinton. It sent me into one of those echo-chamber vortexes where I began to wonder if any more than a few dozen Ohioans would be voting for Clinton at all.

I stopped at a diner for lunch before the interview. (Yes, a literal "diner in Ohio," one of the great clichés in the media's clumsy quest to "understand" Trump voters in the Rust Belt; I'm including this paragraph to embarrass myself.) The waitress, Martha, asked where I was from. Washington, I said. She figured I was in town for Hillary.

"Not a fan," Martha said. Of Hillary or Washington. She had been a Democrat, but liked Trump and had really come to hate politics. "It's all such bullshit," she said. Trump was an antidote. She knew he had issues, but Trump was refreshing in that it felt as if he were telling them the truth. I heard this time and again: that Trump was a truth teller, despite his lying.

Martha also said she was certain Trump would win. She didn't know a single person who believed Hillary would. I realize this was hardly scientific (but it's a diner in Ohio!). Still, anyone who's spent any time around these parts would have a hard time saying Martha felt unrepresentative.

I headed over to the alternative bubble, the Hillary rally. There was no way she would not win. Just like that, my certainty was restored.

The national press in attendance were citing new polls showing her lead bulging. I spoke to confident campaign aides who were discussing scenarios where Clinton could win red-tinted Georgia and North Carolina. Parents drove long distances from college enclaves like Ann Arbor, Michigan, so their kids could lay eyes on the first woman president in person. They talked about the thrill of witnessing history.

I waited for Clinton in a backstage office space with a bunch of her traveling staff. They seemed especially excited about Trump's latest self-immolation—a fat-shaming Twitter assault against a Latina beauty queen. This was also right around the time Trump faced a blizzard of revulsion over a 2005 video obtained by *The Washington Post* in which the candidate was heard making lewd and predatory claims about grabbing women "by the pussy" to the *Access Hollywood* host Billy Bush.

Nick Merrill, Clinton's personal press aide, stepped out into the waiting area.

"The doctor will see you now," Merrill said, directing me into the candidate's holding room. I imagined her washing her hands and scrubbing up for my arrival.

Clinton is always funny and engaging in close-in settings, but her eyes hung heavy, and she appeared somewhat worn down; she'd been diagnosed with pneumonia a few weeks earlier, and she was still feeling some effects. Over the previous few months, Trump had managed—in that gross and sexist way of his—to make his opponent's health, fitness, and stamina an issue. He did this despite being roughly fifty pounds overweight himself. He was barely able to climb a dozen stairs without gasping for breath (or descend without clutching a banister for dear life).

Trump was "just asking questions," he said, just as he was about Obama's birth certificate. He tried to make us smarter every day.

He had been suggesting for weeks that Clinton was "not well physically," a conceit stoked by a Greek chorus on the internet and a few well-placed "medical experts" on Fox News ("Get Dr. Giuliani on the air, stat!"). We were well past the quaint days where if a candidate fell ill, the other candidate would simply wish the opponent well and respect their privacy.

At a speech in Cleveland a few weeks earlier, Clinton unleashed a few coughs between sentences, which soon degenerated into a full-on gagging fit. Clinton tried to continue her remarks, gamely if not wisely. She was unable to choke out any words for several seconds. She popped lozenges and gulped water. You could sense dread in the crowd—and see cringing eyes among the Clinton staff—over what would become of this moment. This is your brain on Trump. The episode was all over TV that afternoon and inspired a screaming *Drudge* headline about Clinton's "violent coughing fit."

She was much better now and had resumed a full schedule, but it was clear Clinton did not share the buoyancy of her staff or even the certainty of the experts. She kept saying how confident she was, and seemed to mean it to a point, but the magnitude of what losing could actually mean seemed to impose its own burden. That was another kind of Trump factor that stripped this campaign of any fun or uplift. Too many people were too busy being scared shitless by the unspeakable.

"I don't go there," Clinton said, referring to the unspeakable. But clearly she did, if not always out loud.

Losing in a presidential election would be hard enough. Now imagine being the person who lost to Donald Trump. Imagine the aftermath of that. Do you ever recover? *"I don't go there."*

Candidates are always declaring that "the most important election of our lifetimes" is at hand. Usually this is true only for the person running (no doubt 2012 was the most important election of Mitt Romney's lifetime). But this year's stakes felt unnervingly off the charts. "Near existential" was how Clinton's running mate, Tim Kaine, described the campaign, and this did not feel hyperbolic.

"There is a dread that people have about what it would actually mean if he were to actually be elected," John Podesta, Clinton's campaign chairman, told me, also not speaking the opponent's name. As much as Obama's team and supporters wanted to see the president reelected in 2012, Podesta said, "they didn't feel that the country was going to fall into the abyss if Mitt Romney was president of the United States."

Clinton's deep contempt for Trump was more intense in person than it even appeared from afar. It went well beyond the competitive fervor with which one general-election candidate might speak about another. "It does feel much different," she told me. "If I were running against another Republican, we'd have our disagreements," she said. "But I wouldn't go to bed at night with a knot in the pit of my stomach."

Given that, I asked Clinton if Election Day—only five weeks away—scared her at all. "No, not really," she said slowly. I clarified that I was talking about the prospect of her losing. She said she knew exactly what I was talking about. "I'm not going to lose," she said. Reassuring, that's what a leader tries to be.

But she said this with an obvious lack of serenity, an apparent pit in her stomach. Before I left, I asked Clinton what she was hearing most often from voters she meets on her campaign rope lines.

"'Don't blow this,'" she said. "I hear it over and over: 'Don't blow this.'"

In certain ways, Clinton's long quest had wound up with an almost poetically perfect opponent. Because of course the first woman to breach the ultimate men's sanctum of the American presidency would first have to defeat someone who actually boasted about the size of his penis on a debate stage.

Who could dream up a better cartoon villain? Perfect caricature had been achieved. If only he was funny.

As it turned out, Clinton, who began her campaign intent on breaking the last barrier—the glass ceiling—found her most compelling rationale in her own role as a barrier, a bulwark against the unspeakable alternative.

As I was leaving our interview, Hillary smiled, looked me in the eyes, and left me with a casual reminder. "As I've told people," she said, "I'm the last thing standing between you and the apocalypse."

CHAPTER 5

APOCALYPSE 45

———

November 8, 2016

Yes, he won. Still seems unbelievable. I tried to convince myself—and all the distraught liberals in my life who believed Trump to be an irredeemable buffoon—that we were not all screwed. My heart was not in it, but I tried.

I tried to make the case that the political system might benefit from an overhaul like this, despite the industrial park of red flags that preceded the overhauler. It was conceivable someone like Trump, for whom there was no pertinent antecedent in American life, might have more success transcending the partisan ghettos than the other would-be change agents who came before.

If you could get beyond the bluster and menace of Trump (and, okay, the cruelty, bigotry, lunacy, criminality, incompetence, and so on), his message did contain kernels of cogent defiance against Washington's permanent syndicates. You could make an argument that he did offer a version of the "they're screwing you" critique that the likes of Bernie

Sanders and Elizabeth Warren had been tossing out. Both Sanders and Warren used the term "rigged system" long before Trump ever did.

From the start, Trump's main trick was not to convince anyone that he was pure but rather to convince people that everyone else was dirty. Everybody lied and cheated at golf, on their spouses, and on their taxes. Trump was just better at being dirty, proving how smart and savvy he was. Only losers got hung up on the unspoken rules of the capital. Bless their hearts.

So, now that Trump had pulled this off, it was theoretically possible to view him as an outside security contractor called in to protect the bullied and the overlooked from Washington's establishment drug lords. Who better than the *ultimate* kingpin to stick it to the pikers? This was the so-called political class, whose rich, slick, and entitled likes were perfectly embodied by a name—Clinton—that happened to belong to Trump's opponent.

If nothing else, Trump's dark message and the general aura of victimhood around his campaign was well suited to the moment. He was by no means a purveyor of hope, optimism, or "Morning in America." But the resentment he stirred was palpable, and the idea that so many well-off and well-educated people were oblivious to it should have been its own detector of a powerful gas in the air.

A number of Republican consulting types mentioned Clinton's infamous "basket of deplorables" line as a key episode in the race. This was the remark—uttered by Clinton at an LGBT fundraiser in September—in which she dismissed half of Trump's supporters as having views that were "racist, sexist, homophobic, xenophobic, Islamophobic, you name it." It didn't help that the statement drew heavy applause from the New York City crowd, or that Barbra Streisand sang an adapted version of "Send in the Clowns" that was written specially for Trump ("Is he that rich? Maybe he's poor. 'Til he reveals his returns, who can be sure? Who is this clown?"). Honestly, no writers' room could have drawn this up any better.

Charles Murray, the conservative political scientist, called Clinton's statement "emblematic of the disdain with which the new upper class looks at mainstream America." He added that "mainstream America notices this" and responded forcefully and in kind on election night.

That was another underappreciated aspect of what Trump represented, Murray said. They did not so much love Donald Trump or care to defend his character. His main appeal, simply, was as a tool of revenge. "He's our murder weapon," Murray said, channeling Trump supporters. "And I think that is a pretty short, accurate way of saying what function Trump served."

Trump, of course, loved the idea of himself as an unlocked firearm. "Killer" had always been a term of high admiration inside the Trump family. He was not short on his own revenge fantasies, either as a proxy conqueror for his loyal members or in response to his endless personal catalog of slights. Cliff Sims, a Trump campaign and White House aide, described the newly victorious candidate backstage on election night, accepting congratulations from all over when he suddenly paused and took a moment to express this tender sentiment to no one in particular. "When I get to Washington," Trump said, "I'm gonna shove it up Kasich's ass!!!"

Trump, or his speechwriters at least, were sporadically capable of giving voice to the contempt that many Americans had come to feel about their leaders. "For too long, a small group in our nation's capital has reaped the rewards of government, while the people have borne the cost," Trump said in his inaugural address. "Washington flourished, but the people did not share in its wealth. Politicians prospered, but the jobs left, and the factories closed. The establishment protected itself, but not the citizens of our country. Their victories have not been your victories."

Everybody, though, knew exactly whose victory this was. His name was everywhere, writ large in brass and in lights. I kept thinking about a line from a spoof Trump inaugural address that Christopher Buckley composed for *The Wall Street Journal* in 1999. "My fellow Americans," the great satirist wrote as he imagined Trump looking out over the National Mall, "this is a great day for me personally."

What was somewhat reassuring, to me at least, was that Trump appeared stunned at his election-night victory party. At least early on he did. As the newly unveiled president-elect walked gingerly onto the stage at his New York headquarters, his face bore a newfound weight. He'd just been declared the forty-fifth president of the United States—"President-elect Donald J. Trump," as Mike Pence would be the first to say, introducing the All-Powerful. Trump stared out at the crowd as if he were in a trance and absorbed his altered reality like initial drips of anesthesia: his existence had changed irreparably, and so had ours.

THE HEADQUARTERS CROWD KEPT CHANTING, "U.S.A." THE CANDI-date started clapping along, thanking everyone. It was as if he could now, finally, receive the "U.S.A." chant as synonymous with adulation for the triumphant Donald. The U.S.A. was now officially Trump, and Trump was now officially the U.S.A. The union had now been sanctified. When he hugged the flag, he hugged himself.

Trump told the crowd that Hillary Clinton had just called to congratulate him and was "very gracious." A few Pavlovian "lock her ups" rang out from the audience, but didn't catch on. (Clinton later told Howard Stern that when she called Trump to concede, "he was so shocked he could barely talk.") The incoming president's face betrayed that amazed "What do we do now?" gaze that Robert Redford's character wore after his victory in *The Candidate*.

Trump thanked his family, friends, and biggest supporters. As he started talking, his master strut returned, as if he were breathing and talking life back into himself. Suddenly Trump was again fully inflated and appeared even bigger than he was before.

Trump singled out Reince Priebus, who was standing in the lineup of VIP supporters. Trump gave special deference to the party chair, and deservedly so, after all the RNC had done for the campaign, which was nearly everything. Trump ordered Priebus up to the microphone. Reince shook his head, but Trump insisted, and Priebus did as he was told. This was classic Trump—a bizarre, spontaneous gesture that carried the added benefit of debasing someone.

After Priebus arrived at the lectern, Trump added a final humiliating touch and made him speak. "Say a few words, Reince." Priebus's eyes bulged as Trump shoved him to the microphone. "Ladies and gentlemen, the next president of the United States," Priebus managed to say.

"Thank you, it's been an honor," he added. His words were mildly slurred, understandable given what Reince had been through. No doubt, he was pouring Baileys into more than just his cereal at this point. Priebus coughed out a few garbled "God blesses" and "thank Gods" before fleeing the mic as if it were in flames.

Priebus and the Republican Party had also availed themselves of Trump, the murder weapon. It had been a while since they'd held one. They'd been losing not only a lot of presidential campaigns but also, seemingly, the thread of America's cultural future, or so they'd been told for years now by all the faculty lounge and greenroom geniuses. It had always been left to the functionary likes of Reince to somehow try to autopsy his party out of its demographic oblivion.

But then Trump came along, and suddenly the task was not so thankless after all. He didn't bother with niceties about tolerance or big tents or "diversifying the party." He just went all in and fired away with ruthless white grievance, which came naturally. I once asked Trump, during the primaries, whether his campaign even bothered to conduct focus groups. He smirked.

"Yeah, I got a good focus group for you," he told me, jabbing a finger from each hand into his orangey temples. "Right here."

And now, just like that—boom. Trump's message hit, and everything was shaded through victory-tinted glasses for the people around him. Priebus suddenly looked not so hapless. At this moment, there was no doubt that Priebus was getting something out of this deal. He was, for now, part of a protected class.

Murder weapons can also be dangerous and unnerving. They don't always hit the intended target. Handle with care. But Priebus at least had access to a weapon, and for the moment he was powerful.

"It felt amazing," Priebus told me later, of that moment. "Like, wow." (He was suddenly dropping more "likes" than a teenager.) "I felt ten feet tall up there."

Never underestimate how taxing it is to be told you're a loser, again and again. Now look at him. Look at them all.

I KEPT PANNING THE ELECTION-NIGHT STAGE, FOCUSING ON THE Washington or Washington-adjacent characters—the Priebus, Christie, Rudy, Jeff Sessions, and Kellyanne Conway types. They had all, to varying degrees, made it already. They all had their brand names and sweet gigs to fall back on. Kellyanne had her firm, Christie (as soon as he escaped Trenton) his paid gasbag deals, and Sessions his safe Senate seat.

No unemployed steelworkers in this bunch. They had all existed cozily for many years in the winners' circle of D.C. life and its various Acela-accessible studios.

But now this entourage all had *calculations* to make, in a way that a lot of Republican leaders did. Would they "go in," as in to the White House? Could they make this work for themselves, and at what cost? Would they still get their favorite tables at the Palm and Cafe Milano? Who knew how long the Trump Hotel would be there? Ideally, they could avoid total disgrace, social ostracization, and (worse comes to worst) prison.

It wasn't much of a decision, actually. When the president-elect asks, you say yes. They had all made their long-shot bets, and this would be their big dopamine payoff. For this sweet and dizzy moment on the stage, they could be lottery winners, never mind how scared and even miserable they might have looked.

Priebus wanted to be the White House chief of staff. No other president had ever asked him, or probably ever would. This was his shot. So, yes, of course he would "go in," follow the vanquisher to the White House, with full privileges at the hotel.

Priebus knew his time at 1600 would likely end quickly (it did—six months). He assumed it would not end well (it didn't; he was fired by tweet). He read the news of his firing during a final flight on Air Force One while Trump tapped out his lethal Twitter missive from a few feet away. "I would like to thank Reince Priebus for his service and dedication," the president wrote, by way of wishing him well.

When the plane landed, Priebus stepped onto the rainy tarmac and into a waiting car to take him out to pasture. But that would be later. This was now, and it was, as Trump kept saying, *unbelievable*.

Trump then pointed a few places down the cabaret line and started gushing over Sessions, the first senator to endorse him during the primary season. Trump hailed Sessions as being "highly respected in Washington" and "as smart as it gets." Neither was sincere or true. Sessions was in fact a not terribly well-respected backbencher in the Senate, and his endorsement would not be coveted by anyone outside Alabama. Nor did Trump think Sessions was "as smart as it gets." (He would refer to him later as "mentally retarded" and a "dumb Southerner.")

But it didn't matter. They were all in business together now. They could make their own rules and tell their own stories and destroy whom they wanted, even each other.

Trump asked Sessions to be his attorney general, an offer that no past or future president of the United States would ever in a million years extend to Jefferson Beauregard Sessions III. When Trump called him out on the stage, Sessions raised his short arms over his head and applauded for the weapon. Respect, respect!

Sessions also looked terrified and shaken, like a beagle in a thunderstorm. Maybe, on some level, Sessions had an intuition (like a beagle before a thunderstorm). He had to know that something dark could be coming and that holding on to his safe Senate seat might actually have been the more prudent choice. But you get swept up in the vertigo of winning. Sessions kept clapping over his head for Trump, as if it were the only thing he could think to do in the moment.

Christie stood a few paces down, next to Conway, his fellow Jersey wiseass. They both wore mischievous grins, as if they'd been shit-talking among themselves all through Trump's ejaculatory speech. They all had to sense, too, that this was a treacherous expedition they'd hopped on, and who knew where it was headed?

But they could worry about that when the sun came up, if it ever did, because Trump was still talking.

CHAPTER 6

THE PUNCH LINE

—

January 20, 2017

The forty-fifth president had just kicked off his term with what instantly became known as his "American carnage" speech. No one was expecting a JFK "Ask not what your country can do for you" speech or an FDR "Only thing we have to fear is fear itself" speech. But this was Trump setting a big mood; hope was not exactly springing eternal here.

Rain fell through dark clouds as the new president strutted out, as if in a purple robe. Paul Ryan looked as if he were about to cry. Michelle Obama looked as if she had not slept in days. Everyone kept peeking at each other, exchanging uh-oh glances. When Hillary Clinton arrived, in her ceremonial capacity as a former First Lady, she was greeted with a "Lock her up" chant from the crowd. A clot of embedded protesters blew whistles and yelled "Not my president" while Trump was taking his oath.

Trump's speech read like an autopsy for America. From a messenger who lived in a three-level penthouse in a Manhattan skyscraper named for himself. Yet Trump knew intuitively—from TV—just how grim things were. He described a nation of mothers and children "trapped in poverty in our inner cities," where "rusted-out factories" were "scattered like tombstones across the landscape." His biggest supporters, which included some of the country's wealthiest people, cheered as Trump declared an end to the horror show they had apparently all been enduring.

"HOPEFULLY THIS WILL ALL DEFAULT INTO SOME SEMBLANCE OF normal," Ed Rogers, Republican lobbyist and D.C. wise guy for all seasons, was saying. We were having lunch at Tosca, a popular downtown trough for lobbyist and D.C. retainer-class types, where Ed had his own corner table. It was a few days after the inauguration, and he did not sound confident.

Sure enough, the "default to normal" fantasy died a quick death on the first full day of the new president's administration. Sean Spicer, the new White House press secretary, officiated at the funeral.

The burial took place in the White House Briefing Room, site of a rare Saturday press conference the day after Trump's inauguration. Spicer's first official briefing was supposed to be held that Monday, but Trump had become enraged as he absorbed the coverage of his American Carnage concerto from the day before, especially the observation that his inaugural had drawn far fewer people than Obama's did eight years earlier. Overhead photos juxtaposing the two crowds—Obama's much bigger—circulated all day.

Finally, Trump could take no more and summoned Spicer, the newly minted chief of staff, Reince Priebus, and other stupefied White House aides to the Oval Office on a Saturday to vent about the blatant distortion and injustice being visited upon himself.

"The president was clear," Spicer would write in his White House "memoir," *The Briefing* (based on his *brief* time at the White House). "This needed to be addressed."

Bottom line, Trump's feelings were hurt, his mood was in ruins, and someone had to pay—Spicer in this case.

Spicer represented a Washington crossover figure, someone who comfortably inhabited the old Tokyo-on-the-Potomac before Godzilla was elected and put him to work. He also embodied a particular neurosis of Trump-era Washington, where the lizard-brain logic of making a name for yourself collided with the ever-present threat of the capricious force in the Oval Office.

He had spent his entire career trying to get to this most exalted workplace. Spicer worked his way up to become the assistant for media and public affairs at the Office of the U.S. Trade Representative in the last years of George W. Bush's presidency. There, he was known as an advocate for free trade, a cornerstone of Republican policy throughout his career until Trump took over the GOP and became the most protectionist president in decades.

Finessing this would call for nimbleness on Spicer's part. It required that he argue the exact opposite of the position he had spent years promoting. In general, he was known as a competent, generally upbeat functionary, always willing to "eat rocks," to use a go-to Reince Priebus phrase, meaning that he was willing to countenance a great deal of inconsistency and indignity. Once, at the end of the Bush administration, Spicer even volunteered to dress up in a white bunny suit for the annual White House Easter Egg Roll. This was not typically part of the job description for the spokesman to the U.S. trade representative, but Spicer liked being around the White House and seized whatever chance presented itself.

Whenever Spicer was asked about his willingness to defend Trump, he was ready with some variation on this pat answer. Problematic clients are an occupational hazard in his business. "There are doctors who help people who have done bad things," he told *The Washington Post*'s Ben Terris. "There are lawyers who defend bad people," he added. "I don't think it's unique to my profession."

Spicer had a knack for these explanations, which he would deliver with racing self-assurance. Then, when you caught up to his words, you realized Spicer was comparing his patron to a "bad person" who did "bad things." His rationale, essentially, was that even Jeffrey Dahmer was entitled to representation.

As with nearly all his RNC co-workers, Spicer hoped Trump would vanish quickly after Hillary dispatched him. After the unspeakable happened, Spicer faced "the Decision," as many conflicted Republicans around town were calling it. He could either quit or adapt and eat a lot of rocks. *Bon appétit*, sir.

So here Spicer was, on his first full day of work at the White House, getting yelled at in the Oval by the livid new president. Trump ordered Spicer to call a press conference to correct the media's assessment of the inaugural crowd. The president had conjured in his mind that his crowd was bigger than Obama's, and it now fell to his surrogates to convince the world that these delusions were factually correct.

Aides tried to convince the president that this could go badly. There were in fact many photographers present in January 2009 to document the throngs at the National Mall to welcome the first Black president to this overwhelmingly Democratic capital.

They tried to remind Trump that maybe he should not be concerning himself with such a trivial matter as crowd size on Day 1; that it might strike some as a petty and distracting way to kick things off.

"You're really big. That's really small," the counselor to the president, Kellyanne Conway, told the new commander in chief. Conway, whom Trump tended to listen to more than most, trotted out that line whenever he was lashing out over his latest narcissistic injury. She trotted out this line a lot.

Spicer made cursory efforts to echo Conway's point: he told Trump that focusing on a crowd size was beneath his dignity. Left unsaid was that (1) nothing was beneath his dignity and (2) Spicer himself was going to be the ruddy face of this debacle.

The crowd size episode was idiotic, but contained its own autocratic foreboding. "The point was to demonstrate the party's power to proclaim and promulgate a falsehood," wrote Anne Applebaum in a cover story in *The Atlantic*, "History Will Judge the Complicit." Applebaum, who has reported extensively on European tyrants, described the crowd fiasco as a kind of authoritarian's flex. Trump perpetrated this bizarre claim because he could. "Sometimes the point isn't to make people believe a lie," Applebaum said. "It's to make people fear the liar."

"GOOD EVENING, THANK YOU GUYS FOR COMING," SPICER BEGAN. "I know our first official press briefing is going to be on Monday, but I wanted to give you a few updates on the President's activities. But before I get to the news of the day, I'd like to discuss a little bit of the coverage of the last 24 hours."

He then commenced with a career-defining hissy fit over what Spicer called the media's willful efforts to undermine Trump and "lessen the enthusiasm of the inauguration." Spicer called this endeavor "shameful and wrong" and put the Fourth Estate on notice. "This was the largest audience to ever witness an inauguration—period—both in person and around the globe."

This was not true, period. Spicer spoke faster and faster as his scolding gained steam and any remaining speck of his authority dissipated into thin air. "The President is committed to unifying our country, and that was the focus of his inaugural address," Spicer said. (In general, this did not seem to be the main takeaway.)

"This kind of dishonesty in the media," he said, "makes bringing our nation together more difficult." The healing would have to wait until Monday. Taking no questions, Spicer stormed out of the briefing room and into a vortex of ridicule.

Kellyanne Conway went on NBC's *Meet the Press* the next day and kept getting asked by the host, Chuck Todd, why the White House press secretary would go out and "utter a provable falsehood" as his first public statement in the all-exulted *Podium Job*. Conway explained that Spicer was merely offering "alternative facts" to the American viewing public, which became its own epitaph for Conway's credibility.

If it was any consolation, Spicer's star turn from Saturday was now trumped on Sunday by Conway's "alternative facts" master class. But even so, this whole episode felt most instructive as a character study of Sean Spicer, an otherwise replacement-level flack who faced a very public moment of choosing on a big stage.

I went to the White House to visit with Spicer five months into his embattled tenure. Things had only gotten worse after his fiasco of a start. Every day he would go out into the briefing room, his small eyes flared and frightened. He fidgeted and bounced on his feet as the questions were hurled at his head like grenades.

He was not much for soul-searching, but I became fascinated by what Spicer thought about his situation. He was living his dream job, but in this most warped and warping of environments and at such a demeaning cost. Again the question: Was the price of relevance worth it to him? Was the fleeting star power worth the long-term damage to his reputational health?

Spicer was running late and "tied up in the Oval," his assistant explained to me. It was a Thursday afternoon, and I had not seen him since the election.

After about forty-five minutes, Spicer stepped out of his West Wing office and apologized for keeping me waiting. In the same way that a dog can take on a resemblance to its owner, Spicer had acquired the swollen, hopped-up, and somewhat persecuted countenance of a beaten puppy since I'd last seen him.

Given the saturation coverage Trump was receiving, Spicer now had a legitimate claim to being the best-known White House spokesman in history (kind of like the *Titanic* being the best-known cruise ship, but still). I told him that I would come back in a few days and that I wanted to interview him.

"No, you're not," Spicer said quickly. He relented after a bit and agreed to consider being interviewed. But he added that any spotlight trained on him at this moment would not be helpful to "my current status."

This phrase—"my current status"—struck me as a perfectly of-the-moment representation of the city from which Spicer had derived a credible identity for himself until he (and it) had become otherwise occupied. To begin with, it was well known that Spicer's "current status" at the White House had been precarious from the outset, especially after the inaugural crowd debacle. Trump was never sold on him. He lacked "the look," as Trump referred to the lush-haired, sturdy-jawed anchors whom he stared at all day. Spicer also possessed an excitable speaking style that

Trump believed made him appear scared. His declarations had a stop-and-start quality. "Sean can't even complete a sentence," the Audience of One would remark while watching him. "We've got a spokesperson who can't speak."

"Beleaguered" had become part of Sean Spicer's formal name. There was his regular portrayal on *Saturday Night Live* as an irritable, squeaky-voiced twit played by the actor Melissa McCarthy. For a male character to be played by a woman actor was an unforgivably emasculating fate in Trump's eyes.

Spicer had other issues. He suffered nonstop abuse and incredulity from much of the press corps. In a job where every little slipup was ac-centuated, Spicer slipped up regularly. At one point, he claimed that Hitler "didn't even sink to using chemical weapons" (fact check: extremely wrong). His job appraisals were across-the-board brutal. "There's some-thing about Sean Spicer that inspires pity," the *Washington Post* media columnist Margaret Sullivan wrote, and then proceeded to eviscerate him without pity.

Yet in keeping with the Trump-era rule stipulating that "the enemy of the enemy of the people is my friend," the mockery aimed at Spicer propelled him to a golden status with the "base." At Trump's postelection rallies across the country, the press secretary was engulfed by squealing fans and drew a fuss meriting its own headlines (SPICER TREATED LIKE A ROCK STAR AT TRUMP'S NASHVILLE RALLY). His daily briefings became ap-pointment cable viewing for groupies and hate-watchers alike.

Spicer loved how big he had become in MAGA World and boasted about all the new friends in red caps he was making. He was a small-town Rhode Island guy who relished the celebrity encounters—people run-ning up to him in airports, thanking him for his service. But he would marvel only privately, because to be caught trumpeting your fame was a cardinal sin in Trump's White House, where attention was zero-sum, and the forty-fifth president was not one for sharing.

By early June, Spicer had taken several turns in the revolving doghouse of the administration. The press kept listing possible replacements for him at the lectern. The reports were based on "sources close to the president" or in some cases "the president" himself.

WHEN I STOPPED BACK AT SPICER'S OFFICE LATER THAT WEEK, I found him at a standing desk, flanked by TVs replaying his just-completed briefing. He appeared changed from how he was in the good old days of the Campaign from Hell. I did not remember him as such a put-upon toady, besieged and upregulated.

Spicer used to "get the joke," in a relatively benign way. Now he appeared convinced that many of his old Washington friends and colleagues had written him off as a joke himself, given how he'd beclowned himself on Donald Trump's behalf. Spicer's default bearing was now cringe-inducing defensiveness. He gave the impression of someone whose fight-or-flight response had been permanently activated.

I asked Spicer about his "largest audience to ever witness an inauguration—period" debut. In retrospect, this maybe was not the best icebreaker.

"I'm not here to relitigate every fucking number," he said, and then launched into a lengthy relitigation.

Spicer's assistant stepped into his office to remind him that he had a TV interview with Fox in a few minutes. Spicer walked over to a small desk in the corner and started rubbing foundation onto his face. I made a verbal note of this into my tape recorder—that Spicer was putting on makeup.

"Don't you dare!" Spicer said. "Just so we're clear."

"Clear about what?" I asked.

Spicer demanded to know whether I planned to report that he was applying makeup to himself.

"Well, you *are* putting on makeup, aren't you?" I said.

I assured Spicer that this would not exactly be a Watergate-level revelation on my part. (ALL THE PRESIDENT'S YES-MEN—AND THEIR MASCARA!)

Spicer seemed concerned that if I disclosed that he was wearing makeup, it could further emasculate him in the eyes of the president. I mentioned—by way of more reassurance—that Trump himself probably wore more makeup than Tammy Faye Bakker. But Spicer had lost interest in the argument. He patted his cheeks a few more times with a makeup puff and was out the door.

CHAPTER 7

BONFIRE OF THE
GENUFLECTORS

———

June 12, 2017

The Client was requiring more special care and feeding than usual. As always, it was not much more complicated than simply managing his fickle feelings and moods. That had become the definitional battle of the West Wing and much of Republican Washington.

Trump had hit another rough patch—rougher than the usual patches. He was spending hours in his dining room, just off the Oval, not only staring at the TV but yelling and tweeting at it, too. Why, he wondered, was he not being thanked more? For all the unbelievable, amazing, historic things?

All he heard about was *"Russia, Russia, Russia!"*

"Mueller, Mueller, Mueller!"

"Already, at this stage of his term . . . Obama, Obama, Obama!"

When Trump wasn't bunkered down in his private dining area, he was venturing out more into his public dining area, the BLT Prime at the Trump Hotel. His dinner forays occurred with more frequency as his days in office became rougher. The visits seemed to buoy him, especially the excited receptions he would receive from his neck-craning customers.

Trump would dillydally, flash the thumbs-up on command, and let the restorative power of the scene wash over him. He might reside in the most fortified house in America, but Trump seemed to find a truer sanctuary in his eponymous leisure property down the block. Photographers would cluster themselves into a makeshift paparazzi swarm and jockey to get close to the starlet.

"Thank you, everybody," Trump said to cheering patrons as he departed BLT one night. This felt more like a home game to him, with the love of the crowd—such a nice departure.

"WHAT DID YOU ORDER, SIR?" one red-carpet media sleuth cried out. Trump paused, looked his inquisitor in the eye, and replied simply, "Steak."

I happened to catch the tail end of this. There appeared to be some kind of fuss, possibly a disturbance, so I became curious and stopped in to look. No disturbance—just the Client himself, escaping the pressure cooker of the most stressful office in America.

Trump had turned the heat up on himself considerably by firing his FBI director, James Comey, in May. This was quite obviously provoked by Comey's refusal to end the bureau's investigation of Russian interference in the election, which in turn triggered Trump because it diminished his great victory and made him look "like a bad guy" ("*I'm not a bad guy!*").

I visited the White House again in June, this time to see Hope Hicks, the White House communications director, a former Ralph Lauren teen model, and one of the more stalwart day-to-day conductors of this ordeal. She also had a dark sense of humor and knew full well the absurd predicament she found herself in, not to mention the insanity of the object at the center of it all. This last bit was, if not Hope's saving grace, certainly a mitigating grace.

I had gotten to know Hope during the 2016 campaign and had also become friends with her dad, Paul Hicks, who had been a top PR executive at the NFL when I was writing a book about the league. Hope was then just twenty-eight years old and not remotely qualified to be a communications director for any White House except this one. But she had a distinct superpower in her ability to manage Trump, not unlike how a day-care provider might have a special knack for managing a particular toddler.

Hope was also wise beyond her years in terms of "getting the joke" about Trump. She could describe the perfect idiocy she confronted every day while also defending him with some of the most solid-gold bullshit ever disseminated by a White House. "President Trump has a magnetic personality and exudes positive energy, which is infectious to those around him," Hope gushed to *The Washington Post* as part of a lengthy statement she gave defending the boss for a story that described his penchant for demeaning his staff. "He has an unparalleled ability to communicate with people," she continued. "He is brilliant with a great sense of humor."

This was so perfectly over-the-top that I remember giving Hope shit about it the next time I spoke to her. Did she dictate her statement from a Pyongyang prison cell? Her response was a non sequitur but nonetheless made for a concise summary.

"You have no idea," she said.

After about fifteen minutes of catching up in an ornate West Wing conference room, Hope asked me if I wanted to "say hello."

"Say hello to who?" I wondered. "Reince? Spicer?"

"POTUS," she said.

Huh. It's usually not this easy to just infringe on the president's schedule, at least in my experience.

"Uh, sure," I said.

Hope walked me into the Oval. And there Trump was, sitting in his little dining area doing his usual thing—watching the sixty-inch flat-screen TV he had installed as soon as he moved in. His cheeks were a pale, slightly washed-out hue of pink, not the usual glowing orange.

"You remember Mark, from *The New York Times*?" Hope said, as if these random drop-by sessions were a regular part of his routine.

I hadn't seen Trump since the election, so I congratulated him on his victory. He thanked me and pointed out that "you treated me very badly" during the campaign and that the "failing *New York Times*" had been "so unfair" to him. He was perfectly pleasant about it, though.

It was 12:30 p.m., and the president had been watching a DVR recording of *Fox & Friends* from about five hours earlier. Apparently, Trump had missed his favorite morning news massage the first time around, or maybe he just wanted to rewatch and meditate upon the show again—in the way that some film historians feel they must savor *Citizen Kane* at least twenty times before they can begin to really appreciate its artistry.

Trump pressed pause on his clicker, extending his arm the way old people do, as if that might make the TV respond faster.

He then went into his usual repertoire about how he "inherited a mess" from Obama, was doing "historic, unbelievable things," and would have won the popular vote over Hillary by "close to a landslide margin" if not for the "unbelievable voter fraud that everyone was talking about" (no serious person was talking about this). I had heard this all before and was ready for it to end after about two minutes—noteworthy when you consider that for most people an Oval Office visit would be a pinnacle experience that they'd want to draw out as long as possible.

Trump then started talking about how his approval ratings were "setting records" for a first-year president (also not true, though Trump's 36 percent approval in that day's Gallup tracker was in record-low territory). He talked about a great new poll that had just come out and then asked Hope what his "number" was in that one. She promptly replied, "Seventy percent," which made Trump happy.

I was confused. "Really?" I said. That sounded, uh, high.

Hope shot me a nasty look. This line of questioning from me was "not helpful."

"Where was that poll from, Hopey?" Trump asked her; he sometimes called her Hopey. "That 70 percent poll?"

"Tennessee," she replied.

This made more sense, given that Trump had beaten Clinton by twenty-six percentage points in Tennessee. But Hicks then added that the Tennessee poll was "of Republicans," which would have in fact been quite low because Trump's approval ratings among Republicans nationwide were generally over 85 percent. Trump didn't seem to process this, only that his historic popularity had once again been affirmed by "the data."

My visit ended after a few more minutes. I thanked the president for his time, and he said it had been "an honor" to receive me. He then resumed his *Fox & Friends* viewing, and Hope walked me out. As soon as we were outside, I asked her what the deal was with that Tennessee poll. "I mean, I had to give him something, right?" she said. "Whatever."

THE PRESIDENT'S TEAM OF CODDLERS DID THE BEST THEY COULD, but he was definitely in turmoil, not at all pleased with what he saw as he flipped between the cable segments of his soul. He had many questions, all generally on the same theme: Why was everyone betraying and disappointing him?

Why were they not building the wall as he promised? Or killing Obamacare, which he vowed throughout the campaign "would be so easy"?

Or locking Hillary up? The way they were all chanting for him to do! Why was this all so difficult? Why was this so unfair?

"No politician in history—and I say this with great surety—has been treated worse or more unfairly," Trump asserted that May during a commencement address to graduates of the U.S. Coast Guard Academy. The speech was meant to be inspirational.

Chief of Staff Reince Priebus thought the president could use some cheering up. Priebus was himself in a precarious state. TRUMP GIVES PRIEBUS UNTIL JULY 4TH TO CLEAN UP WHITE HOUSE, said the headline in that day's *Politico*, three weeks before July 4.

Priebus's many Republican friends kept asking him if things were as chaotic at the White House as they'd been hearing. "No" was Priebus's response. "It's a hundred times worse than you've been hearing." Around this time, Priebus had unburdened himself to Bob Woodward about his workplace. "When you put a snake and a rat and a falcon and a rabbit and a shark and a seal in a zoo without walls, things start getting nasty and bloody," Priebus said. "That's what happens." That sounded bad.

Not shockingly, being the zookeeper of such a nasty, bloody habitat was no easy posting. Priebus later said he had settled on a simple self-preservation strategy. If he could remain in his job for at least six months—ideally a year, but six months would probably be enough—it would be a decent minimum tenure he could cash in on for life. In general, the most lucrative private-sector jobs in Washington are held by people with "former" in their titles—for example, a "former White House chief of staff."

The key to Priebus's continued survival in the West Wing was to improve the president's day-to-day state of mind. On June 12, the full cabinet was scheduled to assemble for the first time. Participants knew to hold nothing back in their stroking of the Client. There would be an opportunity at the start of the meeting when TV cameras were present.

Praise was of course elemental to Donald Trump's existence, like water to a fish. So maybe, the thinking went, a special go-round from Trump's palace guard of former CEOs, generals, governors, senators, congressmen, and a brain surgeon would help the situation. That seemed to be the president's own view as he himself commenced the grand homage.

"Never has there been a president, with few exceptions, who's passed more legislation, who's done more things than I have," Trump boasted. (He had signed no significant legislation to this point, but it's not as if someone in here were going to correct him.)

Enough about him, though. Trump wanted to hear from his cabinet: about how grateful *they* were to work for him.

"It's just the greatest privilege of my life to serve as the vice president," Mike Pence said after Trump gave him the honor—and greatest privilege—to open the testimonials. Not just any vice president, Pence said, but one serving "the president who's keeping his word to the American people and assembling a team that's bringing real change, real prosperity, real strength back to our nation."

An excellent start!

Heads bobbed around the table. As the emergency circle jerk gained ardor, social media became crammed with allusions to Shakespeare's

King Lear, the deteriorating ruler of Britain who invites his three daughters to tell him how much they adore him.

Pence was the unquestioned maestro of this top-level symphony of sycophancy. No one did complete submission the way Pence did: the hushed voice, the bowed head, and the quivering reverence for "my president," "this extraordinary man." He was constantly referencing Trump's "broad shoulders," which was weird. The former altar boy could always deliver when called upon, until the bitter end.

Trump looked on, nodding studiously, like a gymnastics judge. Pence went on about the daily gift to America that was "my president." The scene resembled the one from down the street a few nights earlier—the same mood as in the Trump Hotel. If this was BLT, they'd have applauded.

As for Pence, he was laying it on especially thick for this very special customer. It was always a bit of a puzzle with Pence. Why would this most conspicuously moral of Christian men attach himself so utterly to one of the most depraved creatures ever to inhabit our public life? "Phyllis Schlafly deciding to elope with Larry Flynt would have made more sense," Bret Stephens wrote in the *Times*.

Pence didn't just attach himself to Trump in the standard sense of being a loyal vice president. Pence stood by his man in the most nakedly servile of ways. Old friends from Indiana and colleagues from Congress would try to get Pence to break character, just a little. They understood that Trump expected his vice president to be a perfect doormat at all times. But they wanted just one glimpse of acknowledgment from Pence that he saw what everyone else saw, that he got the joke. *You in there somewhere, Mike?*

"You have to know this is nuts, right?" one former House colleague would ask the VP whenever they spoke. Every Republican in Washington who knew better—which was nearly all of them—was cognizant that the situation with Trump would only become more precarious. So, what did Pence think? How could he keep doing this, with such a straight face and ramrod posture?

But Pence would never betray any daylight between himself and Trump. I talked to about a dozen friends, colleagues, and old House pals of Pence's about this, and many of them said basically the same thing. Pence is "an all-or-nothing guy," as one House member put it. "He can't let any doubt or temptation creep in, because once it does, things get confusing."

The former colleague mentioned Pence's custom of never drinking alcohol unless he was with his cherished wife, Karen. Mike and Karen were married in 1985 and became evangelical Christians shortly after they met. After they'd been dating for eight months, Karen was so certain Mike would propose that she started toting around a gold cross engraved with the word "yes." When he did pop the question, Pence presented Karen with a loaf of bread that was hollowed out in the middle to contain a bottle of champagne and a ring.

Now, thirty-six years later, it's easy to view Mike Pence as a hollowed-out vessel of his own. Once you're in the throes of devotion to Trump, something else overtakes your identity. "Mike just chose the easiest path, like a lot of people did," another former House colleague told me. He likened Pence's demeanor of total subjugation to Trump to the dead-eyed disposition of an abuse victim.

But that also grants Pence a passive and powerless status he does not deserve. It undersells his capacity for opportunism and careerism, the colleague said. Real saints tend not to grow up to be politicians. And being a VP could be one hell of a lifetime achievement medallion, and almost certainly more than he was in a position to hope for otherwise. This was "the Calculation" of Mike Pence.

IN THE CHRONICLES OF THE TRUMP PRESIDENCY, THIS CABINET TES-timonial was an event horizon. "Event horizon"—an astronomy term that refers, essentially, to a point of no return—was applied to many situations during these years, but this was a particularly vivid spectacle: one after another, the cabinet members attempted to outdo each other.

"Mr. President, it's been a great honor to work with you," gushed Secretary of Housing and Urban Development Ben Carson.

"I am privileged to be here, deeply honored," said Secretary of Labor Alexander Acosta.

"I can't thank you enough for the privileges you've given me and the leadership that you've shown," added Secretary of Health and Human Services Tom Price.

The outlier to the praise parade was Secretary of Defense Jim Mattis, who was seated directly to Trump's right and spent much of the session staring down at his hands. When it was his turn to speak, Mattis pointedly did not mention the president and could barely manage to look at him.

"Mr. President, it's an honor to represent the men and women of the Department of Defense," Mattis said. Trump turned away, not pleased. After a few seconds, Trump shifted back and leaned in close to Mattis's face in an attempted LBJ-style intimidation move.

"We are grateful for the sacrifices our people are making," said Mattis, staring straight back. He spoke in a determined monotone, then raised his voice slightly as if to accentuate his nonparticipation in this debasement. Mattis stood alone.

For a few seconds, the pool camera cut to Mike Pompeo, the CIA director and future secretary of state, who nodded along with a trademark shit-eating grin that betrayed how pathetic he thought this all was. Pompeo was a particular kind of Eddie Haskell figure among the Alpha Lapdogs, dutiful in sucking up to Trump and prodigious in trashing him behind his back, per several White House and Hill sources.

"He is so full of shit," Pompeo would later write in a note to National Security Advisor John Bolton, referring to Trump during a summit meeting with the North Korean fascist Kim Jong-un. (Bolton's memoir lays out Pompeo's two-facedness pretty clearly; Pompeo of course denied all of it.) Trump always reserved special awe for Pompeo, in large part because he had a JD from Harvard Law School, and few things moved Trump's populist heart more than an Ivy League affiliation.

As with many of Trump's most determined cabinet-level supplicants, Pompeo had been an open critic of Trump back when it was safe. He was a Rubio endorser in 2016, and in a speech before the Kansas caucuses that year Pompeo predicted that Trump would be "an authoritarian president who ignored our Constitution." Pompeo also quoted Trump saying that he would have no problem telling a soldier to commit a war crime, and that if he did, he would expect them to carry it out.

"He said, 'They'll do as I tell them to,'" Pompeo said, quoting Trump in a video clip unearthed in 2019 by *The New Yorker*'s Susan Glasser.

Pompeo, a West Point graduate, was appalled by this, though over four years he had become adept at just that brand of obedience.

"Thank you for the honor to serve the country," said Rex Tillerson, the former ExxonMobil CEO who was enduring a particularly unhappy tenure as secretary of state. This came shortly after Tillerson had privately derided his boss as "a moron," according to NBC News. Tillerson declined to confirm or deny the report, though multiple sources said the actual quote was "fucking moron" (so Tillerson could plausibly deny the stand-alone "moron" quote). He had reportedly said much worse.

This was true of pretty much every other cabinet secretary otherwise showering POTUS with rose petals. Various accounts had Secretary of Homeland Security John Kelly calling Trump an "idiot," National Security Advisor H. R. McMaster calling him a "dope," Director of the National Economic Council Gary Cohn calling him "dumb as shit," and on it went.

Trump would dismiss such disparagement as bitterness coming from "sources that don't exist" and "traitor leakers" who "should be thrown in jail." Another of Trump's operating assumptions was that anything that displeased him (say, a "nasty" quote in the paper) was a criminal act, on a par with treason.

If nothing else, two White House sources (who exist) told me that this ego pep rally and intervention appeared to cheer up the president for a time. That is, until he learned that the session had been ridiculed in the media, and he immediately began lashing out at aides about "the fucking leakers," though it was not clear why something carried on multiple cable outlets would require "fucking leakers."

THE NEXT MORNING, WASHINGTON'S CHIEF NEWS DIGESTER, MIKE Allen of *Axios*, gathered his blue-blazered minions around the virtual campfire to remind them of the wonders we had all been witnessing. "In 18 years of covering presidents, we have never seen a Cabinet meeting like the one yesterday," wrote Allen, who invented the predawn political tip sheet when he started *Playbook* for *Politico* more than a decade ago. "Remember that we're living through history that will be studied and debated until the end of time."

This itself was debatable. I would venture it's unlikely that come the end of time, anyone will still be "studying" whether, say, Priebus could ever have saved himself with his performance in the Cabinet Room. He certainly did register an outstanding effort; that was agreed upon.

"On behalf of the entire senior staff around you, Mr. President, we thank you for the opportunity and the blessing that you've given us to serve your agenda and the American people," Priebus said. This was Employee of the Month–level customer service, no question. But it was too late for Reince, who was gone six weeks later.

CHAPTER 8

SNOWFLAKE CITY

—

January–June 2018

The deluge of leaks at Trump's expense had become a story of its own. On a random morning in the first half of the second year of his term, the top political stories all testified to how porous the White House had already become.

In a communications meeting, Kelly Riddell Sadler, a special assistant to the president, dismissed a mention of John McCain, who had been diagnosed with brain cancer, by supposedly saying that McCain's opinion (in this case, his opposition to Gina Haspel's nomination as CIA director) did not matter because "he's dying anyway." Everybody learned of this because someone in the meeting leaked Sadler's attempted "joke," which was all over the news by that afternoon—competing with a story (also leaked) that Trump had exploded at Secretary of Homeland Security Kirstjen Nielsen in a cabinet meeting the previous day, and another story (leaked the day before) that Haspel had discussed withdrawing her nomination with the White House.

Deep breaths, people. Always remember whom we're here to serve. Gratitude! Okay, back to work.

Spicer's replacement, Sarah Huckabee Sanders, admonished her team of sieves in a meeting the next day, adding for good measure, "I'm sure this conversation is going to leak, too," which ensured the predictable result: ABC News cited "multiple senior White House officials" in reporting on Sanders's scolding, while Jonathan Swan of *Axios* followed with a fuller account attributed "to five sources in the room."

It hardly took a well-placed leaker (or five) to ascertain that the Trump White House was not the most nurturing of workplaces. But things could become even uglier for its embattled lieutenants when they ventured outside the office.

Stephen Miller, the president's top deportation enthusiast, was accosted at a Mexican restaurant by a customer yelling "fascist" at him. Nielsen, the top enforcer of the administration's hardline immigration and child separation policies, met a similar fate at another south-of-the-border bistro. You could understand why their choice of cuisine could be triggering.

"How can you enjoy a Mexican dinner as you're deporting and imprisoning tens of thousands of people who come here seeking asylum?" one female heckler demanded of Nielsen, per *The New Yorker*. The woman led her fellow protesters in a chant of "Shame! Shame!" at the secretary. Nielsen skipped the flan for dessert and departed hastily.

A fellow patron recognized the EPA chief, Scott Pruitt, eating lunch at a stylish Penn Quarter restaurant and kept hounding him to resign. He did a few days later, though there was no indication that the heckler— a teacher who posted a video of the confrontation on Facebook—had anything to do with Pruitt's exit, which had been in the works for a while.

WANTED posters bearing Miller's likeness appeared on lampposts around his CityCenter D.C. apartment. He was a recurring target for such treatment, though Miller also seemed to enjoy his role as the administration's favorite public goon. He was always up for a televised brawl on behalf of his appreciative president.

This became a catch-22 of serving the needy nabob. For as much as defending Trump on TV brought presidential love, it also made the likes of Miller that much more recognizable around town and susceptible to the passions and mischief of local objectors. They solidly believed that the author of Trump's "zero tolerance" immigration policy should himself expect zero tolerance when grabbing a burrito after work.

I once spotted Miller getting hectored out of a downtown sushi restaurant by a bartender who followed him out onto the sidewalk, demanding to know how Miller could live with himself. I admit I felt a slight twinge of sympathy but kept walking.

ALL OF THESE EPISODES MADE THE TRUMP HOTEL EVEN MORE OF a sanctuary for the temporary ruling class of the West Wing. We were almost a year into the incursion when I started to come in semi-regularly. Republicans controlled all three chambers of government, but the hotel had become their main chamber. It was like Cheers for the MAGA set—except instead of Norm and Sam yukking it up over Norm's tab, you had Corey Lewandowski mugging for photos with some leather-faced groupie from the Villages whose grandson might harbor Proud Boy aspirations.

Here, no one would dare harass Secretary Nielsen; she would often dine multiple times a week at the BLT, as if it were her own cafeteria. The iPhone pirates were a small price of entry into the safe house. The hotel was a perfect place for Nielsen to relax and unwind after a grueling day spent separating Central American kids from their mothers and getting abused herself by Trump, who seemed to take special delight in separating Nielsen from her sanity and self-respect.

The president himself was spotted here on at least two dozen occasions during his term, according to *1100 Pennsylvania*, a gadfly newsletter that monitored the various grifts going on at the property. Its author, Zach Everson, would describe the hotel as "a towering granite symbol of Trump's takeover of official Washington—and of his unprecedented for-profit presidency." I once caught Trump at one of these epic drop-bys. I was seated on one of the blue velvet couches across the atrium when the White-Bellied Heron himself swooped in for a snack at the BLT. He was trailed by a chant of "Trump, Trump, Trump" from the lobby patrons and an entourage of bootlickers that included Giuliani, Graham, the former congressman Mark Meadows, and the president's tight-suited Secret Service detail.

The group stopped in the lobby to greet Madison Cawthorn, then a twenty-five-year-old future Republican congressman from North Carolina, who would eventually occupy Meadows's old seat. Cawthorn later attracted negative attention for, among other reasons, a series of Instagram photos he had posted in 2017 documenting a visit he made to Adolf Hitler's vacation retreat in Germany, known as the Eagle's Nest.

Laying eyes on the Eagle's Nest had been on his "bucket list" for a while, Cawthorn shared with his followers. "It did not disappoint," he gushed of the hallowed ground. Cawthorn took care to refer to Hitler as "the Führer." He was always a stickler for proper titles.

A furor ensued. Cawthorn apologized for his "ill-considered" post. He reassured everyone, "I'm definitely not a Nazi."

———

AS A GENERAL RULE, THE TRUMP HOTEL WAS NOT MY KIND OF PLACE to spend time, yet I wound up back there a lot, and it could be worthwhile. I picked up solid intel during my visits to the Benjamin Bar & Lounge, just off the lobby. Minor Trump celebrities and tourists would cavort here in their purest element. They were happy to overpay for candied bacon appetizers ($22) and designer cocktails in glasses coated in caviar (more than $100). When I couldn't be at the hotel myself, guests were diligent about chronicling their visits—the latest poses with the deputy press secretary or the former caddy or the governor of South Dakota.

It was a tasteful venue, to be sure, and also a savvy career move to nourish the boss's bottom line. "People who wanted to suck up to Trump were not exactly shy about wanting the president to know they were at the hotel and giving him their money," Everson said.

The place was teeming with paradigmatic Trump-era figures. I saw Hogan Gidley in here a few times, a deputy White House press secretary whom I'd occasionally run into over the years as he worked for a series of long-shot presidential candidates—Rick Santorum in 2012, Mike Huckabee in 2016. Gidley, then forty-one, was part of an ensemble of serviceable Republican spokespeople who'd hitched their careers to Trump, with mixed results, but at least was able to ride the experience to 1600 Pennsylvania Avenue.

Before entering politics, Gidley worked at a TV station in Little Rock, including a stint as a weatherman. He clearly liked being on TV and was possessed of a polished on-camera presence and customized earpieces molded especially for each ear. "I see you on TV," his admirers would say, running up to him. "Keep fighting the good fight." Can we get a picture?

Yes, of course they can get a picture; Hogan was always a hero at the Trump Hotel.

For any Trump-derivative character, the best way to assert loyalty to the organization was by giving reverence at the shrine. "I spent two years going to Washington and I didn't see the monuments. All I saw was the Trump Hotel," said Lev Parnas, a no-necked businessman who got tied up with Giuliani's project to extort dirt on Joe Biden in Ukraine. This would eventually get the president impeached (the first time) and Parnas arrested, but did nothing to dampen the soiree.

"It's an absolutely stunning hotel," Spicer said on the eve of Trump's inauguration, during which the price of rooms was jacked up to more than $1,000 a night and select bottles of champagne were going for $2,500. Spicer was asked whether it was ethically proper for the U.S. government and Trump-adjacent entities to shell out massive sums to the president's for-profit enterprise. This carried the heavy scent of a grift, did it not? "It's a beautiful place, it's somewhere that he's very proud of," Spicer said. "And I think it's symbolic of the kind of government that he's going to run." These were the rare words from Spicer that nobody would question.

As with many of Trump's top adulators, Kellyanne Conway was deft at suggesting that somehow the chief's willingness to serve as president should be viewed in terms of a philanthropic gesture. The nation owed him its gratitude, notwithstanding what the ingrate media might think.

"The family, beginning with President Trump, have made financial sacrifices to be president of the United States," Conway told CNN.

Like Spicer, Conway was good about plugging Trump businesses while working on the taxpayer dime. "Go buy Ivanka's stuff is what I would say," Conway said after Nordstrom dumped Ivanka's clothing line and the president used his personal Twitter account to trash Nordstrom.

Her cheerleading for "the Brand" brought complaints from the likes of Citizens for Responsibility and Ethics in Washington, just the kind of uptight D.C. outfit this White House loved to piss off whenever possible. That was part of the fun. Kellyanne had a special knack for Hatch Act violations, which she accumulated like parking tickets.

KELLYANNE'S OFFICIAL POSITION WAS "COUNSELOR TO THE PRESI-dent." It was never clear what she did, although several people in this White House fit that description; they included Steve Bannon, Rudy and his son, Andrew, Omarosa Manigault (from *The Apprentice*), Jared Kush-ner, even the princess herself, Ivanka, who would breeze in and out of meetings and announce herself with a simple, authoritative "Hi, Dad." Melania's spokeswoman Stephanie Grisham referred to Jared and Ivanka simply as "the Interns."

As with most of the president's most trusted aides, Conway was not without ambivalence toward Trump but was always a champ when the cameras rolled. Her public loyalty to the president puzzled many of her intimates, including her husband, George Conway, a conservative legal activist and accomplished Clinton antagonist from way back. George, who had been up for a top Justice Department job in the Trump admin-istration, had come to loathe this president and could not understand why anyone could ever work for him, much less his wife and mother of his four children. He complained to friends that Kellyanne had joined a cult.

Just for kicks, he would occasionally tweet out definitions of narcis-sistic personality disorder and antisocial personality disorder in refer-ence to the president of the United States. George went on to suggest that "a serious inquiry needs to be made about this man's condition of mind." There was no shortage of "open letters" signed by no shortage of "concerned" shrinks suggesting the same. It all made for an interesting domestic situation for the Conways, a reality show within the Reality Show, and the marital embodiment of Trump-era Washington—a seething, divided, and bizarre crucible.

George told *The Washington Post* that he was compelled to tweet about the White House "so I don't end up screaming at her," meaning Kellyanne (totally normal!).

The Conways at least got to be celebrities, of a sort, which was no small thing in Trump World. I always half expected the trials of George and Kellyanne to land them some joint TV show (*Living with the Conways*), or book deal (*Reconciliation*), in which the protagonists rediscovered their love for America, God, and, most of all, each other. I still maintain there's a decent chance this will happen.

CHAPTER 9

THE CARETAKER'S DILEMMA

———

It may be cold comfort in this chaotic era, but Americans should
know that there are adults in the room.

—Anonymous senior administration official
in a *New York Times* op-ed

July 2018

They were always pleading for patience and understanding. Trust
them, the president's caretakers would say. They knew how to
handle the boss. Positive reinforcement was often indicated and could
be effective.

"The president put out a tweet last night that was *really* good,"
Speaker of the House Paul Ryan told me when I visited him on the Hill
that summer. He was sitting in a high-backed chair next to his office
fireplace. He had just gotten off the phone with Trump, who had called

to tell the Speaker that he "looked good on *Fox & Friends* this morning"—possibly the highest compliment the president could pay to anyone.

In turn, Ryan complimented Trump on his "really good tweet" from the night before—something innocuous about trade, likely staff written.

It was always delicate with these two. Ryan was a self-described "policy wonk"; Trump was a hyperactive brute whose interest in policy was no match for his ever-present TV clicker. But it was immediately obvious to the Speaker that to defy the president too forcefully would always invite a counterreaction. "It boomerangs," he said about the danger of being too critical of Trump. "He goes in the other direction, so that's not effective." A tantrum could ensue at any second, broadcast in real time via presidential Twitter. This would in turn inflame the "base," including all the aspiring Trump knockoffs in Ryan's caucus.

Ryan was spending a good portion of his time trying to navigate through Trump's moods and not to activate his followers. He was beginning to wonder how much longer he wanted to be doing this. His teenage kids were becoming adults and curious citizens of the world, while his colleagues—not to mention Ryan's main political collaborator down the street—were becoming less serious and mature by the day. Did he really need this? He was thinking seriously about checking out of the Trump Hotel, so to speak.

As a matter of record, Ryan avoided the actual Trump Hotel whenever possible, which he would liken to "the *Star Wars* bar scene." He had more than his fill of Trump in his regular workday. Ryan often spoke about the president in the manner of a frazzled au pair. He was hardly the only Trump enabler to do this, nor was the farcical nature of this lost on any of them. It could be quite embittering.

"It's a shame the White House has become an adult day care center," Senator Bob Corker, Republican of Tennessee, tweeted during one rough go-round with his on-and-off confidant. "Someone obviously missed their shift this morning."

The patronizing tone of Trump's abettors carried a non-subtle message to worried observers. They were providing key supervision. They were the ones trying to help the undomesticated president be "successful." In other words, they were providing a vital service to the country, and everything would all be so much worse if not for all of these caretakers holding this house together.

But it was easy to sense a creeping dilemma among them as the midpoint of Trump's term approached. The elected Republicans I talked to around town were quite torn and miserable at the predicaments they found themselves in.

"You become captive to whatever the latest thing is," said Senator Jeff Flake, another disaffected Republican. Every day brought a new "latest thing," set off by some late-night tweet from the White House or thrown-off threat or new report about Trump's contemplating an invasion of Venezuela or something. They would inevitably be asked about it in the hallways of the Capitol. They rarely stopped walking.

Who needed the hassle of belligerent presidential tweets, primary challenges, death threats? Their dialect was mostly glib ignorance ("didn't see the tweet") and circular nonsense ("Trump's going to do what Trump is going to do," said Senator Chuck Grassley of Iowa).

This was not what they signed up for, and how much longer did they care to stay? For the likes of Corker, Ryan, and others who carried on fraught relationships with the White House—and whose egos were invested in being perceived as serious government stewards—this was an ever-present question.

As a practical matter, the midterms were approaching: Corker and Flake would likely face primary challenges from Trumpier Republicans in Tennessee and Arizona, respectively, while Ryan confronted the threat of losing his speakership if Democrats won a majority in the House, as many were predicting. It was logical to ask when it would be time to leave.

THE ROSETTA STONE OF THE "DON'T WORRY, WE ARE THE ADULTS and we will protect you" genre appeared in the form of an anonymous *New York Times* op-ed whose publication was much fretted about inside the West Wing and speculated about all over Washington. The essay, whose author was later revealed to be the Department of Homeland Security official Miles Taylor, was headlined I AM PART OF THE RESISTANCE INSIDE THE TRUMP ADMINISTRATION, and contained the usual notes of self-congratulation dressed up as reassurance. "There is a quiet resistance within the administration of people choosing to put country first," Taylor wrote. It also proved itself quite fluent in the Toddler in Chief terminology. (The Tufts political scientist Daniel Drezner curated a volume of childlike descriptors that people used for Trump. He titled his book *The Toddler in Chief*.)

"Meetings with him veer off topic and off the rails," he reported. "He engages in repetitive rants, and his impulsiveness results in half-baked, ill-informed and occasionally reckless decisions."

The Mayday from inside the house could have easily been written from inside the House of Representatives. This included the Speaker's suite. Ryan fashioned himself an expert in this emerging field of presidential child psychology. "The pissing match doesn't work," he told me of his rules for engagement with Trump. Rule One: Do Not Provoke.

Ryan told me he preferred to tell Trump how he felt about things in private. He joined a large group of Trump's putative allies, many of whom worked in the administration, who insisted that they had successfully shaped Trump's thinking and behavior *in private*. "I can look myself in the mirror at the end of the day and say I avoided *that* tragedy, I avoided *that* tragedy, I avoided *that* tragedy," Ryan told me. "I advanced *this* goal, I advanced *this* goal, I advanced *this* goal."

Wait, "tragedy"? What tragedy?

My mind recoiled over what Ryan could have been talking about. I asked for an example. "No, I don't want to do that," Ryan replied. "That's more than I usually say."

KEVIN McCARTHY, THEN THE HOUSE MAJORITY LEADER, EXPLAINED to me that Trump and Ryan were "just wired differently."

McCarthy, an eager backslapper and political fanboy, had forged a sporadically productive partnership with Trump. He was cheerful and uncomplicated and telegenic, all of which were key components to being one of Trump's "guys." He also seemed quite starstruck at the idea of being pals with the guy in the White House. In many cases, the key psychological component to why so many top Republicans stayed beholden to the president was simply that it was cool.

In return, McCarthy was more than willing to genuflect before the president, lavish public affection, and be breathless in his praise—certainly compared with Ryan, who Trump felt never appreciated him enough.

Whereas Ryan considered himself a "movement" conservative, McCarthy was a pragmatic conservative. And for any Republican leader hoping to survive in these years, there was no more pragmatic consideration than not getting on Trump's bad side.

"He goes up and down with his anger," McCarthy told me later. "He's mad at everybody one day. He's mad at me one day. This is the tightest tightrope anyone has to walk."

McCarthy kept toggling between on and off the record. I asked him if he thought Ryan wished he could speak out more forcefully against Trump when the president offended him. "On the record or off the record?" McCarthy asked me.

On, I would prefer.

McCarthy paused and proceeded with care. "I think history will show that Paul spoke his own mind," he said.

AT MINIMUM, HISTORY WOULD SHOW THAT RYAN HAD HAD ENOUGH. The Speaker was at this moment just a few months removed from announcing he would not seek reelection, ending his twenty-year run as a member of Congress.

Ryan's departure became inevitable after a certain point. The MAGA types never trusted him. Yet he was still lampooned as one of Trump's chief enablers and portrayed as a weak supplicant.

The Never Trump conservatives—Ryan's natural allies—accused him of deserting his post as a potential conscience of the party, someone who was appalled but still went along. "Ryan traded his political soul," the anti-Trump conservative George F. Will wrote in his *Washington Post* column, "for . . . a tax cut."

"I'm very comfortable with the decisions I've made," Ryan told me. "I would make them again, do it again the same way." He was quick with his counterfactual. What if I did pick a fight with Trump every time the president did or said or tweeted something regrettable? "I think some people would like me to start a civil war in our party and achieve nothing," Ryan said.

The counter-counterfactual was this: Were Republican leaders so unwilling to condemn Trump because their voters supported him so vigorously, or did these voters support Trump so vigorously because so few Republican leaders ever dared condemn his actions? Chicken, egg; egg, chicken.

"I think in the real world, the people in my caucus mostly recognize that we're not in a normal period here," said Flake, who quit Trump early and became a regular target of the president's ire and an instant pariah in his party. I asked Flake, who did not seek reelection in 2018, if his fellow Republican senators even tried to defend Trump to him privately. "No," he said, chuckling. "Not his behavior, his character, or his policies, particularly." If there was any effort at all, Flake said, maybe his colleagues would insist they were supporting Trump in the spirit of GOP loyalty.

"The idea is to just embrace the president and hope he embraces you back," Flake said. "And then try to sleep at night."

This pretty much summed up the governing rationalization of the GOP as Trump devoured it. It became the price of admission to the party. To be fair, it could be quite a party.

Trump would invite his favorite caretakers over to the White House. He loved to give tours. The guests loved to publicize their visits. Right-leaning has-beens and luminaries could light up the place. Maybe they'd ask Lindsey Graham for help getting into the White House. (Sarah Palin and Ted Nugent were all over Instagram, posing with menace under a portrait of Hillary Clinton.) Trump provided a special thrill to a certain kind of political thrill seeker.

Congressman Gaetz, the try-hard Republican from Florida, was living his best life in the Trump years. The president loved "My Matt" for all his attention-grabbing acumen, especially when it worked in the service of

Trump's own grudges and fixations, or whatever delivered Gaetz to the promised land, on TV.

There, he would praise Trump, which made the president feel good. And afterward the president would call My Matt to thank him, which made the apprentice feel good, and everybody won.

FOR MORE SOBER-STYLED REPUBLICANS, THE MOST FOOLPROOF approach to Trump-proofing was to simply walk through the Capitol as if protected by a selectively permeable bubble, filtering out certain unwelcome words (for example, "Trump"). Mitch McConnell was the best at this. I caught the Senate Republican leader one day as he walked off the Senate floor. I asked him a question, about the former FBI director James Comey accusing Trump of lying about something or other.

He kept walking, his face stony and owlish. The McConnell Zombie Walk is familiar to any reporter who has spent time on Capitol Hill, but this was a rare privilege to be *exclusively* blown off by McConnell all the way down an otherwise empty hallway. It was just me alone with him and his security detail. I asked the question twice more, until we passed Lindsey Graham, who was walking in the other direction.

Graham had at that point been a font of Trump backhanded defenses. "He can't collude with his own government," Graham said on *Face the Nation*. "Why do you think he's colluding with the Russians?"

Graham had also suggested to reporters that it was no big deal that Comey had accused Trump of lying, because "everyone in the primary accused him of lying." Laughter ensued.

When I went to see Graham's Senate sidekick, John McCain, some months earlier, he seemed to be in a darker place. McCain, then eighty, had been traveling the globe to the point of weariness, seemingly on a personal mission to reassure allies who were unnerved by Trump. "Make no mistake, my friends, these are dangerous times," McCain said at a security conference in Munich a few months earlier. "In many respects, this administration is in disarray."

McCain was also battling an insidious form of brain cancer that would eventually end his life. But McCain was still ambulatory enough to come to work and impede Trump's agenda—never more than when he cast the deciding vote against Republican efforts to kill Obamacare. This only made Trump loathe McCain more than he already did, and the feeling was quite mutual.

"Whatever, I don't care," McCain said, then caught himself. "I care. But I'm not going to react. I think it was gradual. First shock, then surprise, then Whiskey Tango Foxtrot"—military slang for "What the fuck," or "WTF," both of which were being heard a lot around the capital in these days.

McCain promoted the ideal that it was the duty of a citizen-patriot to take on "a cause greater than himself." This, he believed, was a most righteous undertaking, and the opposite of the only cause Trump ever cared about—the cause of himself. To McCain, the essence of "a cause greater than himself" was finding a worthy tormentor, a proper bully, and fighting like hell against them. He viewed the necessity of opposing Trump in that spirit.

This was obviously not easy for his Republican colleagues to do. They rationalized every which way against it. "This is not supposed to be easy," McCain told me in 2017. He understood self-interest and opportunism. "But it's the right thing to do," he said about Republicans being willing to defy Trump. "It's an important cause. So where is everyone?"

CHAPTER 10

FUNERAL PORN

———

Don't let your coattails hit you in the ass.

—John Tower

August 2018

My last conversation with Senator McCain was about self-respect. As in, what happened to it?

A lot of his Republican colleagues were driving him nuts. They all understood the calamity atop the executive branch, yet they kept kowtowing. "I have no idea what some of my friends are thinking when it comes to this character," he told me. He was not naming his "friends," though it was clear that "this character" resided in the White House.

"It's just unbelievable to me what some people are willing to live with," McCain said. "It comes down to self-respect."

Our encounter took place in a basement hallway of the Russell Senate Office Building. "Hey, what's the difference between a lawyer and a catfish?" I yelled at McCain when I saw him rounding the corner. It's a joke I'd heard him tell a million times. McCain liked jokes, and the "one about the catfish" was my go-to icebreaker. He always humored me with the punch line, regardless of his mood.

"One is a bottom-feeding scum sucker," McCain replied dutifully. "And the other is a fish."

It was December 2017, a few months after McCain had been diagnosed with the terminal brain cancer, glioblastoma, that would later kill him. The six-term senator tried to carry on as normally as he could and had just returned from the wedding of his daughter Meghan in Arizona. A few days later, McCain came down with pneumonia and, soon after, departed Washington for the last time.

I'd known McCain for about two decades, going back to the joyride of his first presidential escapade of 2000. He referred to the media as "my base" and his campaign bus as "the Straight Talk Express." He let pretty much anyone onto the bus and in on the joke. He held forth for long stretches, telling stories, mocking the sound-bite approaches of his opponents and their "professional campaigns," namely that of the front-runner, George W. Bush.

The novelist David Foster Wallace, writing in *Rolling Stone*, described that iteration of Candidate McCain as someone who "acts somewhat in the ballpark of the way a real human being would act." (By contrast, Wallace quoted a CNN sound tech describing Al Gore as "amazingly lifelike.") Central to that human quality was that McCain had survived three plane crashes, cancer, public disgrace, and, above all, five and a half years of torture in a North Vietnamese POW camp that left him unable to raise his arms over his head.

McCain was the ultimate "house's money" politician. When you passed a big chunk of your life in solitary confinement on the other side of the world, you accrue lots of FOMO. You try to be every place at once and say everything you need to say. As Bob Dole said of McCain, "You spend five years in a box, and you're entitled to speak your mind."

McCain spoke his mind. He drank vodka on ice and loved snacking on Chuckles (the fruit jellies). Maybe his public persona could contain shtick at times, but that was true of most politicians. They become captives to their own acts. McCain, for his part, had been captive to the North Vietnamese, and when he was finally free, he had little interest in being tied down any more than he had to be.

McCain had gone through many acts as both a Washington icon and an iconoclast. He was McCain the Maverick for many years. He would later become known as a bipartisan bridge builder, sore loser, sacred cow, old bull, lion in winter, and (sometimes) happy warrior. You lost track of which McCain caricature was operational at a given moment. He did, too. "I think I was the brave maverick when I was taking on Bush, and then I was the bitter old man when I was criticizing Obamacare," McCain told me in 2013. "You know, there are second acts in American politics." I asked him how many second acts he'd had at that point. "I've probably gone through twenty-five, twenty-six, something like that," McCain said, and then laughed his wise-guy cackle, like the Penguin from Batman.

He had a favorite Teddy Roosevelt phrase, "the crowded hour," which the twenty-sixth president used to describe his charge on San Juan Hill. In TR's philosophy, "the crowded hour" referred to a warrior's moment of truth, a seminal and rollicking time that would test their mettle. McCain always claimed to be in the middle of some "crowded hour" of his life, placing him at the center of whatever the mortal drama of the moment was.

He was a regular viewer and guest on the Sunday talk shows and loved that he'd been on NBC's *Meet the Press* more times than any of his colleagues. They, his fellow senators, would ask McCain if he could put in a good word with Stephanopoulos or Schieffer or whomever. McCain loved to advertise this, wielding his high demand in the guise of being magnanimous. Sure, he would do what he could. To whom much airtime was given, much was required.

"The biggest fear John has is not being relevant," Lindsey Graham told me. "He worried after he lost the election in 2008. He worried, okay, I'm done, nobody wants to deal with a loser." McCain had another favorite line, one of his hundreds, which he attributed to the late Texas senator John Tower. "Don't let your coattails hit you in the ass," Tower told him once. "Keep moving."

McCAIN INVITED ME TO STOP BY HIS OFFICE LATER THAT DAY. THIS seemed unlikely to happen, given the fragile state of his health and how protective his staff had been of his time and stamina. Julie Tarallo, McCain's spokeswoman who was with him in the Russell Building, shot me a look, seemingly a signal to wrap up our hallway confab.

"What else, what else?" McCain then said, not ready to wrap up. "You see what our president said today?" Trump had put out some tweet about NATO.

"I understand why so many people in my party are so terrified of getting on the wrong side of the president," McCain said. "They don't want to get the shit kicked out of them by Limbaugh, Hannity, the tweets, all that. It's no fun. I get it. Trump can cost them their jobs, and they like their jobs. I get that, too. Every elected official makes certain calculations." Again, McCain understood the Calculation as well as anyone. Senators can't be effective if voters fire them, right?

"But it's just so over-the-top with this guy," McCain said of Trump. "The Russia stuff, the lies, the bullying, the ignorance, the bullshit. Look, I know I'm not going to be here much longer. But I'd like to think that even if that weren't the case, I would have enough self-respect not to kiss his ass like this."

McCain died on August 25, 2018, at eighty-one, at his home in Cornville, Arizona.

I learned the news from my daughter via an alert on her phone while we were eating dinner. It was no shock, obviously, but it was still as jarring as any politician's passing that I could recall. McCain was such a fixture in the life of Washington. The man lived *conspicuously*. I felt I knew him as well as perhaps anyone I'd covered. Yes, a lot of people felt as if they knew McCain. He was a man of many clichés, including the one about how he was good copy and how many media hacks felt as if they "knew" him. I guess that made me my own cliché.

I'd profiled McCain maybe a dozen times through his various campaigns, crusades, and next acts. He addressed me as "a jerk" and "my boy," both familiar McCain terms of endearment. He would introduce me to people as "a Trotskyite reporter from *The New York Times*" and someone who was "part of a work-release program" and who "just got out of the Betty Ford clinic."

I'd been to McCain's home in Phoenix, out to eat with his family, and a passenger in many cars he'd driven (harrowingly) through the heavy traffic of Washington, Phoenix, and Northern Virginia. I attended Arizona Diamondbacks and Phoenix Coyotes games with him. McCain was one of the few politicians fans would cheer when he arrived at sporting events. "Thank you for your service, Senator," they would yell to him.

"They always say this," McCain told me after another fan at the Coyotes game did. "Usually right before they unload on me."

I had seen McCain heckle professional athletes—actually tell them that they sucked. Politicians don't typically do this.

I had heard McCain go off on a million random asides, which he would deliver as if he were making the most fascinating point of his life. We were on a two-hour car ride from Phoenix to Tucson, and someone mentioned Mike Enzi, his affable Senate colleague from Wyoming, and McCain was launched.

"Have you seen that Geico ad?" McCain said to no one in particular. "Mike Enzi looks exactly like the guy in that Geico ad. He talks like him, too. It's the damnedest thing!"

Another damnedest thing: Fiji, the island nation in the South Pacific where McCain used to vacation. "They are lovely, gentle people," McCain raved about the Fijians, "even though they used to eat each other."

McCain could be opportunistic, full of himself, and, yes, completely full of shit at times. This could be especially true when he was up for election. For as much as McCain was known for his truth-to-power rebellions—calling Jerry Falwell and Pat Robertson "agents of intolerance"—he was not above sucking up to the base as necessary.

There was his reelection campaign in 2010, in which McCain, a pro-immigration Republican for many years, became a tough-talking border hawk. He went off about "all the illegals in Arizona" and said in a campaign ad that it was time to "complete the dang fence." No one recalled McCain ever talking like this in real life, let alone using the word "dang." "John did what he had to do," Graham said.

Nor did McCain even bother to claim Sarah Palin was anything but a straight-up political choice to be his running mate in 2008—a convenient, Alaska-sized loophole in his "Country First" motto.

McCain also had an impressive capacity for grudges. He went years without speaking to *New York Times* reporters after our paper published an article in February 2008 that suggested he'd had an affair with a Washington lobbyist, Vicki Iseman. Both parties denied a romantic involvement, and Iseman went on to sue my employer. (She later dropped the suit, after the *Times* agreed to print a note to readers saying the story did not mean to imply a sexual relationship.)

"I will never forgive *The New York Times* for what they did," McCain told me in 2013, in the first interview he granted to the *Times* in five and a half years. He said he agreed to the interview only because I had "a preexisting condition."

McCAIN SPENT MUCH OF HIS FINAL YEAR RECEIVING OLD FRIENDS on the deck of his family compound near Sedona ("the cabin," as he referred to the multi-dwelling ranch). He despaired over the damage Trump had been inflicting on the country. "We talked about how our international reputation is being damaged and we talked about the need for people to stand up and speak out," said one of his guests, his former colleague Joe Biden. McCain tried to avoid sentimental displays and was loath to treat these visits from friends to Sedona as goodbyes. He would typically end them by saying, "I love you."

He was fond of cold assessments about life and death and legacies. "This will all be over someday, and no one's gonna give a shit who I used to be," McCain would often say, in so many words. But he clearly did give a shit, at least about the choreography of his last act. To ensure a proper send-off, McCain took a direct role in planning his memorial services, all six of them (multiple funerals are an essential flex for any proper D.C. bigwig). There was the service at North Phoenix Baptist

Church, the public viewing at the Arizona Capitol, the ceremony at the U.S. Naval Academy, the one at the U.S. Capitol Rotunda, the wreath laying at the Vietnam Memorial, and the granddaddy of them all at the National Cathedral, preceding the burial back in Annapolis.

Following his terminal diagnosis, McCain convened regular Friday sessions to plan his departure rites. He made his wishes known about pallbearers, hymns, prayers, eulogies, and eulogists. He wanted his program to feature a murderers' row of speakers. They included the forty-third and forty-fourth commanders in chief—George W. Bush and Barack Obama—both of whom had inflicted defeats upon McCain in his two presidential campaigns. "It was almost as if he was planning someone else's funeral," McCain's longtime campaign adviser Rick Davis observed. "He was really excited about it."

Along with his wife, Cindy, McCain dictated who should be invited and, more to the point, who should not be. Palin did not make the cut. Neither, for various reasons, did some of his higher-profile aides from 2000 or 2008 (John Weaver, Mike Murphy). To no one's surprise, the forty-fifth president topped John McCain's final shit list. "I'm sure he would rather play golf," McCain said when the subject of inviting Trump was raised in one of the planning meetings.

Trump's name was never mentioned over the four-day celebration of McCain's life, and no doubt that was the unkindest cut of all for the Viewer in Chief. His prominent non-presence, however, loomed as the embodiment of everything the departed had despised.

The thematic juxtapositions were glaring, especially this one: Washington was not merely celebrating McCain's life; it was contrasting it—or the myth of it—with everything the White House and its saps and weaklings had become under the forty-fifth president.

The narrative was set early. Washington's old, credentialed officers—a government in exile, they'd have us believe—were striking back, forcefully. They were armed with killer eulogies and hot cable takes.

"A sustained rebellion against the president's worldview and his singular brand of politics" is what this was, per Greg Jaffe and Philip Rucker in *The Washington Post*. The full tableau, they concluded, "served as a melancholy last hurrah for the sort of global leadership that the nation once took for granted."

Like everything, the McCain extravaganza became its own Trump-era Rorschach spectacle. It was (I suppose) nice that the right boldfaced leaders could declare this to be some sort of turning point away from the darkness. Speaker of the House Paul Ryan said that McCain's death offered us a rare opportunity to take stock and better our angels and try to be uplifting.

"We have this beautiful thing, the chance to do for this man what he did for us," Ryan said of McCain at the Capitol Rotunda service. "To stand up. To stand up and embrace the cause of his life."

Ryan, of course, had already stood down, having announced his retirement from Congress, at forty-eight, a few months earlier. He went on to reap a fortune in consulting and speaking fees, as well as a seat on the board of Fox Corp.

McCAIN'S CULMINATING VALEDICTION AT THE NATIONAL CATHE-dral took place on a cloudy Saturday morning. It featured a large delegation of Usual Suspects and a heavy concentration of people who knew where all the fun-sized Kit Kats were hidden in the local greenrooms. They lined up and down Wisconsin Avenue starting three hours before the service, alongside satellite trucks and media tent cities. There were designated entrances for the various classes of guests: one door for members of Congress; one for family, media, Senate staff, church staff, military, and special "protectees" (that is, those requiring protective details).

Henry Kissinger hunched over his cane as he entered the sanctuary. Mitt and Ann Romney headed in not far behind hm. The former POTUSes and FLOTUSes George and Laura and Bill and Hill and Barack and Michelle all made the trip. Former/Future Speakers Pelosi and Ryan, Leaders McConnell and Schumer, too.

Gary Hart's hair had gone cottony white (he looked like a cloud), Jay Leno dropped in, Jeff Bezos, too, with his still-wife, MacKenzie. Bezos now owned *The Washington Post*, and he could buy the National Cathedral, too, if he wanted—fully furnished with power mourners, and then send them all into space.

As the service approached, one momentous Washington figure after another soldiered into the elite rows. Dick and Lynne Cheney, Al Gore, John Kerry, all still here, or never left. Bob Dole wheeled in, still hanging on at ninety-five. The camera shots kept landing on Dole in his chair, looking solemn.

The tribute was packed with the full fun-sized assortment behind stained glass: clusters of foreign leaders (presidents of Ukraine and Panama), sprinklings from Hollywood (Warren Beatty, Annette Bening), war heroes, war criminals, and warhorses.

Secretary of Defense Jim Mattis and the White House chief of staff, John Kelly, escorted Cindy McCain from the wreath laying at the Vietnam Veterans Memorial. Trump, who at that moment was tweeting about how he'd been screwed by the courts, apparently took Mattis's and Kelly's presence as an act of disloyalty. How could his generals do this to him? Losers!

Rudy Giuliani was here, too. He liked McCain. They were simpatico once, smoked a few cigars together and shared some laughs. I remember Rudy co-hosting a birthday party for McCain at Cipriani during the 2004 Republican National Convention in New York. This was back when Rudy was still America's Mayor, very much still dining out on 9/11, and not yet dining out at the Trump Hotel.

IN DEATH, AS IN LIFE, JOHN MCCAIN STOOD FOR ANOTHER CHER-ished American asset: media overkill.

The cable networks kicked into their "Special Report: A Nation Mourns" modes. No shortage of *trained observers* were eager to pre-game the National Cathedral service.

"A statement about the bigness of America," MSNBC's Kasie Hunt would declare of this solemn observance. Or maybe, Hunt allowed, it could all be taken as "a funeral for civility." This one could go either way.

The pundit-historian-theologian Jon Meacham, who would eulogize Bush 41 in this same church two months later and would go on to write speeches for Joe Biden, ministered through his live shots. You know it's a momentous Washington ceremony when Meacham gets called in. Where did this Great Deceased Man fit into *the American story?* Only Meacham knew for sure.

I did recall something Meacham had observed in another context. We were discussing how politicians who descend from famous lineages— Liz Cheney, Mitt Romney—tend to place greater weight upon notions of history and reputation than others who do not. McCain, the son and grandson of decorated navy admirals, fit the pattern. "'What will be said of me?' 'What will my character be in history?'" asked Meacham, channeling political heirs. "The people with familial antecedents in the business have tended to understand that a good character in history, a good story, requires standing up to the prevailing sentiments of the hour."

Steve Schmidt, a longtime Republican bulldog who turned hard against Trump and whose emphatic cable diatribes made him a Never Trump icon, was another stalwart of McCain commentary. "John McCain was a great patriot," said Schmidt, who was a top aide to the 2008 presidential campaign. "He more perfectly loved this country than any man I've ever known." McCain, however, did not "perfectly love" Steve Schmidt by the end, for a variety of reasons, and Schmidt, too, wound up among the uninvited.

"This was John McCain's way of shoving it up Donald Trump's ass," the greenroom eminence Al Hunt told me outside the basilica. "Leon Panetta just told me that." Yes, he did, and quite conspicuously. Panetta practically shouted the words and did the old Italian fuck-you arm salute for good measure, drawing stares outside the church.

The pageant called for every sober sage on deck. Tom Brokaw came down from New York. We chatted in front of the church before the ceremony. People kept spotting him and thanking him for his service, though Brokaw himself had never actually served, at least in any wars. He *had*, however, penned a blockbuster book—*The Greatest Generation*—about those who did serve, which was not nothing. At the very least, Brokaw was a commanding officer in the Greatest Generation of TV context givers.

Aside: Brokaw reminded me that we had first met nearly a decade earlier, in Boston, outside the grand memorial of Ted Kennedy. Kennedy, who was killed by the same hideous brain cancer, glioblastoma, that would do in McCain, was another whose proverbial likes would not be seen again. That was another damp day in the late summer, with dignitaries everywhere, a lofty cathedral, and multiple presidents in the front rows.

Mourners kept running up to thank Brokaw there, too. Finally, after about the fourth interruption, Brokaw turned to me and muttered, "It's not easy being a fucking American treasure, you know?" He had me at "fucking American treasure."

AS THEY AWAITED THE ARRIVAL OF McCAIN'S CASKET, THE "PRO-tectees" milled about next to the pews. Ivanka and Jared stationed themselves along the center aisle near the dais, and a loose receiving line materialized. Inviting *them* was Lindsey's idea. He thought it would be a nice gesture to have the First Daughter and First Son-in-Law represent the absent president. He managed to get an okay from Cindy McCain. "I feel like Match.com sometimes," Graham told me.

Ivanka looked self-conscious, as if she felt people staring at her (they were). She smiled a tight petrified smile and tried to blend in, but it was futile. This was not a Trump *property* by any means. This was not her father's funeral.

Everyone fell into brunch mode. Uncle Lindsey kept patting Jared's triceps. Joe and Hadassah Lieberman stopped over. Ivanka seemed to chitchat at one point with Hillary Clinton, though it was hard to tell. (Wasn't Ivanka once friendly with Chelsea? I think I remember reading that.) Dole came over in his wheelchair and wanted a quick word with the president's daughter, while Jared whipped around to get the attention of a Secret Service agent—maybe to order a Bloody Mary.

Random members of Congress hovered around the perimeter. Representative Eliot Engel of New York parked himself just off a main thoroughfare, much as he always did before State of the Union addresses, the better to get in the camera shot. (Voters in his North Bronx and southern Westchester district would remove Engel from the shot soon enough.)

I saw Giuliani chatting with Graham. They were chuckling over something. Senator Schumer sidled up to McCain's close friend Grant Woods and tried to recruit him to run for McCain's old Senate seat. Woods, a former attorney general of Arizona, said this was not the right time or place.

Places were taken. George W. slipped a cough drop to Michelle Obama. Silence fell until it was pierced by a flurry of camera shutters that greeted the arrival of the casket. Hymns and salutes and the wail of thousands of organ pipes filled the church to usher in this Crowded Hour of tributes. They lasted more than two hours, the tributes did, because there was much ground to cover.

"WE GATHER HERE TO MOURN THE PASSING OF AMERICAN GREATness, the real thing, not cheap rhetoric from men who will never come near the sacrifice he gave so willingly," eulogized Meghan McCain, the senator's daughter. She spoke through stifled sobs. "America does not boast, because she has no need to," she concluded. "The America of John McCain has no need to be made great again because America was always great."

John McCain was dead. Subtlety was also dead.

Each marquee speech contained passages that slapped directly upon the unwelcome, unmentioned scourge in the White House. "When all was said and done, we were on the same team," Obama said of himself and McCain. "We never doubted that we were on the same team," he said again. The question hung there: What team was the current president on, anyway? Not theirs, was the clear message. No way Donald Trump belonged in this club.

"It was almost as if it were a meeting of Washington's political underground," my *Times* colleague Peter Baker wrote in his funeral game story, "if the underground met in a grand cathedral with 10,650 organ pipes."

But if it was really a "rebellion against the president's worldview," it would be a brief and bloodless one. You could also make a case that Trump's pariah status at an event like this was precisely why his base loved him so much. The assembled Washington respect payers had collectively nurtured all the notions, false promises, and wars that put Trump in the White House to begin with—Vietnam, Afghanistan, Iraq, deficits, gridlock, cynicism, decadence, and anything that fit under the foul heading of "the Swamp."

In his eulogy, Bush instructed mourners to always imagine McCain whispering over their shoulders. The capital never lacked for dead voices said to be exhorting us to greatness. "We are better than this," Bush said, quoting the mythic figurine of McCain's ghost. "America is better than this!"

That felt unsettled. But we all have stories we tell ourselves.

I WALKED HOME FROM THE NATIONAL CATHEDRAL, WONDERING what to make of it all. The tributes were deemed worthy of their recipient, and McCain was given his full due—if only he could have been there, among the living, to enjoy his last party, or (if you prefer) this "passing of American greatness."

If the latter was true, if this really did spell the end of our national greatness, the power mourners in attendance did not seem that broken up about the demise. Biden, one of McCain's eulogists in Arizona, looked tanned and about ten years younger than he did when he left the vice president's office. He was out of public life for the first time in forty-four years and enjoying his grandkids and finally making some money. And good for Biden, he'd earned the right to live a little. "Call me if you need me for anything," he would say.

George W. Bush would go back to silently painting in Texas; the Obamas (flush with their $65 million memoir deals) returned to the Vineyard. Giuliani would soon be off to Ukraine for his next thing, and ours.

And the navy band played on for John McCain, whose words kept crawling through my brain, these in particular: "It's always darkest before it's totally black, my boy."

CHAPTER 11

STINKBALL

———

I don't like what he says about John McCain. But when
we play golf, it's fun.

—Lindsey Graham

December 2018

Trump in fact did spend the morning of McCain's National Cathedral ceremony at his Virginia golf course, proving himself yet again to be perhaps the greatest self-parodist in history. He could barely bring himself to acknowledge the storied senator's passing. He did manage to tweet that his "hearts and prayers" were with the McCain family, but otherwise Trump played his barstool jackass role to the hilt all week.

He grudgingly agreed to lower the White House flag to half-staff on Saturday but then returned it to full staff on Monday, only to re-lower it after veterans' groups complained. He seethed through days of memorial TV coverage of McCain, which he could not help but consume and naturally took as a personal affront. "He just watched it all, and kept getting more and more mad," one White House aide told me. He described the president's state of mind as "a jealous rage." But at least he offered "hearts and prayers."

He tweeted through much of McCain's grand cathedral adieu: about how the Mueller investigation was rigged "to spy on Barrack [sic] Obama and Hillary Clinton's political opponents" and that "this is the real scandal here." The usual, in other words.

Lindsey Graham, who read from the Gospels at the National Cathedral, called Trump's reactions to his best friend's death "disturbing." But he got over it quickly and was back golfing with the president soon enough.

Where to begin with Lindsey? His sudden solicitousness toward the president had become a persistent curiosity. It had befuddled his friends and colleagues for months. He came to occupy a distinct category of Trump-era contortionist, whose dash from the side of McCain to McCain's archnemesis occurred with breathtaking speed and chutzpah.

No Republican spoke with more contempt for Trump during the 2016 primaries than Graham had. "I think he's a kook, I think he's crazy," he said, among other things ("a complete idiot," "a race-baiting, xenophobic bigot," "unfit for office"). But then Trump became president and deemed Graham fit to play golf with him. And suddenly Graham was getting described in the press as a "presidential confidant." How thrilling was that? His colleagues would ask if he could help get a message to the president about a donor or a birthday call to a family member.

Republicans would seek Lindsey out for help getting an invite to the White House (or some other Trump enterprise, like Mar-a-Lago). "I try to be helpful," he would always say, philanthropically.

By the end of his life, McCain could barely contain his disgust for Graham's servile devotion to Trump. Yes, McCain understood his friend's impulse to have a relationship with a president, especially one from his own party. He recognized the potency of the relevance drug and understood the finesse involved with emphasizing certain base-friendly positions when you're in an election year. If you were Graham running in deep red South Carolina, what could impress the base more than becoming a Gilligan to Donald Trump's Skipper?

Bottom line: any ambivalence Graham had over Trump's conduct (for example, for trashing his best friend to the grave and beyond) was eclipsed by his desperation to remain a U.S. senator. And being close to Trump was extremely "helpful" in that regard.

Now that the midterms were over, Graham was officially "in cycle," meaning he would be on the ballot in South Carolina for his next election, in 2020. He saw what had happened to his Republican colleagues who did not properly nuzzle up to the Almighty in 2018. The principled Jeff Flakes and Bob Corkers of the Senate became instant Trump roadkill. More to the point, they became ex-senators. If Flake and Corker hadn't canceled themselves first (neither sought reelection), it's likely some Trumpier primary opponent would have come along and done the deed for them. McCain knew this as well as anyone, Graham kept saying.

What McCain objected to most in his final months was the theatrical degree to which Graham was willing to submit to Trump. "Do you really have to keep saying how great of a fucking golfer he is?" McCain would ask Graham. Graham was becoming an object of ridicule, McCain told him. Late-night comedians made certain of that: Seth Meyers observed that Graham would wear the same golf clothes as his master, "like a Chihuahua whose owner makes him wear matching outfits."

Graham could lay it on quite thick with Trump, and not just about golf. He would tell Trump how great of a job he was doing as *"my president."*

"God bless you for undoing the damage done in the last eight years." he told Trump during one golf outing in Palm Beach in late 2017. He told the president how "masterful" he was during an Oval Office confab about immigration. He told Trump he was doing "historic" things and "bringing America back" and becoming "the anti-Obama." He stroked all the Trump erogenous zones.

Après golf, Graham would promptly jump on Twitter to pleasure the president about what "a spectacular golf course" Trump International in Palm Beach was. What's the harm in throwing some free advertising to the commander in chief's private business? It was a small price to pay, Graham figured, for those priceless photos of the two of them on the fairway, Graham trailing a few caddy-like paces behind. How many TV ads would he have to buy in South Carolina to get a boost like that? Again, November 2020 got a little closer every day. Graham knew to focus accordingly, inhabit his "in cycle" self.

"Lindsey was really good at this game," one senior White House official said. He did not mean golf. Rather, the game of playing Trump. Graham was a scratch performer. He could be stunningly open about how easy a mark Trump was.

Flattery was always important with Trump, Graham said, but there was an art to it. "If you flatter him all the time, he'll lose respect for you," he told me. If Graham wanted Trump to do something, especially on foreign policy, he would just tell him Obama would do the opposite. "That could be very effective," Graham said. "Obama drives him nuts."

After he got to know Trump, Graham said he developed genuine affection for the man. Trump was a familiar type to Graham, as someone who grew up in the hospitality business. His parents ran a dive bar, called the Sanitary Café, in the rural South Carolina town of Central. "People who are in the retail business, the hospitality business, have a personality like Trump does, if you're any good at it," Graham told me. "He wants you to have a good time."

For his part, McCain thought Graham was having too good of a time with Trump. "Where's your self-respect?" he would ask, in various ways, whenever Graham started gushing over another golf outing with the president.

Graham had no real answer but chalked up McCain's pique to being frustrated about his health. His advancing tumors and aggressive treatments had left McCain isolated and stir-crazy. "If you want to torture John McCain, put him on a cruise ship," Graham explained. And then add brain cancer. "He was not in the best of spirits, let's say."

He knew the end was coming, but McCain's death still leveled Graham. He was left adrift and disoriented. Nearly every Graham story of the last two decades involved McCain. The two of them, along with Joe Lieberman—the so-called Three Amigos—would go on madcap international tours, zipping into volatile countries, rarely spending more than a night in the same hotel. "They were inseparable," said Susan Collins, the Republican senator from Maine, speaking about McCain and Graham. "John's death really left a hole in his heart. It seemed like Lindsey had lost a father."

Like McCain, Graham had a preternatural desire to be in the middle of things. He hated being alone and subsisted on adrenaline. "The most important goal to Lindsey is staying in the game," said Jim Hodges, a former South Carolina governor who attended law school with Graham at the University of South Carolina. That was one of the big draws of McCain. He was all action and friction. It was always exciting.

"John's favorite game was dice," Graham said. "If you spend any time at a dice table, it's like crack addicts. Everybody is around there waiting for the next roll, and it has its own energy. So there's a sort of frenetic feel. There's nothing that makes you more alive in my view than being involved in something of consequence. It's almost addictive."

So was being a player in the Senate. You do what it takes to keep the fixes coming.

GRAHAM SOBBED HIS WAY THROUGH A SENATE FLOOR TRIBUTE TO McCain—"my political wingman," he called him. "It's going to be a lonely journey for me for a while," Graham told his colleagues. He appeared wobbly.

"Lindsey is one of the most engaging country lawyers I've ever seen," said Senator Chris Coons, Democrat of Delaware. "He is agile on his feet. But he was so flattened by John's passing, I found those remarks to be scattered and broken. It gives you a window."

People who have known Graham a long time said that certain politicians are simply born to be sidekicks and second fiddles. Graham was a prototype. He was happy to reap political nourishment from a guardian. This can be a debasing look, but Graham was okay being debased. It became part of his shtick.

Graham's Senate colleagues described him as a kind of sitcom sidekick with a knack for finding himself in sad-sack situations. It struck many people who know him as apt that Trump would decide to yell out Graham's cell phone number at a campaign event in 2015 after Graham had said Trump was a "jackass." He urged everyone to call. Graham later made a video dramatizing all the ways to destroy a cell phone. After their eventual détente, he told Trump that the entire episode was "the high-light of my campaign."

Trump and Graham both loved this story and repeated it often. It reinforced both of their roles, the bully and the bullied, the king and the jester. Graham found this dynamic good for business. It got him teased onstage at Trump rallies. It got him into the clubhouse. It got him on TV.

Graham freely admitted that he needed Trump to survive. Trump kept him fed and employed. He did not care if his approach could seem parasitic. He could live with the unflattering assessments from the Never Trumpers. Graham said they themselves were parasites, for they derived lucrative media profiles from their own cultivated hatreds of Trump. In that sense, Trump kept *them* fed and employed, too.

"It is a mistake to think there is inconsistency between the McCain era and Trump Era," said Steve Schmidt, the former Bush and McCain adviser. "Graham is essentially a pilot fish. They eat parasites and live off the detritus of larger fish. McCain was a noble shark who sustained his pilot fish. This did not make the Pilot fish noble though, just well fed. Sometimes Pilot fish move on. They are not loyal or faithful. Just hungry. Today he lives off of the vile detritus of his new host, Trump. He is indifferent to the disgustingness. He just wants his little piece."

GRAHAM WAS ALWAYS A TAGALONG FIGURE, GOING BACK TO HIS boyhood spent around the family saloon. Short and pudgy, he played the child mascot to the small-town characters who passed through the Sanitary Café. "I was conscious," Graham wrote in his 2015 memoir, *My Story*, "that I was giving a performance." The regulars referred to young Lindsey as "Stinkball."

He always gravitated to custodial, larger-than-life figures. "Alpha dogs," Graham called them. He followed his father everywhere. "I came along late in my dad's life, and he made the most of our time together," Graham wrote. "Whatever he did, he did it with me."

Graham's parents both died when he was in his early twenties. He never married or had children, and his sexuality has long been the subject of whispered speculation around the capital—pretty much what you'd expect about any sixty-five-year-old bachelor in the Senate.

With his practiced shrug, Graham would always insist that he wasn't, you know, gay. "Don't believe anything anybody tells you about my Air Force exploits," he once joked about his tour of duty in Paris and Rome. "I was very heterosexual, that's all you need to know."

He later held out the possibility that he might be sleeping with Ricky Martin. Nah, kidding, KIDDING! "I know it's really gonna upset a lot of gay men—I'm sure hundreds of them are gonna be jumping off the Golden Gate Bridge—but I ain't available. I ain't gay. Sorry."

Just as Graham had described the Sanitary Café regulars as his extended family growing up, he relied on the Senate as a surrogate brood in his adulthood.

"Lindsey would be lost and irrelevant without the Senate," said Grant Woods. "What's he going to do, practice law in South Carolina or something? He couldn't deal with that."

In that equation, the ailing McCain was less useful—less relevant—to Graham than Trump was. It might sound callous, Woods said, but Graham was simply playing a long game. "He knew John was a short timer," he said. "Trump was Lindsey's new meal ticket. John knew exactly what he was doing. I can't say he was happy about it, but he definitely knew."

Graham had minimal regard for Trump as a serious thinker and moral human being. That was evident to anyone Graham spoke with privately. But he also reserved a certain awe for his new patron. He couldn't believe how Trump could endure the crises he did or got away with what he got away with. It created a mystique around Trump, especially among politicians, who tend to be rule-bound by nature, mindful of precedents, and terrified of being shamed. Trump had no such inclination toward rules or common respect and no capacity for shame or embarrassment. He was a pure and feral rascal. It gave him the advantage of being bulletproof in his own scrambled head.

Some of the most hard-boiled politicians I knew, people who dealt with all kinds of schemers and scoundrels in their careers, reserved a perverse curiosity about this president. "Trump is an interesting person," said Harry Reid, the former Democratic Senate leader who did battle with Las Vegas mob bosses as Nevada's gaming commissioner in the 1970s. "He's not immoral, but he is amoral. Amoral is when you shoot someone in the head, it doesn't make a difference. No conscience." Like many of his former colleagues, Reid spoke of Trump as a textbook sociopath. A hint of boyish curiosity crept into Reid's tone, which he seemed to catch and correct.

"I think he is without question the worst president we've ever had," he said. "He'll lie. He'll cheat. You can't reason with him." Once more, Reid's voice assumed a flash of wonder, as if he were describing a rogue beast on the loose in a jungle that he knew well.

Stinkball Graham also knew it well. He clung to Trump as a political bodyguard and ringleader and new identity.

Whenever I watched Graham in Trump's presence, he would stare up at his supervisor with a kind of swooning grin. I saw them heading to dinner one night at Trump's hotel, along with a top-level Greek chorus that included Pence and Secretary of the Treasury Mnuchin. Graham kept his eyes fixed on the president like a moon-faced high school nerd who couldn't believe his good fortune that the class bully was letting him hang with him. He had to know the bully would take his snack money soon enough, but still, wasn't this a trip?

He often spoke breathlessly about their conversations. "I just was talking with him this morning," Graham volunteered to me as I sat in his Senate office early one evening. This was shortly before Trump was scheduled to deliver his State of the Union address in early 2019. "He wanted my advice on what tone he should take in his address," Graham said. "Should I go conciliatory or to-hell-with-it?" Graham's voice assumed a strange, racing cadence, like an exhilarated Little Leaguer describing a big hit.

"He once asked me if he should invade Venezuela," Graham added, chuckling (Graham said he advised against it). Trump also dispatched Graham to Pakistan. "When I talked to the people in Pakistan, they know I'm close to the president, and that I'm going to be able to report back to him." His head shook up and down.

"I've never had that kind of influence before. To me, it's exciting."

It was also, as Graham likes to say, "helpful." In a political sense, certainly. Graham had always been a figure of suspicion among Republicans in South Carolina. They were wary of his friendships with Democrats, his bond with that troublemaker McCain, and his checkered history with Trump. One party activist used to drive around the state with a Graham effigy stuffed headfirst into a toilet.

Since Graham became Trump approved, however, the distrust from the Republican base became less of a problem. "I've never been more popular than I am right now in South Carolina," Graham told me. "The people at home like what I'm doing with Trump."

Graham's tone with me reflected a mixture of amazement and

amusement, with a dash of giddiness. "It's weird, and it's flattering," Graham told me of the attention he received from Trump. "It creates some opportunity. It also creates some pressure."

I asked Graham if he considered himself part of the wider Trump orbit or the more select one. "Well, I'm getting into the smaller orbit now," he said. I asked him who else was in there. He mentioned Melania, Ivanka, Jared. "He's got a bunch of old friends that still have a say, New York types," Graham said. "But the circle is small."

THE DAY BEFORE, GRAHAM HAD BEEN IN GREENVILLE, SOUTH CARO-lina, to address a luncheon of local Republicans, many he'd known for decades.

Graham began his speech in his familiar lounge-act mode. "I'm from the federal government, I'm here to help," he said—a Ronald Reagan line that he'd been leading off with for years. He also trotted out McCain's lawyer and catfish joke but botched the punch line. "One's a slimy bottom-feeding scavenger, and the other is a lawyer," Graham said. (The other's *a fish*, dummy!)

After a few minutes of repartee, Graham's tone acquired an edge. "To every Republican, if you don't stand behind this president, we're not going to stand behind you," he said. As the room fell silent, Graham's voice grew soft, even grave. "This is the defining moment of his presidency," he said, referring to the Democrats' effort to thwart construction of Trump's coveted wall along the Mexican border. "It's not just about a wall. It's about him being treated different than any other president."

Graham continued: "This is a fight between the people who are *so smart* and the rest of us." Heads bobbed over unfinished plates of meat loaf drowned in barbecue sauce. The Democrats and their media partners were trying to sabotage *their* president. "Why? 'Cause they hate him," Graham said of Trump. "They hate *us*.

"They hate *us*," he said again. The crowd stood and applauded.

Back in his D.C. office later in the week, Graham was collapsed behind a messy desk, sipping a Coke Zero and complaining of exhaustion. Politics, he explained, was the art of figuring out how to get what you want. "I've got an opportunity up here, working with the president, to get some really good outcomes for the country," he said.

One outcome of great interest to Graham was winning a fourth term in the Senate. This required him to speak one way in South Carolina and another way when being interviewed by a reporter in Washington who was onto him. "You just showcase your issues, right?" Graham said.

Well, sure. Graham was hardly the first politician to "showcase" different themes and postures before different audiences. But Graham spoke out of both sides of his mouth with such gusto it was rather audacious. He could squeeze Trump like a teddy bear in South Carolina and then—safely back with the people who are *so smart* in Washington— boast of playing him like a tuba on the golf course.

Graham was happy to lay out exactly the game he was playing. He knew I was versed in the election-year "showcasing" he was now engaged in—that I was one of the "people who are *so smart*" that he derided earlier in the week. I was also one of the convenient devices "who hate *us*," although nothing about Graham's cozy manner with me suggested that he really thought I hated him or his constituents.

He knew that I knew that he had been using me and my ilk as a narrative foil. He seemed confident that I wouldn't hold it against him.

"What's odd to me is that Donald Trump's base is kind of 'the little guy,'" Graham said. He felt he could relate, he said. There was a strong whiff of southern populism to this, a proud anti-elite that was looked down upon—"the people who felt like the smart people write them off."

What was odd to me was the ease with which Graham could avail himself of Trump's little-guy credibility while speaking *"to the rest of us"* in South Carolina, and then turn around and talk about his constituents like native critters he had brought to heel in his electoral petting zoo.

Graham knew I got the joke, and he knew that I understood the only principle that guided him.

"If you don't want to get reelected, you're in the wrong business."

Okay, fine, fine. I had a few things I was curious about, though.

"Does it bother you that so many of Trump's associates keep winding up in jail?" I asked Graham. I mentioned Trump's former campaign manager Paul Manafort and his former lawyer Michael Cohen.

Graham questioned whether Trump was all that close to these people, borrowing from Trump's risible defense that he barely knew his closest aides (usually right after they get arrested). "He attracts an unusual crowd," Graham said of the president. Trump could be a "handful," no question, Graham often acknowledged. Lovingly, like a whipped caretaker.

I tried the "as an American citizen" tack with Graham. "As an American citizen," I asked earnestly, "do you ever get a little puzzled, or maybe concerned, by all the dealings Trump's campaign seemed to have with Russians?"

Graham was fast to invoke the amateur-hour defense. "They didn't know what they're doing; they'd never run for city council," Graham explained. "I don't think that campaign could have colluded with *any-body*. I mean, to be honest with you, at first I was suspicious, but the more I'm around these folks . . ." He shook his head and laughed. I'd heard a million versions of this excuse: that Trump was too inept to shake down a key ally (Ukraine), too undisciplined to plot to overturn an election, too naive and childlike to abide by basic governing standards.

"He's entertaining as hell," Graham said of Trump. Part of what was so entertaining was watching the "smart people" get all bent out of shape in response to him. This included some of Trump's top White House wet nurses. Everyone needed to just relax and appreciate the big gag, as Lindsey did.

"He's good for business," Graham said, continuing in his Trump-explainer mode.

"And he knows he's good for business. What's going to happen next? Stay tuned. Any tweet he sends is like crack cocaine for this guy."

It was not clear that Graham realized it, but he could come off quite cocky about how easy and riveting this game had become to him.

"The point with Trump is, he's in on the joke," Graham said. I asked Graham if he was in on the joke, too.

"Oh, a hundred percent, a hundred percent." He laughed. "Oh, people have no idea." I asked him to explain the joke to me. "If you could go to dinner with us," he said, shaking his head. I was never invited to dinner.

McCain understood the joke, too. But unlike Lindsey, he had no desire to spend a minute with Trump, let alone have dinner or play golf. Nor would McCain ever stray too far from his "cause greater than himself." If he spoke his truth and stuck to basic principles—country over party, patriotism over ambition—McCain believed he was serving the cause, if not always the base.

Graham was a grateful sidekick to McCain, but I always suspected he was along more for the ride and the political benefit than for any cause. The virtues that made McCain a global icon always felt like more of a posture or even a nuisance with Graham. In that sense, McCain's death was liberating to Graham.

"The knock on me and John was that we were too high on our horse, too idealistic," Graham said. That was no longer an issue. "I'm a very practical guy." He looked at me as if he thought I understood, just like all of his smart friends and colleagues in D.C. understood, even the ones who now hated his guts. He figured they would all joke about it one day, maybe after 2020.

CHAPTER 12

BRISTLING, EXPLODING IN RAGE, AND INCREASINGLY ISOLATED

———

Trump has retreated into a cocoon of bitterness and resentment.

January 2019

et's start with the state of Donald Trump," Fox News' Chris Wallace said, asking the president to kick off his White House interview, in the manner of a support-group facilitator pausing for a brief check-in before unpacking recent events. "How dark is your mood?"

Presidential interviews have not traditionally begun this way. It is important to pause and note this, too, because after a few years people had come to view these exchanges as normal, or "normalized," to use the Trump-era parlance. Wallace's eagerness to lead his interrogation with the ever-present "How dark is your mood?" question reflected the extent to which the state of our politics had become dominated by the moment-to-moment state of Donald Trump.

Tracking the president's moods had become an obsession inside the

White House—and, as such, its own reporting beat. This became especially true after Republicans lost Congress in November, and the indulgence that Trump had enjoyed from Republican-led committees on the Hill was set to expire. Client One would not take well to Democratic oversight, it was believed.

Sure enough, he did not, and considerable news coverage was being devoted in the early weeks of 2019 to how ill-tempered the forty-fifth president was becoming. Trump was "privately fuming," went the evergreen assessment, according to multiple sources familiar with his feelings. He was alternately "bristling," "emboldened," and "embittered"; "lashing out," "exploding in rage," and "increasingly isolated."

There was also a subgenre of media coverage about the media coverage of how the White House was coping with their spiraling supervisor. "The latest dispatch from the child monarchy of Donald Trump comes via *Politico*'s Tara Palmeri, who conveys the methods used by Trump's staffers to manipulate his delicate and damaged psyche," reported *New York* magazine's Jonathan Chait.

"Should Trump's Mood Swings Be a Top Story?" was the subject of its own meta-segment on CNN's *Reliable Sources*. In fact, the network had answered its own question in the previous few days. "Yes, he's pissed—at damn near everyone," CNN quoted "a White House official," who concluded that "the mood in the Oval Office is darker than normal this week."

These accounts typically began with some anecdote about the president's being upset about something. The same themes and stories repeated, with a revolving cast of Trump explainers at the ready to guide us through the foggy mood maze. By reflex, Trump would take issue with these "sources close to the president" when they portrayed him as anything short of a stable genius overseeing a well-oiled machine. He continued to maintain that these "sources" did not exist.

But Wallace was now positioned to go directly to the primary source, who was sitting here before him in full flesh and makeup. I remember thinking this was another event horizon of this presidency, a complete melding of character and caricature. As Democrats gained power, Trump felt instantly "cornered"—another recurrent presidential feeling. Wallace read off a bunch of these recent media diagnoses about Trump's mental state and asked the president to respond. Was it true, as the *Los Angeles Times* had reported, that Trump had "retreated into a cocoon of bitterness and resentment"? ("Are you listening to a lot of Radiohead?" would have been my dream follow-up.)

The exchange proceeded from there as you'd expect. "Disgusting fake news," Trump protested. He reassured Wallace that his mood was in fact "light" and that he was "extremely upbeat."

I TALKED TO SEVERAL HOUSE MEMBERS WHO DESCRIBED ANOTHER overlooked consequence of Trump's outsized profile and the obsessions he attracted from both supporters and detractors. "He has led a lot of copycat behavior among my colleagues," said Tom Rooney, a Republican congressman from Florida who was close to Ryan and not running for reelection either. "They see how Trump has been rewarded for acting out like he does, even worshipped, and they figure it can work for them, too."

Rooney, who had been in Congress since 2009, mentioned a few of his colleagues as examples. Greg Gianforte, a Republican of Montana, won a 2017 special election that featured an incident in which the candidate body-slammed a reporter, Ben Jacobs of *The Guardian*, after

Jacobs had approached him to ask a question about his health-care plan. Gianforte, a tech millionaire endorsed by Trump, was charged with misdemeanor assault and pleaded guilty to the charge. He was sentenced to four days in jail, but a judge later adjusted the punishment to forty hours of community service, a $300 fine, and twenty hours of anger management classes.

Gianforte was easily elected to Congress the day after the assault. He also became a MAGA folk hero for daring to get tough with "the enemy of the people," as Trump called the press. Trump later hailed the congressman as "my kind of guy" and "a tough cookie" at a rally in Missoula, adding that he believed the assault helped Gianforte win. He went on to be elected governor of Montana in 2020.

You could look at this result and say, "Okay, it's Montana," super red state, Wild West mentality. Everyone kept trying to convince themselves the results were a fluke, just as Trump was. This was NOT WHO WE ARE!

Rooney mentioned another colleague who had launched a long-shot bid for governor of Florida, Ron DeSantis. Rooney was more amused by the prospect than anything else, mostly because DeSantis was known within the House Republican caucus as a socially awkward weirdo who had minimal profile outside his district. He was given little chance in the GOP primary against the Florida agriculture commissioner, Adam Putnam, himself a respected former congressman.

But then DeSantis, who graduated from Yale and Harvard Law School, undertook a simple strategy of transforming his identity into that of a panting and performative Trump-worshipping fanatic. His strategy was to get on as many Fox News shows as he could and defend Trump as hard as possible. DeSantis also released an ad in which he was seen reading a bedtime story to his infant son. "Then Mr. Trump said,

'You're fired,'" the loving dad reads. Bingo. The Almighty himself took notice. Trump endorsed his favorite Sunshine State superfan—now known as Governor Ron DeSantis.

So maybe it was *who we are*, at least in Florida.

"It looked silly and embarrassing to me at first," Rooney said of DeSantis's campaign antics, which coincided with Rooney's own retirement. "But what can you say, the formula worked, and it was pretty straightforward as far as showing what you needed to do to get elected as a Republican these days. MAGA is the dogma."

The formula had little to do with building a local following and accumulating life achievements, the things that used to burnish credentials. It had everything to do with what DeSantis was willing to do to prove devotion. No matter how degrading it was, it worked.

"We've created a whole entertainment wing of the party," Paul Ryan said. "This has given rise to amoral opportunists who have found they can scale politics much faster than the meritocracy of proving yourself. Instead, they just become quick celebrities and entertainers."

No shortage of Republicans was willing to do it. The ones who were not, like Ryan and Rooney, fell away and were replaced by Trump-enthralled Republicans like DeSantis and Gianforte.

Even Republican members who a few years earlier had enjoyed reputations as relatively serious lawmakers were transformed. Devin Nunes, a former protégé of House Speaker John Boehner's, once derided his GOP House colleagues as "lemmings in suicide vests" over their efforts to shut down the government until Obamacare was repealed, in 2013. To his later regret, Boehner even made Nunes chair of the House Intelligence Committee before he left Congress.

From the outset of Trump's ascent, he cast a powerful spell over Nunes. Nunes became one of Trump's earliest supporters and shared

Trump's willingness to entertain paranoid conspiracy theories. He also held a long-standing suspicion of the national defense and intelligence establishments—the so-called deep state.

Nunes was always an enigmatic figure within the GOP, "but not really anything beyond the pale of misfits we get around here," one GOP leadership aide said. House members, particularly Republicans, always took a certain pride in portraying the House as a haven for oddballs and outsiders. "The Senate is like a country club; we're like a truck stop," Kevin McCarthy was always saying. This overlooked that the Republican side of the truck stop was attracting more and more racists, freaks, and extremists who once would have been consigned to darker corners of the rest area. Trump's iteration of the party had little interest in casting any of them out, so long as they liked the president. In return, Trump would enthusiastically support the likes of Roy Moore, a Republican Senate candidate in Alabama who was credibly accused of sexual assault against multiple underage girls, though he still lost, by just 1.63 percent of the vote.

McCarthy acknowledged that the truck stop could get a bit scary. He added, though, that he still preferred eating at a truck stop, "a free-wheeling microcosm of society," where he would much rather fit in than try to impose order.

PART OF THE APPEAL OF TRUMP WAS THAT HE DID, IN HIS OWN WAY, impose order. This despite the never-ending disorder he created. Another colleague said that Nunes was similar to a lot of House Republicans in a fundamental way: he was sick of being pushed around and condescended to in Washington, even when they were in the majority. Trump drew in a lot of the same disaffected characters, the member said, whether they were unemployed mine workers in Pennsylvania or back-bencher Republicans in Congress who felt powerless. "Trumpism is not the philosophy of free-market and limited-government conservatives like me," *National Review*'s Kevin Williamson wrote in *The Washington Post*. "It is something more like group therapy for conservatives and others who feel alienated from, and hostile toward, the progressive social consensus . . . Trumpism is, at heart, not a philosophy but an enemies list."

It was easy to see how Trump could invite fierce loyalty and appeal to those hungry for something to fight for and identify with.

"When Devin's all in, he's all in," Representative Tom Cole, an Oklahoma Republican, told my *Times* colleague Jason Zengerle. "And when he is on your side, he is on your side. If there was a bar fight going on and Dev walked into the bar and saw one of his friends, he would immediately get in on the side of the friend. And when it was over and they were walking out, then he'd say, 'What was that all about?'"

Nunes proved himself a worthy Trump combatant from the start. His most notorious action became known as Devin's Midnight Run, in which Nunes made a mysterious late-night visit to the White House to view classified reports that supposedly confirmed Trump's claim, made a few weeks into his term, that Obama had been tapping his phones.

"What I've read seems to me to be some level of surveillance activity," Nunes told reporters the next day outside the White House. Instead of briefing the rest of the committee on his "findings," Nunes took them directly to Trump, who promptly claimed vindication.

"I had a duty and obligation to tell him," Nunes explained later of the president. "As you know, he's taking a lot of heat in the news media."

Nunes was forced to temporarily step down from the House Intelligence Committee's investigation of Russian meddling in the 2016 campaign until the House Ethics Committee investigated his conduct.

Lindsey Graham, who had not yet gulped down his full dosage of MAGA Kool-Aid, mocked Nunes's behavior at the time and compared him to the bumbling Inspector Clouseau in the *Pink Panther* movies. (Fun fact: Graham loved the *Pink Panther* movies. He used to exchange lines with his fellow *Pink Panther* fan John Kerry back when they were in the Senate together.)

A former dairy farmer, Nunes was elected to Congress in 2002 and would later be subjected to what became a familiar lament about certain Republicans who fell hard for Trump—some variation on the "Didn't Nunes used to be, you know, normal?" question.

"He was not an ideologue," Representative Adam Schiff said of Nunes, with whom he said he had worked relatively well for many years on the Intelligence Committee. Schiff, a Democrat and fellow Californian, likened Nunes to Ryan and Boehner, "kind of an old-school moderate Republican," he called him.

But after Nunes was forced to step down from the Russia inquiry, with all the ridicule he took over the Midnight Run, it marked an unhealthy turning point. "It ended up bonding him to MAGA World, because MAGA World was the only one offering a life raft at that point of disgrace," Schiff said. "And he's been part of that world ever since. It's been a rather shocking transformation and quite a sad one, from my point of view."

Trump granted the likes of Nunes a notoriety they could never have dreamed of. Like Sean Spicer and Corey Lewandowski, he became another derivative hero in MAGA World, a coveted guest, a magnet for selfies, and always on Fox. Steve Bannon hailed Nunes as the Republican in Congress with whom Trump had the second-strongest relationship.

(People in the White House kept track of these things, apparently.) "Only Mark Meadows," who was still a member of Congress at the time, "has a stronger relationship with Trump," Bannon said.

Unlike other junior Trump disciples Nunes was driven not so much by the need for attention as by true belief. Trump gave him an identity and a cause greater than himself. Trump also awarded Nunes a Presidential Medal of Freedom. Nunes's once-promising career in Congress had been given over fully to being a house organ for Trump.

He wound up quitting Congress in late 2021 to lead Trump's start-up media and technology company. "Professional disseminator of Trump propaganda Devin Nunes makes lateral move," is how *New York*'s Jonathan Chait announced the news in a tweet.

"It happens one day at a time, one small concession at a time," Schiff said. "It's one small lie, followed by a demand for a bigger lie and a bigger concession, a bigger moral lapse, until, you know, these folks that I admired and respected, because I believe that they believe what they were saying, had given themselves up so completely to Donald Trump."

By the middle of 2019, the patterns had become entrenched. The exodus of Republicans in the House and Senate was consistent throughout the Trump years. When Trump took office in 2017, there were 241 Republicans in the House, David Wasserman of *The Cook Political Report* pointed out. "Since then, 115 (48%) had either retired, resigned, been defeated or at that point had signaled plans to retire in 2020."

Anecdotally, the single biggest reason these members gave for walking away was they had no interest in debasing themselves in the service of Trump any longer than they had to. "You have a situation where the leader of our party models the worst behavior imaginable," another outgoing Republican member of Congress told me. "And if you're a Republican in Washington, the idea is basically to make yourself as much of a dickhead as possible in order to get attention and impress the biggest dickhead of all, the guy sitting in the White House."

I asked the outgoing congressman—very nicely, even a tad aggressively—whether I could attach his name to this excellent quote. "No fucking way," he said. Why? "Because a lot of these dickheads are my friends. And I might have to lobby them one day, too.

"I know, it's depressing."

THIS DEPRESSION WAS CONTAGIOUS THROUGH THE EARLY MONTHS of 2019. It extended up and down Pennsylvania Avenue and seemed to cut into every sector of our politics. Even the quasi-uplifting traditions of the Capitol, the kinds of things that members of both parties would happily participate in—championship sports teams visiting the White House, the Kennedy Center Honors, the comedy routines at the Correspondents' Association Dinner, or even the National Prayer Breakfast— were now fully colored by Trump's presence, if not ruined or canceled altogether. He could not get through a hokey set piece, like the annual White House turkey-pardoning ceremony in the Rose Garden, without taking potshots at Pelosi or Mueller or Schiff.

President George H. W. Bush passed away at ninety-four, which Trump managed to be minimally gracious about, even though Bush had no use for Trump (and said as much, and voted for Hillary Clinton). Still, Trump couldn't help remaining an inescapable point of tension around the funeral.

Trump was present, if not welcome, at Bush's main D.C. send-off at the National Cathedral. Trump's appearance created a familiar tableau of awkwardness, proving once again the inability of durable Washington rituals to absorb the forty-fifth president in any way that felt natural. Trump's folded arms at the funeral, strained greetings with the Obamas, and the look-away death stare from Hillary would be its enduring images.

One of the few benefits that Trump brought to the Republican establishment was that any GOP eminence who happened to die on his watch (McCain, Barbara Bush) looked that much better, by comparison, in his or her final performance review.

As was the case with McCain, it was hard not to hear in the tributes to President Bush's valor and virtues—combat service, public-mindedness, principled patriotism—a contrast with the sitting, stewing occupant of the White House. But there was also a marked change from the McCain memorial, a sense that Trump had become that much more embedded into the Republican DNA over just three months. It might have been delusional in retrospect, but there was a faint wish that maybe the bipartisan outpouring that greeted McCain's death could somehow portend a fever break, some pause in the delirium.

But Bush's send-off never had the pretense of being much more than a quick courtesy call from the Old Normal. Soon enough, we would plunge back into the New Whatever-This-Is: the perpetual sense that the next shoe was about to drop.

I WENT TO SEE BUSH'S COFFIN AS HE LAY IN STATE AT THE CAPITOL Rotunda, which drew a solemn procession of family, A-listers (the eulogist and biographer Meacham), Capitol lifers (the Democratic whip, Steny Hoyer), and lame ducks (the just-defeated Florida senator Bill Nelson). Bunches of guests were led through, a few dozen at a time, with longer pauses allowed for selected dignitaries and changings of the guard.

The scene was heavy with protocol and reverence, both for the departed and, perhaps, for the antediluvian Washington in which Bush had been a fixture. With the Old Normal lying in state in the Capitol, it was tempting to overglorify it, to forget that voters reviled the Old Normal enough to elect Trump in 2016—or for that matter, to not reelect Bush in 1992.

Bob Dole arrived to pay his respects: President Bush's fellow World War II hero and another politician whose old-timey normalcy was rejected in two presidential elections. The nearly century-old Dole was helped from his wheelchair to offer a last salute to his longtime friend and former rival. He wore bright red Christmas socks, adorned with snowmen. It was a made-for-cable moment, inviting all the usual blow-dried platitudes about this parting of happy warriors.

But there was an intimacy to the visit, too. Bush and Dole had seen and shared and known things that required no words or hearing. It was a nice pause in the procession, but just a pause.

CHAPTER 13

CONTAGION

———

Death threats are not fun.

—Susan Collins

April 2019

While Bush 41 lay in state, Trump 45 spent the morning railing against "presidential harassment" from Democrats and escalating a trade war with China via Twitter as the Dow dropped by nearly eight hundred points in response. Or as we called this during Trump-era Washington, "Tuesday."

Also, Stormy Daniels was in town.

No offense to Stormy, but I consider it a minor feat that I've gotten this far in the book without mentioning her now-household name. But as we've come to learn, Trump has a way of wearing you down. He invades your habitat, like the opossum that gets into the attic, dies, stinks, and attracts derivative nuisances. Okay, it's not a perfect analogy (for one, Trump remained very much alive). It's probably disrespectful, too, to compare the president of the United States to a dead opossum—respect for the office, you know. I used to be mindful of these things. Color me worn down.

Anyway, Daniels, the suddenly very famous porn actor, had dropped into town to promote her memoir, *Full Disclosure*, which was not your typical political memoir in the way that, say, Henry Kissinger's memoir would be. The book included a lot about her difficult childhood, her abusive relationships, and her entry into the world of adult film, where the former Stephanie Clifford would rechristen herself Stormy Daniels. The stuff about her childhood and relationships and professional journey was ignored in favor of the spicier details, such as the part where Daniels compared the shape of Trump's penis to a mushroom ("smaller than average," "unusual," "like a toadstool").

On his show a few nights earlier, Jimmy Kimmel had helpfully presented Daniels with a tray of actual mushrooms and invited her to pick the fungus that best resembled the presidential member (she picked the smallest). At one point, Kimmel referred to Daniels "making love" to Trump, which understandably set her off.

"Gross!" she protested. "What is wrong with you? I laid there and prayed for death." There had to be a metaphor here.

At the very least, the presidential porn paramour's state visit to Washington in the same week President Bush departed the earth would add another layer to what had become a regular series of juxtapositions between the city's dignified old and its tawdry new. Out with the Poppy, in with the Stormy.

While the former was memorialized, the latter discussed her new literary contribution at Politics and Prose, the venerable Northwest D.C.

bookstore and café. Sally Quinn, the former *Washington Post* reporter and widow of the legendary *Post* editor Ben Bradlee, drew hostess and moderator duties. The august pair sat on stools in front of the store's religion shelf while a large weeknight contingent of maybe two hundred filled folding chairs in front of them.

Daniels was pressed for time, because, she said, she had to dash off from her Politics and Prose interview to a scheduled gig at a strip club not far from the White House. The Cloakroom, the club was called. As Bradlee always used to say, "The caravan moves on."

AS TRUMP'S TERM FALTERED ON, THE STORY WAS GETTING ONLY darker and darker. Despite losing their House majority in the midterms, the Republicans who remained were cooked more and more viciously into the Party of Trump. If anything, they were emboldened by their purer ranks and, in many cases, welcomed the departures as a necessary cleansing.

To proclaim oneself an anti-Trump Republican at this point had a certain Jews for Jesus disconnect about it. There was at least a critical mass of this resistance ilk in 2015, 2016, and 2017, but their ranks steadily dropped off. They died (McCain, George and Barbara Bush), retired (Corker, Flake), made their rationalizations and adapted (Cruz, Graham), or were primaried out of their misery (Representative Mark Sanford).

Their departures were often lamented by former colleagues, but quietly, as Trump mocked them on the way out. "Of course, people like Flake and Corker were just saying publicly what a lot of people were saying privately," said Representative Charlie Dent, a Republican of Pennsylvania. But they spoke privately for a reason, he said. Maybe they weren't the type to rock the boat, or they didn't need the hassle, or they did need the job. "A lot of them were just worn down," Dent said. A lot of them simply gave up.

"I'm not going to pretend that I'm not disappointed that we've had this attrition," added Charlie Sykes, a longtime conservative radio host in Wisconsin who would become the editor in chief of *The Bulwark*, an online redoubt of anti-Trump conservatism. "It's been this rolling, soul-crushing disappointment, watching people that you thought you knew."

The likes of Corker were replaced by dynamite-tossing GOP House alums like Marsha Blackburn (in Tennessee), while centrist red state Democrats such as Claire McCaskill (Missouri) and Heidi Heitkamp (North Dakota) were supplanted by the hard-core Trumpists Josh Hawley and Kevin Cramer. The few even moderately Trump-ambivalent Republicans who remained were embattled outliers.

I visited one of them, Senator Susan Collins, the Republican moderate from Maine, in her D.C. office shortly after the midterms. I've always had a warm spot for Collins, originating from my love of her state. My family owned a nineteenth-century farmhouse in southern Maine, on the Saco River, between Portland and North Conway, New Hampshire. We would make the two-and-a-half-hour drive north from our Boston-area home, and I spent many childhood weekends around the typical villages—Cornish, Hiram, Limerick—of the place Collins has represented in the Senate since 1997.

I have always been impressed by Collins's deep knowledge of these towns. We had a running conversation about an old family restaurant in Cornish, the Enterprise, home to something called "Johnny Floggers"—essentially deep-fried rolls, the size of tennis balls, served in baskets.

Okay, back to our darkening Washington story.

"I mean, it's not fun," Collins was saying in her office. "Death threats are not fun. Protests are not fun. Being mobbed—sorry, I know the media hates that word—being mobbed when I go to vote. I do not enjoy that at all. I find that exhausting."

Protesters were regularly getting arrested in Collins's office; her staffers were quitting over the death threats; a letter laced with white powder had just been sent to her Bangor home; and a fax had come in from someone promising to "slit Collins' throat and sever her limbs."

You could see where Collins, then sixty-five, would not quite be radiating fresh-start and renewal vibes for 2019. She was especially bummed out over the defeats of McCaskill and Heitkamp, two of her closest friends. Heitkamp, who once described Collins as her "role model," lost her race by eleven points to Cramer—whose most conspicuous contribution since landing in the Senate was a tweet calling Nancy Pelosi "retarded." (Cramer later deleted the tweet and apologized, claiming he meant to say "ridiculous.")

Collins was up for reelection in 2020 and already had a (figurative) bull's-eye on her back from both directions. Her openness to bipartisanship had, paradoxically, made her a bipartisan target. Republicans readily cataloged Collins's RINO apostasies, as when she cast one of the three GOP no votes against the Obamacare-repeal bill in 2017. Democrats hailed her "heroic" and "courageous" vote against the repeal, until they lacerated her for voting in favor of the Republican tax cut. For good measure, many women will forever regard Collins, who favors abortion rights, as a traitor over her support for the nomination of Brett Kavanaugh to the Supreme Court.

Collins stood out as a red speck in the deep blue Northeast. Of the thirty-three senators and members of Congress from New England, Collins was at the time the lone Republican. She despised Trump, and very publicly did not vote for him in 2016 (she wrote in Paul Ryan instead).

But Collins was ever vulnerable to a primary challenge from the right and vigilant about not going out of her way to activate the state's heavy MAGA contingent. I would periodically email her for comment about some Trump-related outrage, which yielded replies such as this: "Thanks but no thanks. I was the graduation speaker at Sacopee Valley High School 10 days ago and thought of you as I entered the town." Nice of her to respond at least.

Collins had become a kind of caricature of the solemn centrist, always *deliberating very carefully* or being *deeply saddened* or *troubled* over something or other.

She had been maddening people across the political spectrum for years, which went with the territory of being a "moderate." The main difference now was that people had become, generally, madder.

"It saddens me," Collins said (sure enough) of the dimming state of affairs in the capital. I tried to get her talking on the record about Trump, which was always a recipe for sadness in its own way.

"There is no doubt that the president and I have extremely different styles," Collins said. It was always amusing to hear elected Republicans who were plainly appalled by Trump try to paper over their differences with him as a matter of "style"—if only he wore different shoes or something. Or the ever-present, ever-lame "I don't like his tweets" complaint, as if Trump's use of the medium itself were the issue.

Collins took a deep breath and said little of consequence about Trump. This was no great loss, and I didn't press her. What was most notable to me was her despair, which was obvious, and her foreboding over what was next.

———

WE WERE NOW NEARLY FOUR YEARS INTO TRUMP, IF YOU START the clock with his escalator descent into our lives in June 2015. "Where does this end?" I asked Trump a few times during the early curiosity months of his campaign.

"I have no fucking idea," Trump would typically answer. "But I'm here now. And it's beautiful."

Trump kept blowing through the guardrails that, theoretically, were supposed to keep a vehicle like him in check. The guardrails always turned out to be made of paper. The Republican "establishment" and vaunted "party apparatus" did not exist as any functional bulwark. Appeals to human decency fell on deaf ears. GOP voters were the opposite of Trump's kryptonite; they were his superpower. They gave him crowds, ratings, votes, and the popular affirmation that maybe he really did reflect *who we are*—or at least enough of us.

As soon as I started going to his rallies and forcing myself to watch more Fox News than I normally would, it was clear that Trump truly was speaking for a big and determined swath of the GOP.

A lot of it was right there in the polling. In 2015 and 2016, more than half of Republican poll respondents were still saying that they believed Barack Obama was a Muslim, and probably not born in the United States, too. The instinct—by the media, by the GOP grown-ups—was always to consign this to a fringe view, or a "settled question" (which of course only required "settling" because Trump had previously questioned Obama's country of origin nonstop). It was not a polite or uplifting topic. It hardly mattered that they were ugly and demonstrable lies. But the reality was, these views, or "suspicions," existed solidly in the Republican mainstream, even after Obama had been president for nearly two full terms.

"We had a Muslim president for seven and a half years," said Antonio Sabato Jr., the underwear model, reality show character, and big Trump supporter. Sabato made this claim in an interview with ABC, just before delivering a speech on the first night of the 2016 Republican National Convention in Cleveland.

"It's in my heart," Sabato said, when asked what the source of his claim was. "I see it for what it is. I believe that he's on the other side . . . the Middle East. He's with the bad guys."

The constituency that Trump had branded as his Nixonian "silent majority" had become anything but silent. On the contrary, they were emboldened and could be downright menacing. They terrified elected Republicans. They made Trump Teflon, just so long as he could keep his MAGA army entertained and stirred up. Elected Republicans usually felt their safest path to reelection was to protect Trump. In return, he protected them, or at least made it safe for them—with his blessing—to move about the world without getting harassed by the president's tribal foot soldiers.

Paul Ryan told me a story about going to a Metallica concert in Texas with his son after he left Congress. "This guy was sitting in front of us," Ryan recalled. "He said, 'My wife likes you, but I'm a conservative.'" Ryan countered that he was in fact a conservative, too. "Yeah, but Trump doesn't like you," the man said. Ryan didn't bother trying to win the man over with his favorite Ayn Rand and Jack Kemp quotes. He was thankful not to have to worry about these encounters much anymore. "But if you're a member of Congress, that rattles you. The intimidation factor. If you're below 97 percent on the fealty scale, Trump's going to come after you. It's like a mass sociology experiment." Ryan said he never believed that such mass intimidation could ever take hold in American democracy. "It just surprised me so much," he said. "The idea that just one guy—one guy could just Luca Brasi you, and all of these members would be so afraid." (Luca Brasi was the loyal Corleone enforcer in *The Godfather* who winds up sleeping with the fishes.)

NANCY PELOSI RECLAIMED THE SPEAKER'S GAVEL IN EARLY 2019, and maybe *she* would prove to be Trump's undoing. It took a grandmother, right? Maybe she would be the guardrail. "She's going to get us," Steve Bannon predicted about Pelosi early in 2017. "Total assassin."

If all else failed, there was always the designated guardian of all things proper and adult in Washington, Robert Mueller. "In Mueller we trust" became the catchall for much of the Trump resistance in both parties and in the media. They portrayed the special counsel—appointed to investigate Russian meddling in the 2016 election—as a white knight of awesome and competent authority who would finally be the one to end this disgrace.

Upon his assignment, Mueller was hailed as a bipartisan beacon of integrity, just the kind of honest broker the situation called for. "A superb choice," Newt Gingrich tweeted about Mueller the day he was named, or before Trump could wind his adorable little Newt doll in the other direction. ("Republicans are delusional if they think the special counsel is going to be fair," Gingrich tweeted four weeks later.)

But Trump did not end with Mueller, either. The former FBI director's long-awaited, 448-page, redacted report was plenty damning to those who bothered to read it—which was not many people in the scheme of things.

By contrast, many more people (tens of millions, probably) were privy to Attorney General William Barr's predistilled, prescrubbed, and misleading summary of the report. Barr's headline: Mueller's "investigation did not establish that members of the Trump Campaign conspired or coordinated with the Russian government in its election interference activities."

This would quickly become "Total EXONERATION," in Trump's oft-tweeted words. Hey, wait, but Mueller explicitly claimed the opposite; he even complained to Barr in a dreaded *sharply worded letter*!

I WALKED PAST THE TRUMP HOTEL ON AN EARLY SPRING DAY, JUST after Barr undercut Mueller with his four-page whitewashing and Trump went into immediate victory-lap mode. A small pep rally was under way outside the hotel, with a larger than usual contingent of red MAGA-hatted tourists gathered on the sidewalk. They posed for photos in front of the bright gold Trump International Hotel sign. The hotel had become a stop on the tour for Trump-loving tourists, the logic being if you schlepped all the way to D.C. from, say, Tennessee and couldn't lay eyes on the Man himself, you might as well see the next best thing—in the same way that if you went to Disney World and you couldn't see Cinderella herself, you might as well take some pictures at the castle.

The sidewalk gathering also drew reporters eager to chronicle the "scene" on this Trumpian holiday of Total EXONERATION. The media people surveyed the varied "takes" on the Total EXONERATION from the Trump faithful. In fact, the takes were not so varied at all and tended to fall into three categories: (1) no, they hadn't read the Mueller report, and probably wouldn't; (2) no, it wouldn't have any impact on their devotion to Trump, regardless of what it said; (3) no, they didn't think any of this mattered, and besides, they'd heard that Trump was *totally exonerated* anyway, so what was the big deal?

They'd heard No. 3, in large part, thanks to the new attorney general.

Barr had come into the job a few weeks earlier and was viewed, in certain circles, as a potential grown-up and *enforcer of norms*. The hope was he could lend professionalism to Trump's Lord of the Flies operation.

In addition to having served as AG nearly three decades earlier under Bush 41, Barr boasted impeccable bona fides as a mainstream conservative of establishment lineage. He grew up on the Upper West Side, attended Horace Mann and Columbia, and his dad was headmaster of the venerable Dalton School. Even Trump's fiercest critics held out some hope at first that Barr could serve as a quasi-honest broker to a White House deeply in need of one. Barr "deserves the benefit of the doubt," the former FBI director James Comey said on CNN. "He's an institutionalist and loves the Department of Justice, and the only thing he has to lose at this point in his career is his reputation."

In retrospect, the threat of reputational harm was not enough to keep Barr on the straight and narrow. The honest-broker/benefit-of-the-doubt crew was naive to expect otherwise given that Barr had spent the first half of the Trump administration campaigning for the job. His approach amounted to a virtuoso performance in how a GOP has-been can get back in the game and impress a president who otherwise wouldn't know him from Adam (Schiff). Barr essentially turned himself into a Yo-Yo Ma of White House toadyism, with Trump as his cello.

His sheet music was straightforward enough. Barr criticized legal challenges against Trump and the special counsel investigation in general and, in June 2018, sent an unsolicited twenty-page memo to the Justice Department about why Mueller should not be investigating the president at all. He provided copies to Trump's own lawyers. Big surprise: Trump completely agreed.

As Trump spent the better part of two years performing the Twitter equivalent of holding Jeff Sessions naked by his feet over the Truman Balcony, Barr ramped up his donations to the National Republican Senatorial Committee.

Sessions walked the plank officially the day after the midterms. Less than a year before, there might have been hell to pay over this, which were the exact words Graham used in warning Trump there would be consequences if he got rid of Sessions. Now, with the broken AG gone, Graham's reaction was appreciably short of "hell to pay." "I look forward to working with President @realDonaldTrump to find a confirmable, worthy successor," Graham tweeted, "so that we can start a new chapter at the Department of Justice." Who knew that hell could be such a supportive and nurturing environment?

Barr was perfectly positioned to glide into the job. In total, he had given roughly $10,000 a month between October 2018 and February 2019 to the NRSC, despite previously having criticized Mueller for, among other things, hiring prosecutors who had donated to Hillary Clinton's presidential campaign in 2016.

Democrats derided Barr's activities—mainly his various statements and writings critical of Mueller—as a "job application" for the AG role. His application was accepted by Trump in December, and the beneficiaries of Barr's NRSC largesse voted to confirm him in February.

AFTER BILL BARR'S CAMPAIGN FOR AG WAS COMPLETE, HIS FIRST task in the job was to essentially kick off his boss's campaign for re-election.

"It's not hard to figure where we're going to go with this," a Trump campaign official told *The Atlantic* after Barr released his friendly preemption of the Mueller report. "We're still in victory-lap mode, but it will turn into a message that [Democrats] will say or do anything to stop us from making America great again, including making up lies about the president and ruining a lot of people's lives."

The other big theme at the Trump Hotel on this day of Total EXONERATION was, of course, payback.

Someone needed to be punished, and *VERY STRONGLY*, for this Total Witch Hunt. "No president should go through something like this!" the victimized viceroy tweeted roughly three million times after Barr kicked off the orgy of absolution. (Future presidents were of paramount concern to Trump, no one doubted that.)

A few days later, *The Atlantic*'s Peter Nicholas and Elaina Plott found Giuliani in the Trump Hotel lobby, sipping a Diet Coke, consumed with revenge. He said he had already pivoted to his next mission. "We're now trying to prove who did it," Giuliani said, like O.J. finding the real killer.

"The premise is somebody had to have started the 'He colluded with the Russians' narrative," Giuliani said. Nicholas and Plott then asked Giuliani whether Trump himself wanted an investigation to get to the bottom of this terrible injustice.

"Goddamn right he [does]," Rudy said. "This is not, 'Oh, gee, it's over, let's forget about it.'"

A few weeks later, Barr confirmed his devotion to the errand by announcing an investigation into the great national riddle, the so-called *origins* of the Mueller investigation. There had already been a separate probe into the matter, but it didn't seem to be getting anywhere, so Barr jumped in.

In announcing his inquiry, Barr parroted Trump's concern that the FBI had spied on him. Trump was pleased by his new AG's decisive action—tough and loyal, not like that *total disaster*, Sessions. Strong start for Barr, no question.

He was well on his way to becoming, arguably, first among equals when it came to the president's bagmen. He proved to be a faithful protector and buster of norms. Barr even booked the Trump Hotel for a two-hundred-person holiday party that December, signing a contract with his boss's business that required a minimum of $31,500 in spending and a $10,000 deposit, according to a review of the document by *The Washington Post*. The cost of the soiree could go higher depending on the menu and whether Barr was willing to keep the bar open for four hours. (Spoiler: He was.)

The *Post* later reported that Barr rescheduled the party to another date, which a DOJ spokesperson did not reveal, probably to keep the protesters away. A handful of demonstrators showed up at the hotel anyway on the originally scheduled Sunday night. They flashed signs, meant for Barr—who was not there—but they made their point, anyway.

YOU'RE ON THE WRONG SIDE OF HISTORY, said one placard, attempting to taunt the attorney general, likely to little avail.

THE HALLOWED "VERDICT OF HISTORY" WAS ALSO A FAMILIAR SCOLD during these years. It felt beside the point in this warped realm of "alternative facts," where something as tactile as, say, an inaugural crowd size could be disputed despite clear visual evidence. How would the "verdict of history" ever be adjudicated in a hundred years?

Not a lot of Trump's protectors seemed all that hung up on their historic grade, no matter how many of them saw their reputations incinerated in service to the sovereign. I once asked Kevin McCarthy some variation on the "Do you worry about how history will judge you?" question, and he looked at me as if I had three heads.

"I don't care about my legacy," Giuliani told *The New Yorker*'s Jeffrey

Toobin, who had asked him if he was concerned that his antics on behalf of Trump might harm his legacy. "I'll be dead."

Rudy had a particular knack for making exactly this point in seemingly every interview he did. "My attitude about my legacy is: Fuck it," he told *New York*'s incomparable Olivia Nuzzi, who noted that he was drunk on Bloody Marys at the time (so maybe he didn't really mean it, though I tend to doubt it).

Trump wielded the same brush-off. "My legacy doesn't matter," he said. "If I lose, that will be my legacy."

There were quasi-erudite versions of this, too. "Everyone dies," Barr said in response to the legacy question, posed by CBS's Jan Crawford. "I don't believe in the Homeric idea that immortality comes by, you know, having odes sung about you over the centuries."

It was always the same glib rebuff. And emblematic of the sunken-eyed contempt that Trump's most committed conspirators had learned from the expert. They took special delight, at least outwardly, in their disdain for the lofty judgments that the *very serious people*—the self-important reporter types, the academic historians, the biographers—would try to impose on them. Why would any of them care what their obituaries said?

"Don't care," Lindsey Graham told a reporter on the Capitol subway platform who asked whether his reputation suffered because of Trump. There was a lot of this going around. As 2019 wore on, a kind of resigned nihilism had overtaken the GOP. You felt a lurch into the deep recesses. The blur of events imposed its own tyranny: What would today bring? What happened yesterday? How could tomorrow be worse?

"The ball got rolling from Day 1 and it just didn't stop," said Charlie Dent, a former chair of the House Ethics Committee. "You had the Great Crowd debate after the inauguration, the immigration ban, which was horribly executed, and then Trump fired Comey, and there's a bunch of intervening events—Charlottesville, whatever. There was always something; it just rolls on." People lost their will to engage with it, Dent said. They created their own boundaries for self-protection. "It's just human nature," he said. Because why bother? Dent quit in 2018.

"Jeff Flake is one of my better friends here," Dent said. "We used to play paddleball together. When I announced I wasn't running for reelection, he sent me a text: 'Nooooo, you can't leave.' There's this expectation that if you really have principles, you should stay and fight the good fight.

"And then, when Flake said he wasn't running, I sent him a text back that said, 'Noooo, you can't leave.'"

And then they were both gone.

CHAPTER 14

THE FIFTH AVENUE CROWD

———

November 2019

Who could care less?

Entering the home stretch, Lindsey Graham had become hard to beat. No one worked as hard at caring less. "Don't care" had become his all-purpose rejoinder to any number of Trump-related shenanigans. He had a habit of staring straight at the floor as he said this.

"I don't care if they have to stay in these facilities for 400 days," said Graham, after visiting an overpacked and foul-smelling Texas Border Control facility that contained hundreds of kids in cages.

"I don't care if we have to build tents from Texas to Oklahoma," he told Fox.

"It's all theater, it doesn't matter," Graham said, this now referring to Trump's attempts to impede the various Russia investigations.

After a while, Graham was practically begging to be called out. His flamboyant hypocrisies became like taunts.

"I want you to use my words against me," Graham said in 2016, asserting that Obama should not fill the Supreme Court vacancy after

Antonin Scalia died. The next president should nominate his or her own judge, Graham said, and insisted that he would say the exact same thing if a Republican was in office.

"You could use my words against me, and you'd be absolutely right," Graham said. Everyone knows what happened after Ruth Bader Ginsburg died in 2020, and how Graham helped rush through Judge Amy Coney Barrett's nomination to the bench just a few weeks before the election, and how the "use my words against me" clip was played everywhere.

And how Graham could care less.

Graham's "I don't care" mantra was a variant of a Trump credo that was literally spelled out on the back of one of the First Lady's jackets. Melania Trump wore a coat reading "I Really Don't Care. Do U?" during her own border junket. When the predictable uproar followed, her spokeswoman, Stephanie Grisham, complained that the "dishonest" media was reading way too much into "I Really Don't Care." "There is no hidden message," she insisted.

It was not clear where "LOL, Nothing Matters" began, but the refrain started popping up on Twitter in the early Trump years. The phrase packed an exasperated tone, an acknowledgment of the consequence-free environment that Trump had fostered.

The longer Trump survived without ramifications, the easier it became for him. No scandal could ever be processed before the next one came along. Outrage fatigue was his best enabler.

Before, when Trump did something that was once considered egregious, it would be met with a certain heart-racing anticipation that maybe *this* would be the thing that did him in. But now fewer and fewer former critics even bothered to summon disgust.

His most loyal defenders, like Graham, showcased their indifference with the zeal of converts. "I don't care" had morphed from brush-off to war cry.

Trump had achieved full "nothing matters" status in his party by late 2019.

His onetime pains in the asses had all been anesthetized into numbness—with certain exceptions (Lindsey) who seemed strangely aroused by the naughtiness.

By lashing themselves so tightly to Trump, elected Republicans acted as if the president's impunity extended to them. His GOP facilitators felt petrified of Trump and protected by him at the same time—the essence of an abusive codependency. His strut of cavalier disregard for oversight became their own.

I WAS HAVING A DRINK WITH SOME COLLEAGUES ON A LOUD AND notably boisterous night at the Trump Hotel. We noticed more White House appendages around the atrium than usual: the law firm of Gidley, Gorka, and Gaetz; Rudy with his shirt untucked and a woman with a purse dog, possibly Mnuchin's wife. POTUS and FLOTUS were rumored to have been in here earlier. Security seemed to be heavier than normal.

News had broken around this time that White House national security officials were privy to a *concerning* phone call that Trump had placed to his new Ukrainian counterpart, Volodymyr Zelensky. Initial reports suggested that Trump had tried to strong-arm Zelensky into helping him and Giuliani find dirt on Joe and Hunter Biden as a condition of Ukraine's receiving its congressionally authorized military aid. If Zelensky played his cards right—if he did Trump the "favor" he was requesting—maybe there'd be an invitation to the White House in his future, too. As a rule, this is not typically how a U.S. president speaks to a key ally, especially one so vulnerable to Russian aggression.

As was often true, the scheme's origin story featured key scenes set at the hotel. This included a fateful private dinner in April 2018 that included Trump, Don Jr., Giuliani, and two Soviet-born businessmen/fixers, Lev Parnas and Igor Fruman, who had gained access to the president by donating to Republican groups and pro-Trump super PACs.

At the dinner, Parnas shared the rumor with Trump that the U.S. ambassador to Ukraine, Marie Yovanovitch, had been bad-mouthing him. She had also not been helpful to the efforts to destroy Biden via Kyiv. "Get rid of her," Trump replied in a video captured on Fruman's phone and provided to ABC News. "Get her out tomorrow," he continued, addressing his words to an aide. "Take her out. Okay? Do it."

Yovanovitch, who denied ever trashing Trump, was abruptly recalled from Kyiv in May 2019. Parnas and Fruman were arrested and charged by prosecutors in Manhattan with federal campaign finance violations. Trump followed his normal playbook: he denied knowing them.

The White House then released a readout of the Trump-Zelensky call, essentially confirming the worst. Assessments of the president's performance included terms such as "national security blackmail," "diplomatic extortion," and the devastatingly simple "shakedown." This smelled like a legitimate scandal, at least in a world where anything *mattered*.

"Holy shit," Adam Schiff wrote in his memoir, *Midnight in Washington*, summarizing his initial response to the call record. "The ease of Trump's corruption was stunning." Schiff compared Trump's behavior on the phone call to a racketeering operation. He also contrasted this with the Trump campaign's dealing with Russia in 2016. Back then, Trump was merely a candidate. "Now he could use the full power of the office to browbeat the leader of another nation into helping him cheat in an election," Schiff said.

Trump smeared Yovanovitch ("that woman") as "bad news" on the call. "Her attitude towards me was far from the best," Trump said. He added, grimly, that the U.S. ambassador was "going to go through some things." He also promised Zelensky that Barr and Giuliani would reach out to him and follow up.

"I have no idea how they're going to explain or defend this," one disgusted GOP House member told me after the initial readout of the Zelensky call was released. There were cursory efforts to admonish Trump by the few Republicans still obliged to go through such motions. Representative Mac Thornberry of Texas, the top Republican on the House Armed Services Committee, said it was wrong for a U.S. president to enlist a foreign leader to smear a political rival. "I believe it was inappropriate," Thornberry told ABC's Martha Raddatz. "I do not believe it was impeachable."

Now safely out of office, Ryan urged his successor, Kevin McCarthy, to say something similar. That would allow Republicans to at least disapprove of Trump's conduct on the record while maintaining that it still did not rise to the level of an impeachment. McCarthy seemed open to this at first, but then Trump did not react well to the initial "inappropriate but not impeachable" statement from Thornberry. McCarthy promptly retreated to his usual posture—surrender.

Trump defended his conversation with Zelensky as a "perfect phone call," which became his officially branded line. Nancy Pelosi announced an impeachment inquiry, new details of the White House's pressure and intimidation campaign in Ukraine emerged, and it all sounded quite damning, theoretically.

And everyone knew exactly what consequences Trump would suffer from his party: none.

His partisan media barkers praised his "strength." His GOP wingmen on the Hill cowered, insisting that Democrats were bent on impeaching the president from Day 1. All the boxes were checked; wagons were circled. The whole story was freighted from the start with inevitability, like a cruise-controlled drive to nowhere. Trump suffered zero erosion of his base. *LOL.*

THE IMPEACHMENT PROCEEDINGS THAT DOMINATED THE DARKENing months to come brought a certain clarity about where the Republican Party was now and where it was headed. The significance of the impeachment process went beyond merely revealing, or confirming, Trump's willingness to abuse his office.

What the hearings laid bare was the sad state of the Washington "debate," such as it was. Trump's Republican attendants barely bothered to contest the most basic claims of wrongdoing against their proprietor. No one suggested this phone call was not 100 percent in character for him: the facts underscored it, and a parade of witnesses confirmed it.

The president's protectors cobbled together their "defense" almost entirely from grievance and debunked conspiracies. Again, they learned from the best. Trump was both their martyr and their teacher. Nunes, the ranking Republican on the Intelligence Committee, dismissed witnesses as pawns in "the Democrats' scorched-earth war against President Trump." He said they were all "auditioning" for the right to play in "the Democrats' Star Chamber." He called the hearings a "show trial" and predicted "low ratings," the ultimate insult in the eyes of the Audience of One. (This weaponization of "low ratings" was one of the weirder ways the president's followers had "absorbed Trump's couch-potato mentality," *The Atlantic*'s David Frum pointed out. "Reality only exists to the extent it's watched on TV.")

Republicans accused Democrats of trying to "overturn the results of an election," of being blinded by their hatred of the president and, yes, by their hatred of his supporters and their "way of life." This was another common theme of the Republican defense. That any attempt to check or punish Trump's flagrantly corrupt conduct amounted to contempt for anyone who voted for him.

In a floor speech, Representative Bill Johnson, Republican of Ohio, invited his colleagues to stand and please observe a moment of silence "to remember the voices of the 63 million American voters" who backed Donald Trump. It was not clear when they all died, but what a moving tribute this was all the same.

"This is truly a sad day for America—it's a sad week for America," said Representative Louie Gohmert, Republican of Texas, his voice choking with emotion when he invoked the president. "He has hung in there, it's amazing," he marveled.

Gohmert was one of several House members who were there to watch the proceedings, even though he was not on the Intelligence Committee—or possessed of much intelligence. "There's not a functional brain in there," was former Speaker Boehner's succinct assessment of Gohmert. Gohmert would pigeonhole reporters and call for Democrats to apologize to *my president* for the ordeal they had put him through. No apology appeared to be forthcoming.

But at least Gohmert could renew his membership in the president's fan club. There was a good chance Trump would be watching and would see "My Louie" perform and he would be proud.

"A sham circus," Gohmert declared, and snapped a selfie from the gallery with the hearing table in the background.

CORRECTION, THIS WAS NOT A CIRCUS, THE COMMITTEE DEMOCRATS insisted—sham or otherwise. Presidential impeachments must be treated as somber occasions, not circuses. The Republican Doug Collins of Georgia was dubious, scoffing at what he called the Democrats' fake solemnity—or "solemn-*enity*," as he kept calling it.

"There are few actions as consequential as the impeachment of the president," proclaimed Schiff, the chairman of the Intelligence Committee. His voice oozed with solemn-*enity* as he welcomed witnesses into the hearing room, each greeted by ritual camera bursts. They embodied the professional class of the capital—diplomats, civil servants, and servicemen—whose norms and traditions Trump had so gleefully disrupted.

"I am not here to take one side or another or to advocate for any particular outcome," said the first one to testify, William Taylor, the top American diplomat in Ukraine. One after another, the witnesses kept asserting they were loyal to their country, not to any one president or party.

And one after another, every Republican on the panel was unmoved. They had their line and dared not depart from it. Representative Steve Cohen, a Democrat of Tennessee, wandered out into the gallery during a break and said he was resigned to the inevitable.

"These Republicans, they have their roles," he said. "They will perform for Trump." Cohen said he took theater and drama courses in college and learned how important it was for a performer to suspend disbelief. "The Republicans, they obviously took that course over and over and over again," Cohen said. "They're not the Fifth Avenue crowd."

Cohen's "Fifth Avenue crowd" referred to Trump's probably accurate assessment that he could stand in the middle of Fifth Avenue and shoot somebody and it would cost him no support. The giddy future president delivered the line in Sioux City, Iowa, a few weeks before the caucuses in 2016. He pantomimed the shooting motion with his fingers. It was met with applause and a "We love you."

"We love you too," Trump replied.

"My people, they stay," Trump then summarized. "Like, incredible. My people, I have the most loyal people."

Cohen said he questioned whether "loyalty" really applied. That sounded too noble. "I see it as something else," he said, pointing to his colleagues. "I just see a willingness to suspend disbelief." Whatever it was, Cohen said again that he was resigned.

"We've seen this act before," he said. "We know how it ends."

The Fifth Avenue line was mostly taken as an absurd exaggeration when Trump first said it. Four years on, it sounded entirely plausible. Putting the legal particulars of presidential immunity aside, if Trump literally did shoot someone on the street (say, in downtown Palm Beach), here's what likely would happen: He would immediately cry self-defense, make up some claim that his victim was a "protester" and was "harassing" him. Citizen Trump was simply exercising his "rights" as a peace-loving gun owner. He felt threatened. He did nothing wrong.

Within hours, some pro-Trump media outlet would perhaps find a picture of the victim at a Black Lives Matter rally from a few years ago. Within days, the victim would be dubbed "a dangerous radical protester," or some such, by a Fox host. The various pro-Trump smear brigades would assume their positions. Blizzards of lies about the victim would blow through social media. Don Jr. would "like" a bunch of them.

Hannity would blame the "radical woke police," Cruz would blame "the protesters," and the mourning family would be inundated with death threats. Trump would hail the "record-breaking crowd" at his next rally and brag that he was fighting back against being "canceled" over this latest hoax. A majority of Republican voters would remain "loyal" to Trump and an even bigger majority of elected Republicans would desperately try to avoid the issue. Senator Grassley "didn't see it," so he couldn't comment.

By now, Trump's assumption of impunity was perfectly obvious. He enjoyed full faith that his party would protect him, no matter what he did or what precedent he murdered. During impeachment, Trump would boast of doing exactly what he was being accused of and then push it even further. A pool reporter asked him outside the White House what Trump hoped Zelensky would do about the Bidens.

"I would think that if they were being honest about it, they'd start a major investigation," Trump said, adding that "China likewise should start an investigation."

To review, President Trump was asking two foreign governments to investigate his political rival on live television—just as Candidate Trump had urged Russia to help surface his opponent's private emails. Hillary Clinton went on Twitter herself to point out the obvious after the China comment. "Someone should inform the president that impeachable offenses committed on national television still count," Clinton wrote.

But who was counting?

CHAPTER 15

TROUBLEMAKER

———

Oh, everybody gets the joke.

—Mitt Romney

February 5, 2020

Impeachment became part of Donald Trump's historic record at the end of 2019. Only two previous presidents had been sanctioned as such, and you could see how Trump might be haunted by the notion of "that very ugly word." Impeachments are not easily brushed aside, like subpoenas. They are meant to be rare, and were rare, at least until Trump.

The first clue that Trump was having a hard time with this occurred just before the House impeachment vote when he tweeted that Nancy Pelosi's "teeth were falling out of her mouth." Not presidential!

Trump then fired off a six-page harangue likening his impeachment to an "attempted coup," "an election-nullification scheme," and a "lynching." He compared his impeachment to the Salem witch trials.

All in all, none of this read like the reaction of a fully balanced, self-actualized individual, let alone one with access to the requisite nuclear codes. (People would inevitably invoke "the nuclear codes" whenever Trump kicked it up to next-level bonkers.) "Concerning" was how Senator Mitt Romney assessed the situation in general.

This was not normal, the Utah Republican reiterated, although it had come to feel perversely so. Romney had seen enough. "It has become quite familiar," he said on a late January morning at the Capitol. The Senate "trial" of the just-impeached president was under way. And while there was little doubt how it would turn out—conviction required sixty-seven Senate votes, and that was not happening—some drama still rested upon the well-barbered head of Willard "Mitt" Romney. Romney was considered the one Senate Republican who might be the wild card to thwart the unanimous absolution that Trump had demanded, and usually received, from his own party.

Over the previous few days, Trump had engaged in a curious kind of charm offensive to win Romney over. He called him a "pompous ass," a "fool," and a "bitter loser." He called for *Romney* to be impeached. He decried the general ilk of Never Trump Republicans as "human scum."

Romney was largely unbothered, mainly because he couldn't respect Trump less at this point. This was true of most elected Republicans in Washington, though Romney was one of the few willing to say so in public.

But this was no easy call for Romney. He found himself agonizing awake most days at 4:00 a.m. "My personal and political and team affiliation made me very much not want to have to convict," he told me. "I know myself well enough that if there's an outcome I really want, I will rationalize that outcome." That's a tendency Romney had seen in people faced with big, public decisions, including himself. "The mind is biased to the easier result," he said.

In his case, the easier result—to be a good soldier—would spare him considerable grief. "I've in the past convinced myself to make decisions based on avoiding discomfort," Romney said. Looking back, in many cases, they were decisions he would regret. "I've learned that if you don't follow your conscience, it haunts you for a long, long time," Romney said. "At this stage in life, I'm not going to do that anymore."

Romney had traveled a long and checkered political path. He was the son of a three-term Michigan governor, George Romney, a maverick Republican and rare figure of conscience in his party during the civil rights and Vietnam eras. Mitt ran for Senate in Massachusetts in 1994, lost to Ted Kennedy, was elected governor of the Bay State in 2002, and ran twice for president, becoming the Republican nominee in 2012 before losing to Barack Obama. Romney often said that his deep Mormon faith, close family bonds, and many decades of political rigmarole—particularly the experience of losing a general election campaign for president—had somewhat inured him to the petty nuisances and menaces of Donald Trump's Washington.

"As Mitt once said in some context, 'The worst thing that could happen to anyone in politics has already happened to me, I lost the presidency,'" said Stuart Stevens, his top campaign strategist in 2012. "It's like the guys in Vietnam said, 'What are you going to do, send me to Vietnam?'"

There was a time, after Obama defeated him in 2012, that Romney expected to live out his days in quasi-exile. That had been the precedent for party nominees after they lost general elections. "Mike Dukakis can't get a job mowing lawns," Romney remarked in *Mitt*, the Netflix documentary about his two presidential campaigns. Romney said he had resigned himself to being known as "a loser for life." He had watched his father suffer in the political wilderness.

After George Romney left public office, he found himself flailing around for relevance. "I remember my dad becoming quite frustrated," Mitt told me. "He used to say that Washington is the fastest place to go from 'Who's Who' to 'Who's That?'"

Mitt Romney expected the same would happen to him. He was not running for anything and considered himself semiretired. He tended to his investments, posed for selfies at gas stations, and fought Evander Holyfield in a charity boxing match.

But then Orrin Hatch vacated his Senate seat in Utah after forty-two years; Romney, who had moved to the state in 2014, was bored. He was elected in 2018.

Now ensconced in the Senate, Romney had been gifted by the forty-fifth president with a dose of late-career purpose. He had become the highest-profile specimen of that rarest of breeds: the Republican with enough spine to criticize Trump.

Romney was hardly a natural-born troublemaker. "I don't want to be the skunk at the garden party, and I don't want the disdain of Republicans across the country," Romney told me. It was too late for that now. But the position suited this late-career iteration of Romney. Or maybe it was just the vacuum of principle he had come to abhor in his party and was now trying to fill. Sometimes a moment finds an unlikely leader, no matter how depressing that moment might be. You don't always get to pick your moment, or your skunk.

———

THE MOST FASCINATING ASPECT OF WATCHING ROMNEY IN THE Senate was seeing him toss an increasing number of fucks out the window. (He would word that differently.) This occurred in conjunction with Romney's watching Republicans he had known for years tossing him overboard.

A blatant example involved Kelly Loeffler, a GOP donor from Georgia who got herself appointed to that state's vacant Senate seat by Governor Brian Kemp after the incumbent Johnny Isakson retired in late 2019. Loeffler began her new job just in time for the impeachment trial and was clearly in way over her head. She strode around the Capitol with a shell-shocked expression and barely knew a soul on Capitol Hill. One exception was Romney, whom Loeffler and her husband had gotten to know during his two runs for president. They gave $750,000 to Romney's super PAC and hosted fundraisers at their $10.5 million Buckhead, Georgia, estate, located in a gated community known as Tuxedo Park.

"We'd never known anybody that was running for president and actually had a friendship with them," Loeffler's husband, Jeffrey Sprecher, said in a 2013 interview with *Atlanta* magazine. "And so, it was easy to support a friend."

It became less easy in 2020. Loeffler was eager to make a name for herself, and her old "friend" had been deemed a traitor by the president of the United States. So, when Senate Republicans were debating whether to call additional impeachment witnesses—something Romney supported but virtually no others in his caucus did—the new kid in the middle school cafeteria saw a chance to hurl a fruit cup at the unpopular dork.

"Sadly, my colleague @SenatorRomney wants to appease the left by calling witnesses who will slander the @realDonaldTrump," Loeffler wrote in a tweet that landed exactly as Senate Republicans were meeting to discuss the witness issue.

Romney, who had no advance word of the attack, was taken aback. One senator described Loeffler's move as a "sucker punch." Senators rarely disparage each other publicly by name, or by tweet; that's more of a president thing.

On the Senate floor the next day, Loeffler approached Romney, appearing sheepish. She said something to the effect that politics is a tough business. According to witness accounts from the gallery, Romney smiled tightly for a few seconds before walking away.

"Kelly was in an unusual situation," Romney conceded later. "We'd probably done three fundraisers at her home, and she and Jeffrey were friends as well as strong supporters. And it's like, really?"

Future senator Bill Hagerty of Tennessee, another old friend who served as Romney's national finance chair in 2008, was also happy to plant a kiss on Trump's backside by placing a boot in Mitt's. Hagerty took the step of returning a $5,600 donation to his Senate campaign from Romney's super PAC. He also attacked his former pal and future colleague by calling Romney "indistinguishable from Obama" and one of the "most despised names in Tennessee."

Romney insisted that he'd long since learned to shrug off such ham-handed opportunism at his expense. If the Loefflers and Hagertys of the world needed to kneecap him to make themselves look tough, whatever. That's just politicians doing politics. Romney had logged plenty of time in this cafeteria.

Loeffler wound up having a brief and unmemorable Senate career, whose most notable episode was probably a campaign ad (not convincing) in which she compared her ruthless style of conservatism with that of Attila the Hun. She lost.

Hagerty won easily in redder Tennessee, and I was curious if it was now awkward for Romney to share a workplace with him. What does he say when he sees Hagerty in the hallway? Romney looked at me as if this were something he literally had never thought about before. He shrugged and grimaced before finally answering my dumb question. "Hi?" He chuckled.

Romney said he has long experience as an outcast. He was the only Mormon in his high school class. "Look, we all want to be approved by the group; it's a natural thing," Romney said. "No one wants to sit alone in the cafeteria. And yet there comes a time."

One of the lessons of his youth, Romney said, was that he could live without the affirmation of the pack. "I grew up being different," he said. "Kids drove Mustangs and Camaros. I drove my mother's Rambler station wagon. I was not a great athlete. I was not cool."

As a young adult, Romney completed a church mission in France and became accustomed to having doors slammed in his face. "I knocked on 200,000 doors, I was there five months, and I didn't convert a single person," he said. But he's come a long way since. "I got invited to Evander Holyfield's wedding," Romney said, relishing the oddity of this.

"It's in Hollywood, Florida. I can't wait. It's black tie."

IN GENERAL, ROMNEY SAID HE GETS ALONG FINE WITH HIS FELLOW senators, including the leadership of his caucus. "Mitch has let his hair down with me," Romney said of McConnell—an interesting image.

"He has said what he thinks about prominent members of our party. Namely the president."

This was true of most of his Republican colleagues, Romney said. Privately, everyone is fully aware of what Trump is about. "Oh, everybody gets the joke," Romney assured me. "They still are very aware of his, uh, what's a good word, 'idiosyncrasies.'"

For Romney, dealing with the Trump-infused grass roots of his party posed a greater challenge. The Republican rank and file had acquired a cruel, often bigoted edge. Romney was confronted by Trump-activated supporters whenever he ventured out of the relatively mannered bubble of Washington. They turned up at his events in Utah, getting in his face about something Sean Hannity or Mark Levin had said about him. They would repeat—word for word—some insane claim that Trump had just made about "Loser Mitt Romney." People could become relentless. Their leader in the White House had no restraints, so why should they?

None of their grievances appeared to be grounded in any set of ideas, and certainly not conservatism as Romney knew it. It was pure tribalism. He had spent the weekend in Florida at the height of Impeachment One. He was in a parking lot, unloading groceries, when a pedestrian started unloading on him. He railed against Romney as a "traitor" and ordered him to "leave Trump alone" and, while he was at it, leave the Republican Party.

Mitt had observed this growing populist strain within the GOP well before Trump came along. They were hardly his natural base when he ran for president in 2012. But he noticed they were more pervasive and vocal than they had been even in 2008, when Romney first ran, especially with the explosion of social media that occurred in the intervening years.

After 2012, Romney said he was surprised that he managed to win the Republican nomination that year, given what the party was clearly becoming. There's a reason Trump could attract such a big following with his birther lie about Obama in the early 2010s. Seventy-two percent of

Republicans in 2016 said they believed Trump's smears about Obama's citizenship. That tracks almost identically to the 71 percent of Republicans who in January 2022 said they believed Trump's Big Lie that Joe Biden was not a legitimate president.

I VISITED ROMNEY IN HIS HIDEAWAY OFFICE AT THE CAPITOL ON THE Wednesday morning of the Senate impeachment vote. He had agreed to give me advance word of his decision on the condition that I not report it until he started his floor speech a few hours later. This would allow me to write up a story in advance and put it online as soon as Romney took the floor, at around 2:00 p.m.

In the scheme of things, this was not the most earthshaking scoop of my career. I would essentially be alerting readers to something that would be revealed two or three minutes later, or however long it took for Romney to get to the point. But it was always satisfying to reveal something just a little bit early and then watch it career around the internet. Even cooler was to have the cliff-hanger solved directly from the mouth of the human scum himself (a term of endearment from me, surely Romney understood).

Romney seemed genuinely unsure of his decision in the days leading up to the vote. If I had to predict, I'd probably have guessed he would vote not guilty, mostly because we'd seen this act before, too. Expecting a Republican to do the tough and right and uncomfortable thing in the face of Donald Trump was like betting on the Washington Generals. And for all his anguish and deliberation, this was still Mitt Romney, whose long rap sheet of political expedience had been exhaustively documented over many years and campaigns.

Romney sat on his hideaway couch, with bags of peanut M&M's piled on a shelf. He greeted me with minimal chitchat and jumped right into Topic A. He said he would vote Trump guilty on the first count of impeachment, abuse of power.

He added a "not guilty" on the second count—obstruction of Congress—which came out like the afterthought that it was. What was significant was that Romney was willing to strike a clear blow against the volatile ruler of his party. He would become in fact the first U.S. senator in history to vote to remove a president of his own party: a flicker in the GOP's moral darkness of the Trump years.

"NOT VOTING MY CONSCIENCE IN ORDER FOR ME TO HAVE A BETTER political and personal benefit would subject my own conscience to its censure," Romney said. His words came out halting at first, and it took a minute for Romney to get rolling, but once he did, his tone acquired real acidity.

"Attempting to corrupt an election to maintain power is about as egregious an assault on the Constitution as can be made," Romney said. "And for that reason, it is a high crime and misdemeanor and I have no choice."

Romney kept pausing, as if he kept getting newly surprised to hear himself saying what he was saying. Or I might have just been projecting, too, because this expression of authentic outrage rang so exotic in a world so soaked in the fake kind.

Romney's face was a mix of determination and dread. The latter was merited, given the bear he was about to poke and the world of crap he was about to endure. "I recognize there is going to be enormous consequences for having reached this conclusion," Romney said. "Unimaginable."

Within a few hours, there would come fresh threats and harassment, censure motions, and Twitter assaults from Trump and his protectors, including Romney's own niece Ronna Romney McDaniel, the RNC chairwoman. Don Jr. called for Romney's expulsion from the Republican Party, and the president would brand him a "Democrat secret asset."

If it was any consolation, I told Romney as we were walking out of his hideaway, he would soon be lavished with "strange new respect" from all the Democrats and media types who used to abuse him when he ran for president. "Great," Romney said, which I took to be sarcastic. He then headed back to the Senate floor and into history.

I went back to my office and told a few colleagues what Romney had told me about his plans. They seemed shocked, more than I expected anyone to be. Again, in the scheme of things, this was but a single strike of defiance that would have no bearing on a result never in question.

Romney said he even expected Trump to be reelected that November, as most people still did then. He knew the essential bleak story remained the same, except that Romney had a tweak to the ending. He declared in his floor speech that Trump was "guilty of an appalling abuse of public trust." He sounded nervous and shaken, and his voice cracked a few times.

"I will only be one name among many, no more, no less, to future generations of Americans who look at the record of this trial," Romney said. "They will note merely that I was among the senators who determined that what the president did was wrong, grievously wrong."

As the vote came up, Romney sat staring straight ahead, talking to no one, his hands clasped in his lap. When he stood up and declared the president "guilty," he did so quickly and sat right back down. His vote was met with a brief stir in the gallery followed by a second of pure silence. Senator Brian Schatz, a Democrat of Hawaii, dabbed at his eyes. "I had an instinct," Schatz said afterward, "that this might be a moment."

Here's what lingered most for me in this moment: After the president's acquittal was sealed, Romney shook hands with his seatmate, Senator Mike Braun of Indiana, and rushed off. Romney was the first senator to depart the chamber. I noticed that barely any of his Republican colleagues even looked at him as he walked out. It was as if they were afraid that Romney might meet their eyes and some acknowledgment might be called for, something they could not face.

CHAPTER 16

HELL, IN REVIEW

———

I'm really not a bad person.

—President Donald J. Trump

February–March 2020

Trump gave his annual State of the Union address on the same day that a new Gallup poll showed an 84 percent gap between Republican and Democratic approval of the president. His speech elicited a corresponding split screen of reactions.

When Trump announced that he would be awarding the Presidential Medal of Freedom to the cancer-stricken Rush Limbaugh, the Republican side of the chamber jumped to its feet and applauded, while Democrats cried out "*NOOOO*" as they realized what was about to happen. Melania Trump—seated with Limbaugh—placed the medal grandly around the ailing radio host's neck. Speaker Pelosi, whose hand Trump refused to shake before the speech, tore up her copy of the prepared text as the president departed the dais. So, there's your state of the Union.

Graham would call these "the good old days of impeachment." Indeed, at least no one was marauding through the Capitol yet. No one had heard of hydroxychloroquine, either. And a woman in a cowboy hat stood alone outside the Capitol, belting out "Silent Night" into the cold. I chose to focus on that.

With a particular kind of contempt for any rational listener, the GOP's solemn elders continued to speak of imminent "pivots" and "resets" from the White House. They persisted with their pro forma hopes that Trump might finally heed the counsel of his "better angels," despite little evidence they existed. Perhaps impeachment could be a valuable teaching moment for him.

"I believe that the president has learned from his case," Senator Susan Collins said on *CBS Evening News*. After a blizzard of ridicule, Collins clarified that the idea of Trump's being chastened was perhaps "more aspirational on my part."

"We simply cannot let factional fever break our institutions," Mitch McConnell said in an address to the Senate that Wednesday afternoon, just before the Senate voted officially to formally acquit Trump. "I hope we will look back on this vote and say this was the day the fever began to break." Again, skepticism was warranted.

The next morning, the president spoke for an hour in the East Room of the White House, unleashing a free-associative torrent against his expanding roster of political enemies—or, as he called them, "the crookedest, most dishonest, dirtiest people I've ever seen." Let the healing begin, this was not.

Trump's West Wing caregivers had arranged for this post-acquittal pity party to rally the troops after these difficult months. They packed the room with his most ardent supporters, which was important not only for the president's state of mind but for the general optics of the moment. Trump was not alone in this epic fight was the message.

"You've been incredible!" the president said, looking out upon the room, moved. "Unbelievable."

This came a few hours after Trump served up yet another outburst at another National Prayer Breakfast. In between, Pelosi held a news conference and observed that the president seemed "a little sedated" at the State of the Union. If true, the sedation had worn off by the time Trump landed in the East Room to deliver his wild, whiplashing journey of a diatribe.

"I'm really not a bad person," Trump said, interrupting his own riff against the "top scum" of the FBI. "This is a day of celebration," he declared—which would have been a fine and hopeful note to end on. Instead, he opted for "We've been through hell."

ON THE SAME WEEK THAT TRUMP WAS ACQUITTED, LIMBAUGH WAS honored, and hell was declared, the Democrats kicked off their presidential nomination contest by botching their Iowa caucuses after their custom-designed software or app failed. The results remained a muddled mess for days. Trump deemed the caucuses an "unmitigated disaster," which turned out to be the rare White House statement that no one disputed.

Also indisputable was that Joe Biden lost and lost badly. He finished fourth in Iowa, behind Bernie Sanders, Pete Buttigieg, and Elizabeth Warren. This was no surprise, because the top three finishers had all been drawing large and enthusiastic crowds and had built strong organizations across the state. Not so much for Biden, whom I had followed around off and on for months. It was always a dreary spectacle, as if someone had roused the retired VP from a nap to run for president and we were all forced to watch.

In addition to the visible indicators (listless audiences, rambling speeches), Biden expressed little rationale for why he was even doing this again. I would periodically make a nuisance of myself, join his post-event press scrums, and ask Biden directly why he was running for a third time. "How badly do you want to be president?" was how I asked the question after one rally in Prole, Iowa.

The answer would be self-evident with most candidates ("very badly"), especially someone like Biden who'd been running pretty much since kindergarten. But the query seemed to come at Biden as a bit of a curveball. He paused for a second.

"I think it's really, really, really important that Donald Trump not be reelected," he said, and then launched into a classic Biden Roller Derby of verbiage in which he listed all the reasons Trump was so unacceptable. He landed on a rhetorical question for himself. "Could I die happily not having heard 'Hail to the Chief' play for me?" Biden asked. "Yeah, I could. That's not why I'm running."

So, again, why was Biden running? I was not sure that the unfitness of the incumbent would be enough to convince voters that Biden's moment had finally arrived. Biden, smartly, did not pretend that it had, or that at seventy-seven he was the one everyone had been waiting for. He did not try to pitch himself as some repackaged progressive or elderly version of AOC with hair plugs.

"You know, I've been around a long time; that's the bad news," Biden told me. "But the good news is, I've also been around a long time." He was fond of these bad news/good news constructions. "The bad news is that everybody knows me," he said. "The good news is everybody knows me."

It was always easy to whiff obligation around Biden. There was something passive about the whole enterprise. "We didn't really intend to be going on this journey," Jill Biden said at a fundraiser in Sun Valley, Idaho. "But when it came down to it, too many people were saying, 'Joe has to run,' 'Joe has to run.'"

The state of the Democrats in general resembled its own gloomy story of flattened ambitions. At the very least, Biden was a known quantity who seemed to scare the fewest number of people. He was much older than you'd ideally want in a standard-bearer. He was rusty and musty and gave the impression of treading gingerly into a world of trolls and Twitter vigilantes who did not exist the last time he ran. But Biden was not a bad guy, or a total idiot, and he talked a lot about basic decency, and that sounded fine to a lot of exhausted voters in 2020.

"I think the fact that he is an older white man kind of has a Santa Claus soothing effect on a lot of traditional voters," Representative Alexandria Ocasio-Cortez told me in an April 2020 interview. She said she believed that the comfort Biden engendered could buy him ideological latitude. "I'm convinced that Biden could essentially adopt Bernie's agenda, and it would not be a factor," she said. "Just as long as he continued to say things like 'malarkey.' And just not be Trump."

"MY DAD USED TO KID," BIDEN WAS TELLING ME DURING A HALF-hour drive from Des Moines to a rally at a college in Indianola, a few weeks before the caucuses. "He said, 'Joey, don't compare me to the Almighty. Compare me to the alternative.'" (Biden had, on other occasions, credited this line to the former Boston mayor Kevin White; he could be sloppy on attribution.)

Biden said that too many of the *"smart as hell"* people—by which he seemingly meant bubbled-off media elite types—were missing that simple calculation about his candidacy. If Biden was going to win, this election had to be about the alternative. His simple message: Biden was hardly perfect, but he was much better than Trump and probably best suited to beating him. "Electability" always won out as the chief quality Democratic voters were seeking in a nominee.

Trump would be tough to beat and in distinct ways. He attracted a passionate brigade. On the drive to Indianola, we passed at least two dozen Trump signs, billboard-sized in many cases. There is always a tendency to mistake the ubiquity of signs for a candidate's real strength, but Trump banners seemed to wave everywhere for four years. They popped out in plain sight, as did those monster Fox News ratings and overflow rallies.

And they remained fastened down on lawns and farms whether an election was coming up or not. They signaled that this president was more than just a seasonal candidate to his supporters. He was also a permanent identity marker and lifestyle brand. And it was not as if anyone were about to take their signs down if Trump happened to say something "problematic"—a word they never spoke in those houses.

Maybe, at a minimum, Biden really was best suited to clearing the do-no-harm bar and eking out a win. He was asking Democrats to set aside their grand plans and Green New Deals and let him extinguish this garbage fire before it burned out of control and the neighborhood became uninhabitable. In case of emergency, why not Joe Biden?

Or, alternatively, why bother?

That was the unavoidable question for Biden out of Iowa, and even more so after New Hampshire, where he finished fifth. Biden put in a dutiful week of campaigning in the Granite State before escaping early to South Carolina. I caught him ducking out a side entrance of the Double-Tree hotel in Manchester after the campaign canceled its primary night "celebration" and the candidate was attempting to distribute Dunkin' Donuts to his traveling press.

"Who wants one?" Biden said. "Who likes jelly? We have a lot of chocolates left." He was having a hard time finding takers. Eventually, he bolted for the airport.

WE'LL SKIP AHEAD, PAST THE EARLY PANDEMIC DAYS, THE MOBILE freezer morgues, Trump's inability to feel, or even fake, empathy, Biden getting resurrected in South Carolina, then clinching the nomination from the sealed-off safety of his home in Wilmington.

The obligatory "key takeaway," for our purposes, was that the forty-fifth president fell into a tailspin in which he became his absolute worst self at the worst possible time and made everything more terrible for everyone. Every single day. It was a leadership miscarriage the likes of which no corporate board or oversight body would ever tolerate in any chief executive, although the U.S. electorate just might.

I had often wondered how Trump would handle a genuine crisis like this that happened on his watch, one that called for compassion and warmth. I asked Trump about this once, when I was writing about him during the 2016 campaign. We were aboard his jet and the candidate had been fixating on his own image on a flat-screen TV in front of him. I mentioned those "presidential empathy" moments, like Obama had after the mass shooting at the Black church in Charleston, South Carolina, or George W. Bush at Ground Zero in the days after September 11. How would Trump perform in such situations? His face remained still and distant, as if it was coated in plastic. Empathy, he finally assured me, "will be one of the strongest things about Trump.

"When I'm in that position," he continued, "when we have horrible hurricanes, all kinds of horrible things happen, you've got to have empathy." Trump then returned to watching himself on the flat screen.

Trump's daily coronavirus calamity made for the single worst Rose Garden strategy in history. No need to relive that, either. Or the part where Trump suggested virus sufferers inject themselves with bleach or his promise that the coronavirus would just "disappear" or his insistence on restarting his rallies well before they were safe (RIP Herman Cain). For good measure, he turned the once universally revered infectious disease expert Dr. Anthony Fauci into a culture war bogeyman who required a security detail. "A bit bizarre" was how Fauci self-diagnosed his situation.

The prevailing assumption was that Trump had been dealt a bad reelection hand: that the pandemic wrecked his "beautiful" economy and entertainment presidency. In fact, if Trump could have demonstrated a bare minimum of competence and compassion, the pandemic might have benefited him politically, as it did governors of both parties.

Biden himself emerged fine from the ordeal, despite holding no office and holing up at home. The lockdown allowed him to act like a responsible grown-up while not showing his age in public every day. He happily stood aside and let Trump run against his most lethal opponent of all, Donald Trump.

The president could never just flail around in private. He had to inflict his full blowhard self every afternoon in the White House Briefing Room during live TV marathons. His political team watched in agony.

"We're going to lose in a landslide," his campaign manager, Brad

Parscale, said in a phone call to Jared Kushner, according to an account in *I Alone Can Fix It* by Carol Leonnig and Philip Rucker. "You've got Dr. Trump up there all day," Parscale continued. "We're losing and nothing's changing."

"I know," Kushner agreed. "This is horrible."

Trump also had plenty of help blowing himself up. Kellyanne Conway went out and informed everyone that the virus was "being contained," another "alternative fact" worthy of the maestro. The future press secretary Kayleigh McEnany reassured everyone on Fox News that the coronavirus happened only in other countries.

"We will not see diseases like the coronavirus here," she announced, and yes, we needed to also be grateful to our great president for that.

"Isn't that refreshing when contrasting it with the awful presidency of President Obama?" McEnany asked. Great question.

Among their unique skills, those in the White House also had a gift for setting timelines that would come back to bite them in the most predictable of ways. Trump said in March that the virus would die in warmer weather and churches would be filled on Easter Sunday. Pence predicted that "by Memorial Day weekend we will have this coronavirus epidemic behind us," while Kushner said the country would be "really rocking again" by July.

As it turned out, the only thing that was "really rocking" that spring were street protests after George Floyd was murdered by a Minneapolis police officer. It would be that inescapably gruesome video of the officer, Derek Chauvin, pressing his knee down on Floyd's neck for nine minutes that effectively ended the Trump presidency as a TV show. This was the abuse that brought much of the country outdoors again. Finally, *something* felt as if it mattered enough for millions of Americans to risk exposure to one another.

CHAPTER 17

CARACAS-ON-
THE-POTOMAC

———

I'm late for lunch.

—Senator Rob Portman,
Republican of Ohio

June–August 2020

Part of the beautiful urgency and relief of the George Floyd protests was that they were so much bigger than the daily blundering from the White House. Donald Trump was rendered peripheral.

"He is just a social media personality to us, the guy who told us to drink bleach," said Artinese Campbell, thirty-three, who had come downtown on a Monday afternoon in early June and was watching protesters gather near the White House.

Trump's tangential position quickly became intolerable to him, and he had to seize back the screen in his usual worst-possible way. I was in Lafayette Square, across from the White House, when Trump officially reached his end with this. The president had become fixated on a story, written by my *Times* colleagues Peter Baker and Maggie Haberman, about his being whisked into an underground bunker during a heated hour of protests outside the White House a few nights earlier. He thought the image of himself being cloistered for protection made him appear weak and scared, and he became obsessed with (1) finding who leaked the detail, (2) putting the leaker in jail, and (3) proving that he was not weak or scared.

A large late-afternoon crowd of protesters had assembled near the White House on the first day of June. It felt as if a new level of energy and tension had been building all day. There was a stepped-up contingent of police in place, with few if any identifiers on their uniforms saying who they were or what federal forces they represented. The air was heavy as hell.

And then, like a soccer riot, something went off: a low rumble of footsteps, explosions, a human wall of armored officers shoving protesters into barriers with plastic shields. "Move out, move out," the officers kept screaming. The rumbling chaos of the Trump presidency had now also moved outside.

I ran a block or so away, toward my prepandemic office in the *Times'* Washington bureau on I Street. It was hard to decipher from a distance what was happening, but it became clear soon enough. Police on foot, bike, and horseback used shields and batons, flash grenades and chemical spray to clear the area. A few minutes later, Trump walked across Lafayette Square for a photo op in front of Saint John's Church. He held a Bible aloft. There were many pictures taken of this; it was a photo op. You can google it.

For maybe a few days, there appeared to be some breakthrough shock over what had transpired. This latest case of presidential trauma seemed pretty bad—a true Caracas-on-the-Potomac spectacle. Could this become the latest next-level horror that might somehow register beyond Trump's very large pale? "This felt different," went the recurring Twitter refrain from inside the D.C. humidifier.

It also felt very familiar. As did the trickle of Republican criticism from the usual caucus of the *troubled and concerned*. Collins said she found the episode "painful" to watch and that she thought Trump "came across as unsympathetic."

"What we saw last night was not the America that I know," added another GOP senator, Lisa Murkowski of Alaska. In fact, Lafayette Square was very much what America was becoming, or at least what one major party was abiding.

Reporters trekked up to Capitol Hill the next day to assess any potential weakening of Republican support for Trump. The usual flaccid reactions followed.

I happened upon McConnell leaving his office, and even had him to myself for a few seconds. "Senator, what did you make of the events at Lafayette Square yesterday?" I asked. The usual zombie walk ensued as the majority leader silently made his way to the weekly Republican caucus lunch.

A few yards ahead strode Kelly Loeffler of Georgia, who appeared hypnotized into muteness. She offered nothing but the sound of quickening clacks of heels on Minton tile. (A cord trailed from her pocket, making it look as if her movements were being controlled from a booth.)

"Senator, what did you think of the incident outside the White House?" I asked as she hurried away and an aide brandished a business card, inviting me to follow up with him at a later time.

At this point, I defer to the queen, Kasie Hunt, then of NBC, who had become the preeminent Capitol Hill journalist in the category of wrangling lame GOP comments about Trump's latest act of devilry. Hunt had made a reportorial art form of pressing scared Republican members and then documenting their nonanswers. Her sequence of tweets from that June 2 stakeout read like a dark poem of dereliction scrolled through a screen of our learned national helplessness:

Senator Pat Roberts (R-Kans.): "I don't have any comment on that."

Senator Mike Enzi (R-Wyo.): "Sorry, I'm late for lunch."

Senator Rob Portman (R-Ohio): "I'm late for lunch."

Senator Bill Cassidy (R-La.): "I didn't follow, I'm sorry."

Senator Ted Cruz (R-Tex.), asked if what he saw at the White House last night was an abuse of power: "By the protestors, yes."

Senator Mike Lee (R-Utah) said he had concerns. What were they? "Violence is scary," he said.

Finally, as the Republican lunch broke up, McConnell hosted his weekly leadership press conference in the hallway. He opened his remarks with a passive-voiced statement about the Floyd protests in general.

"Egregious wrongs have been done," McConnell said. "Much of it recorded."

Egregious evasions persisted through the afternoon—much of that also recorded.

IT WAS CLEAR AT THIS POINT THAT LAFAYETTE SQUARE WOULD recede soon enough into the rolling Fog of Trump. Both parties had their nominating conventions planned for August, the Democrats in Milwaukee, Republicans in Charlotte. Trump saw no reason they should not go on as scheduled; certainly his own party's would. The festivities, however, mostly fell victim to the coronavirus. The Ds had a skeletal presence in Milwaukee, and the Rs largely stuck to D.C., with the Trump Hotel serving as a main den of activity.

Mayor Giuliani hosted his convention-week radio show from the hotel, a short walk from the Andrew W. Mellon Auditorium, where many of the grand homages to POTUS were taking place. Washington's indoor COVID restrictions kept many of the usual groupies away, but Rudy was always a destination draw. He was photographed, hugged, and tweeted about at all hours. He could never be thanked enough.

On the second night of the convention, I snagged a lobby table at the Trump Hotel with my *Times* colleague Shawn McCreesh and a D.C.-based Brit correspondent for *The Spectator*, Matt McDonald, who was attempting some Jane Goodall treatment of our crazy American political rituals. The three of us took in the bar scene together. It wasn't much of one, though it was Matt's birthday and a friend of his had baked him a delicious carrot cake, which he shared generous helpings of and we all devoured with our beers.

I stopped in again briefly at the hotel on the next night and happened to catch Rudy in the lobby. He was in full Belle of the Ball mode. An older woman approached and asked to shake *Mistah Giuliani's* hand. Happy to do it, Hizzoner said. He said he was not afraid of getting sick and would not let the virus win, just as he would not let the terrorists win after 9/11.

Rudy had already won this round. No one had seized the moment under Trump with more gusto. His epic career of ups and downs, feuds, outrages, and swift descent into shamelessness and desperation made Giuliani the master creature of the Trump Swamp.

Now he was back on the main stage, speaking in the peak Thursday night slot of the scaled-down convention. Trump granted Giuliani a broad portfolio and room to run. Not some chastened version of Rudy, either. "He's got a boss who is not exactly reining him in," said Andrew Kirtzman, a New York political consultant who wrote the Giuliani biography *Emperor of the City*.

There would be little suspense or drama at this convention, beyond the usual circus acts and third-tier talk show actors.

"DON'T LET THE DEMOCRATS TAKE YOU FOR GRANTED!" Don Jr.'s girlfriend, Kimberly Guilfoyle, the former Fox News anchor, screamed in an address to the mostly empty Mellon Auditorium.

"DON'T LET THEM STEP ON YOU! DON'T LET THEM DESTROY YOUR FAMILIES, YOUR LIVES, AND YOUR FUTURE!

"DON'T LET THEM KILL THE FUTURE GENERATION!"

Whoa!

If there was a crowd here, they'd have been going nuts.

The convention's culminating pageant was of course Trump's valedictory address in which he accepted his party's nomination on the South Lawn of the White House. It was set against an Orwellian backdrop of American flags, massive Trump-Pence billboards, giant jumbotrons, and hundreds of maskless courtiers seated on fifteen hundred folding chairs lined up across the grass.

Trump would have been perfectly attired in a general's uniform if he had so chosen. He had reportedly considered holding his big acceptance speech at the Civil War battlefield in Gettysburg, Pennsylvania, but opted for his own backyard, if nothing else for convenience's sake.

The usual fusspot concerns about ethics were raised, if not legal ones: the use of federal property and employees for such a blatantly political event would be frowned upon in any previous, norm-abiding administration.

"We have the Hatch Act to prevent such behavior," noted Michael McFaul, a former U.S. ambassador to Russia. "It's obviously not working."

House Democrats even deployed their favorite weapon—the *sharply worded letter*—to register their displeasure with the White House Office of Special Counsel. That didn't work, either.

The speech itself was the familiar litany of Trump 2020 fictions. It described a country where the coronavirus had been fully eradicated by the president's own brilliance and the economy hadn't tanked—as opposed to the reality where the United States was approaching 200,000 COVID deaths and had just seen a third of its GDP vaporized. And Trump spoke confidently about the future, in that transparently ominous way of his. "The only way they can take this election away from us is if this is a rigged election," he said. This is what is known in the TV drama business as "foreshadowing."

I WAS WALKING HOME LATER THAT NIGHT AND FOUND MYSELF A few blocks from the White House as the grand finale was breaking up. Waves of Trump supporters were emerging from the perimeter of the complex. They were mostly well-dressed donor types, recognizable public officials, and some who looked more like tourists in shorts, T-shirts, and red MAGA caps.

Departing conventiongoers were in many cases met by hundreds of protesters who had gathered around the White House. They had spent the previous hours chanting, demonstrating, and blaring music in an effort to disrupt the president's climactic performance. Several clashes were reported, including one in which Senator Rand Paul had to be escorted to safety by police into a nearby hotel. "Just got attacked by an angry mob of over 100, one block away from the White House," Paul tweeted later. "Thank you to @DCPoliceDept for literally saving our lives from a crazed mob."

As I walked a few blocks north toward Dupont Circle, the streets became much less populated and suddenly quiet. Entire blocks of businesses remained boarded from the spring and summer protests. Much of downtown had been hollowed out to begin with during this first pandemic summer.

But the fanfare and commotion back at the White House lent an eerie energy to the rest of the capital on this night. Everything was still, yet the Land of Liberty felt anything but peaceful, divided into two perfectly infuriated teams, with Trump in full possession of one of them.

At around midnight, explosions burst from the south. I spun around to see what they were: fireworks, ignited by the president's reelection campaign over the Washington Monument and Lincoln Memorial, spelling out "Trump" and "2020" in the hazy sky.

CHAPTER 18

"WILL YOU SHUT UP, MAN?"

———

RESOLVED: That the Republican Party has and will continue
to enthusiastically support the President's America-first agenda.

—Republican Party Platform, 2020

September–November 2020

Beyond the speeches and commotion, little actual business was conducted at the convention. The GOP's central objective—to comfort
Donald Trump and afflict his enemies—remained much the same, only
more so.

"This Republican party dances to whatever tunes come into Mr.
Trump's head," wrote Edward Luce of the *Financial Times*. The party did
not bother to even produce a new platform, for the first time since 1856.
Their unchanged mission was fired off in a single-page list of bullet
points and "resolutions." This from a party whose ideal was once embodied by rugged individualists, Marlboro Men, and archetypal John

Wayne fantasies. While their Trump-era descendants were now vocalizing their "fuck your feelings" contempt for easily triggered libs, much of their reason for being had now been given over to placating this most overwrought and delicate of presidential souls.

As for the Democrats (being Democrats), they had more ground to cover—progressives to heed, interest groups to pander to, and Trump-averse women in the suburbs to accommodate. Never a beacon of brevity, Biden nonetheless managed to spit out a nifty headline and rallying cry despite himself.

It came at the end of his first debate against Trump in September, as Biden was attempting to answer a question from the moderator, Chris Wallace, about the Supreme Court. Trump kept interrupting him. Finally, Biden closed his eyes, shook his head, and spoke for an audience at wit's end.

"Will you shut up, man?" Biden said. The line was seemingly born on a bumper sticker.

There would be no shortage of perfectly plausible reasons for why Trump was expected to lose. The economy still reeled, and the pandemic still raged. Polls were taken, numbers were crunched, and the president's dismal standing with an exhausted electorate was confirmed again and again.

But the main explanation remained straightforward. Huge numbers of Americans were simply done with this guy. They were sick of his face on their screens and the space he occupied in their heads. Trump had become a burning irritant across every realm, like a national canker sore.

The weariness afflicted Trump's natural allies, too. "It was just too much," Kevin McCarthy recalled a few months later. McCarthy recounted something a Republican House colleague had told him in early 2017, just a few weeks into Trump's term. "The person said to me, 'Oh my God, it feels like two years already. People are just going to be worn out.'"

Speaking four years later, McCarthy said that's essentially what happened. There was too much Trump. "Too much stimulus, too much exposure," McCarthy said. "That got Biden a lot of votes."

Chris Christie recalled running into a Republican friend he'd known for years in the grocery store just before the election. Trump couldn't leave fast enough, she said. "I just can't listen to that voice for another four years," Christie said, relaying what the woman told him. "This is someone who generally supported Trump's policies but who voted for Biden. She just couldn't take Trump's personality anymore."

There were more academic takes on this. "He's a symptom as much as an accelerant," Obama said in an interview with *The Atlantic,* of his successor. "But if we were going to have right-wing populism in this country, I would have expected somebody a little more appealing." The former president added that he would not have expected "someone who has complete disdain for ordinary people to be able to get attention and then the following from those very same people."

There were also purely local explanations for Trump's deficit, all related to his general lack of impulse control. If, for instance, Trump had managed to resist, say, trashing recently deceased Representative John Dingell, the Michigan Democrat who served a record fifty-nine years in Congress, it might have proven decisive in a state that Biden carried by just 150,000 votes. Presumably, Trump's post-death contempt for John McCain (of extremely close Arizona) and John Lewis (of even closer Georgia) was not helpful, either. Trump's own team would occasionally suggest to the president themselves, at their peril, that his act was wearing thin. The president understood his predicament on a certain level. He could be quite blunt and desperate in describing it.

"Will you please like me?" he pleaded from the stage at an October rally in Johnstown, Pennsylvania.

Experts had deemed "suburban women" in particular to be Trump's problem demographic. Fifty-six percent of white female voters said they held a very unfavorable view of Trump in a *New York Times*/Siena College poll released two weeks before the election. These included many independents and former Republicans who self-identified as moderate or conservative and were likely to be put off by the president's boorish inclinations.

Trump's "Will you please like me?" exhortation was addressed specifically to this cohort. "Please, please," he continued. "I saved your damn neighborhood, okay?"

That same week, Sarah Longwell, the founder of Republican Voters Against Trump, tweeted out a clip of his plea along with this retort: "I did a focus group tonight with women who voted for Trump in 2016. Not a single one was planning to vote for him again."

Plenty of anecdotal evidence suggested a definite trying of patience, if not a pending divorce. And there was no question that over four years Trump had turned large numbers of Republicans into former Republicans, drove huge numbers of retirements from Congress, and contributed to sweeping GOP House defeats in 2018. In the history of modern polling, voters under thirty had never been less identified with a major political party as they were with the GOP in 2020.

But it was also clear that what remained of the Republican Party was bonded as tightly as ever to Trump. Newly "former Republicans" were replaced by this new breed of "Trump Republicans," whose energized ranks included previous nonvoters, onetime fringe actors (now main-streamed), conspiracy pushers, white identity fetishists, and the like. Trump kept transgressing, in ways that were more and more egregious, yet their devotion endured. Trump was their party. Not a fusty old entity that espoused some bullshit about "family values" or "compassionate conservatism."

Trump's spool of personal grievances had become their own. In effect, his narcissism did, too. How could the viewpoints or experiences of others ever be valid? How could anyone not vote for Trump? How could he lose? It wasn't hard, given the identity web Trump had woven in this "community," to see where this pathology was headed. As Jonathan V. Last wrote in *The Bulwark* on October 8, "Go write this down: after November 3, the price of GOP politics is going to be an insistence that, actually, Donald Trump did win the election and/or would have won if it hadn't been stolen/rigged."

Still, most commentary explained the fidelity of Trump's supporters in the context of conventional political allegiance to a set of policies. That was always easier to digest than the broader, more incendiary effects.

"We were always asking, 'What would it take to break the camel's back?'" said the former congressman Tom Rooney, Republican of Florida, who withdrew his support for Trump in 2016 after the release of the *Access Hollywood* video. Rooney mentioned an article that had been published in *The Atlantic* a few weeks before the 2020 election in which Trump had derided American combat troops as "losers" and "suckers." The report, denied by the White House, set off the usual cycle of pundit shock ("NOW he's really done it"), which lasted until that shock was muted and blotted out by ten new outrages.

"When the losers-and-suckers thing happened, I asked a friend in

Florida if that bothered him, and he said, 'Nope,'" Rooney told me. All that mattered to his friend was that he thought Trump was a better bet to keep his taxes low. "That was it," Rooney said. "End of discussion."

I SPENT THE CLOSING WEEKS OF THE CAMPAIGN DRIVING AROUND battleground states, hitting candidate and surrogate events, and generally reengaging with the country after months of home confinement. Things were clearly much quieter than they had been in the Before Times. Blocks of businesses were shuttered, many forever. But it was encouraging that at least most places did not resemble the dystopian visages of our pandemic media screens.

About ten days out from the election, I went to see Ivanka Trump speak in a sunlit function room overlooking a pond outside Milwaukee. The First Intern was here on a surgical mission to make nice with a roomful of her father's demographic kryptonite, suburban women.

The president had spent the past twenty-four hours calling Hunter Biden a "criminal," Dr. Fauci a "disaster," government scientists "idiots," and members of the media "real garbage." Ivanka, meanwhile, tried to carve out a pleasant messaging safe zone for herself. Her persona departed from the daily tornado of grievance coming from the White House. She skipped the usual red meat in Wisconsin and went straight to dessert.

"I learned that the first ice cream sundae was created in this amazing state!" she gushed as an icebreaker. Who doesn't love ice cream sundaes? "Wisconsinites eat twenty-one million gallons of ice cream a year," the president's daughter continued. She liked to collect souvenir trivia like this from the road, which she said she would serve up as cool-mom fodder.

"My children, upon hearing this, want to move to Wisconsin," she said. *Woo-hoo.* "So, the Kushners might be coming to town!" (Update: The Kushners have not moved to Wisconsin.)

Adding a final dollop of whipped cream to this sundae, Ivanka delighted the crowd by telling them she'd spent so much time campaigning in the Badger State it had *already* become like a "second home" to her. She was in and out of the function hall in an hour.

I approached a few audience members after the talk. They said they loved hearing from Ivanka, that it was a nice antidote to the vicious lies that the First Family was normally subjected to.

"It was a breath of fresh air," said Joe Krupa, of Franklin, through a navy blue MAGA-emblazoned mask. "I'm really sick of all the Debbie Downers and the negativity," he said. To be clear, Krupa said he blamed this on the "hatred for Trump" from the biased Debbie Downer media ("except Fox"). Hunter Biden's work for a Ukrainian energy company, he said, "should be an even bigger scandal than Watergate." Krupa seemed to be getting slightly worked up but stopped himself, because this was not the right vibe for Ivanka's reception.

Later that week, Donald Trump Jr. would appear on Fox News to talk about Hunter's connection to "human trafficking and prostitution rings." A few days earlier, Wisconsin's Republican senator, Ron Johnson, told a Trump rally in Janesville that Biden supporters "don't particularly love America."

Another Trump supporter in Franklin saw my *New York Times* badge and had questions. Why, he wanted to know, were "all of you in the mainstream media" ignoring antifa, "Fascist Fauci," Biden's senility, and whatnot? The man, about seventy, wore a blue blazer over a dress shirt. He listed a bunch of other reckless and fantastical things related to Biden that he said the press was suppressing. (He attributed his claims of Biden atrocities to "common sense.") He also asked me if I was a socialist and a "card-carrying member of antifa."

His tone was flat but not unfriendly. I told him I left my antifa membership card at home. This even got a laugh. Perhaps a time for healing.

I MARKED THE LAST WEEKEND OF THE CAMPAIGN DRIVING AROUND Georgia and the Carolinas, which were home to three competitive Senate races and two presidential battlegrounds (Georgia and North Carolina). Trump popped in for a Sunday night airport rally in the northwest Georgia city of Rome. Several thousand of his supporters waited in the chill, and every major Republican pol in the state who didn't have COVID dropped everything to be there. And why shouldn't they? The day before, the White House had put out a sheet of its "science and technology accomplishments," beginning with the top one: "ENDING THE COVID-19 PANDEMIC." As *FiveThirtyEight*'s Clare Malone noted, "That day alone, 983 Americans died."

Trump's supporting cast onstage included Loeffler, her fellow Republican senator David Perdue, and Marjorie Taylor Greene, the loony-tunes local congressional candidate and QAnon enthusiast whose long history of racist, anti-Semitic, and generally harassing conduct made her an incendiary character long before she ever arrived in Washington. And yes, you knew she would arrive in Washington soon enough, as surely as her campaign would run up a tab of $717.30 for meals at the Trump Hotel a few days after her election.

Pre-Trump, no Republican standard-bearer would be allowed anywhere near a stage that included Marjorie Taylor Greene. In 2020, however, the president had anointed her a "future Republican star." Based on the loud reception she received in Rome, this star had already been born. "She's somebody that gets a little more publicity than I do," Trump said of Greene, bestowing his highest form of flattery, or envy, upon the protégée.

Trump also talked up his old friend and New Jersey Generals employee Herschel Walker, the former University of Georgia football legend whom he would later persuade to run for Senate. Like Greene, the notion of Walker running for anything with a presidential blessing would have been ludicrous in any before-Trump version of the GOP. His multiple-personality disorders and history of violent behavior and bizarre conduct would have certainly been disqualifying. Not to mention that Walker, a former Dallas Cowboy, was a longtime resident of Texas.

But Trump's imprimatur was more than enough to transcend all of that. Walker has since moved back to Georgia and is the likely Republican Senate nominee in 2022. And he immediately proved his fitness as a blue-chip candidate in today's GOP. "He is no doubt the greatest president to ever, ever hold office," Heisman Herschel said of Donald J. Trump.

Leaving Rome, I got stuck behind a caravan of cars, pickup trucks, and rigs plastered with Trump ornaments, banners, and flags motoring northeast on Interstate 75. Trump had boasted at his rally of these massive highway convoys that kept materializing in his honor (along with their flotilla counterparts on water). They were "a hundred miles long," Trump claimed, which was his typical exaggeration, though true enough in spirit. The demonstrations could indeed be massive and sometimes menacing. Confederate flags were common, as were vulgar stickers aimed at the predictable Democratic targets, usually female. (Hillary, Nancy, and AOC were the usual trio.) A pickup truck driving in front of me hauled a sound system on its roof that blared a Trump speech.

As these cavalcades went, this one in Georgia was tame. But not all of them were. Several states were reporting clogged roads and delays as Trump supporters aggressively announced themselves in these highway gangs. The FBI was investigating an incident in Texas in which several Trump-adorned vehicles blockaded a Biden campaign bus traveling from San Antonio to Austin. In one video, a Trump car bumped up against a campaign SUV trailing the bus. None of the vehicles contained Biden or Harris, and no injuries were reported.

Earlier that day, at another Trump rally in Opa-locka, Florida, Marco Rubio fired up the crowd with an endorsement of these vehicular bullying displays. "I saw yesterday a video of these people in Texas," Rubio said, sounding like an excited teenager. "Did you see it? All the cars on the road?" That happens in Florida all the time, he said. "I love seeing the boat parades," Rubio shouted. (Presumably he was not referring to the flotilla, also in Texas, in which five of the Trump boats sank.)

"We thank all the great patriots," he went on.

And thank *you* for your servitude, Marco!

I heard a clip of this on the radio and couldn't help contemplating Rubio's sad slide into slavish devotion to someone he'd previously called "the most vulgar person to ever aspire to the presidency." He had traveled a steady spiral to defeated Liddle Marco and now fully co-opted minion.

As his own campaign had ended four years earlier, Rubio would often bemoan the thuggish behavior that was in evidence at Trump rallies and declare that the candidate bore responsibility for whipping up his supporters. "There's only one presidential candidate who has violence at their events," Rubio pointed out. He promised there would be a "reckoning" inside the GOP, someday. "You mark my words, there will be prominent people in American politics who will spend years explaining to people how they fell into this," Rubio said.

On the eve of the 2020 election, Rubio was well past explaining anything.

I saw Graham the next day in South Carolina. He was holding a rally in Rock Hill on the Monday before the election. November 3 would be its own day of reckoning for Graham, who appeared to be in a tight race with the Democrat Jaime Harrison for a job he would seemingly do or say anything to keep. "There is no one in this chamber who needs to be in the United States Senate as desperately as Lindsey Graham does," one of his colleagues once told me.

As the two Senate candidates were running even in polls through the final weeks, Graham had taken to going on Fox News programs to literally beg viewers for campaign cash. "Help me," he told Sean Hannity. "Help me. You did last week. Help me again." This was the same day Graham went on *Fox & Friends* and nearly cried.

"I'm getting killed financially," he said that morning. "They hate my guts!"

The Washington Post's Paul Farhi called Graham's performance "an emotional appeal almost as weepy as Jerry Lewis in the later hours of his old charity telethons."

In Rock Hill, I chatted briefly with Graham outside his election eve rally. He stood in a parking lot surrounded by about a hundred supporters snacking from a buffet table of Chick-fil-A set up next to the campaign bus. I asked Graham how he was holding up. He was never one to hide his fatigue or weariness. He resembled a disheveled and disoriented hostage just emerging from captivity.

"I'm pretty much brain-dead," he told me, adding that he was optimistic about his chances the next day against Harrison. Graham wound up winning by a healthy margin. "I'll be seeing you back in D.C.," he said. "We'll visit."

MY PLAN WAS TO HEAD BACK TO WASHINGTON AND SPEND ELECTION night at the Trump Hotel. This felt fitting, if probably a mob scene—and complicated by D.C.'s public-gathering limits during COVID, on the off-chance anyone at the hotel was complying. Trump was also scheduled to be there for an election night celebration, which would have meant a lot of security restrictions.

Apparently, though, Trump bugged out at the last minute and decided to stay back at the White House to watch the returns while his supporters partied on at the Mother Ship. The MyPillow Guy and Ralph Reed were expected to attend the festivities. Promising!

I was still in South Carolina on Monday night, with a flight back to Washington scheduled from Charlotte (not far from Rock Hill). But I had to file a story first and wound up missing my plane, so I kept my rental car and decided to just drive the six hours back to D.C.

An hour or two into my journey, I stopped off in a hotel near the highway to catch some sleep. Lying in bed, I heard the voices of Fox News hosts blasting from an extremely loud TV set in the next room. It seemed whoever was on the other side of the wall was a hard-core Hannity, Carlson, and Ingraham devotee (and quite possibly hard of hearing). I nodded off for a few hours and woke up around 3:00 a.m. as the Fox hosts brayed on in the darkness. I heard thunderous tirades about Hunter Biden, "widespread reports" of irregularities in early voting, and concerns that antifa was plotting all kinds of mischief. I wondered if my neighbor went to sleep with these voices every night, or if this was something that a lot of people did.

By around 3:30 a.m., I was back on the road. I arrived in Washington by dawn on Election Day. I drove into the city via downtown, which was devoid of people and covered in plywood. Radio news was filled with special warnings and precautions. Once a celebration of our tranquil democratic traditions, Election Day was now being dreaded as a hazard on par with a potential terrorist attack or natural disaster. Walmart removed gun and ammunition displays from thousands of stores, due to concerns about "civil unrest." Students at George Washington University received an email headlined "We Suggest Preparing for the Election Day Period as You Would for a Hurricane or a Snowstorm." New Zealand's ambassador to Washington urged embassy staff to keep fourteen days of food and essentials.

"I'm just glad this thing will be over tomorrow," Graham had told me the day before in South Carolina. These had become the most famous of last words in America.

CHAPTER 19

"WHAT IS THE DOWNSIDE FOR HUMORING HIM?"

———

Is there anybody in charge at the White House who was doing anything but kissing his fat butt?

—Nancy Pelosi to General Mark Milley,
chairman of the Joint Chiefs of Staff

November–December 2020

Trump lost. He did not take it well. Seasoned observers of this president were not surprised.

The race was too close to call for a few days, but Biden was ahead late on election night and clearly trending toward a win. Trump, however, was determined to go on TV as early as possible to declare victory. Several aides cautioned him strongly against this. Who could imagine what would happen next?

"This is a fraud on the American people," Trump said in an East Room address in the wee hours of November 4. "This is an embarrassment to our country. We were getting ready to win this election. Frankly, we did win this election."

For those still bothering to keep track of Trump's wildly irresponsible words, he now held the distinction of saying the single most reckless thing ever uttered by a U.S. president on election night. It was obvious to every responsible steward of American democracy that such claims would undermine faith in the vote, cause confusion and embarrassment around the world, sow chaos at home, and possibly incite violence.

Chris Christie called Trump's speech "one of the most dangerous pieces of political rhetoric I have ever heard in my life." He added that it made him "physically sick to my stomach." But Christie was an outlier. He had, finally, reached his end with Trump after years of frustrations, humiliations, and thwarted job ambitions. The final indignity occurred in late September after Christie attended a super-spreader reception at the White House for the Supreme Court nominee Amy Coney Barrett. In addition to the president and First Lady, several high-level officials present wound up infected with the virus. This included Christie, whose multiple comorbidities (obesity, asthma) placed him at high risk and landed him in the ICU.

Trump was being treated concurrently at Walter Reed hospital and called Christie in New Jersey to check in, caring friend that he was. After some chitchat, Trump moved to the real purpose of his call. "Are you going to say you got this from me?" Trump asked Christie. It was important that he not say this, the president reminded him. Contagion, pathogens, ICU—not beautiful associations for the brand.

"It was one of the few laughs I had in the hospital," Christie told me later of Trump's friendly reminder. "I got off the phone and I just shook my head. Like, this guy will never change."

Neither did Trump's usual contingent of co-saboteurs. They lent credence to Trump's bogus election claims almost immediately. "President Trump won this election," Kevin McCarthy told Laura Ingraham on Thursday. "So, everyone who is listening, do not be quiet. Do not be silent about this. We cannot allow this to happen before our very eyes." The House Republican leader did not relent even after every major news outlet declared Biden to be the president-elect a few days later.

Graham was also very much on board with the "What is the downside for humoring him?" approach, famously laid out by a senior Republican official in *The Washington Post* a week after Election Day. Other Republicans asked Graham to intervene, maybe try to talk the president down a little from the more outlandish claims. "He'll get there," Lindsey reassured them ("give it time, give it time!").

In the meantime, Graham went on *Hannity* and announced that he would be donating half a million dollars to Trump's legal defense fund—money derived in part from contributions he had begged for on air a few weeks earlier.

BEHIND THE SCENES, ANOTHER SET OF CONFEDERATES WAS EGGING on Trump to keep working to undermine the result. Rick Perry, Trump's former secretary of energy, sent a text message on November 4 to the White House chief of staff, Mark Meadows, calling for an "agressive [*sic*] strategy" for Meadows to pursue: Georgia, North Carolina, Pennsylvania, and other closely contested states with Republican state legislatures should call the presidential election "BS." And "send their own electors to vote and have it go to the [Supreme Court]."

Like everyone else, Perry knew how destructive this vandalism of the vote tallies could be. As a rival to Trump in 2016, the former Texas governor had also warned about the danger of placing a strongman in the White House who was willing to do anything to keep power. Benjy Sarlin of NBC recalled a speech Perry had given during that campaign in which he described an 1854 attack on Washington by members of the nativist Know-Nothing movement who had been pushing a conspiracy that the pope was planning to overthrow the U.S. government. "They existed to cast blame and tear down certain institutions," Perry said in his speech, describing the Know-Nothings. "To give outlet to anger. Donald Trump is the modern-day incarnation of the Know-Nothing movement."

Perry will never go down as a brilliant historian. Or brilliant anything. After Perry got into the 2012 Republican presidential race, Mitt Romney told friends he received a phone call about him from his fellow Texan George W. Bush. "People thought *I* was dumb," Bush said. "Well, wait till you get a load of *this* guy."

Mike Pompeo was asked at a November 10 news conference about whether there would be seamless transition to the next administration. Yes, the secretary of state promised, "there will be a smooth transition to"—*wait for it*—"a second Trump administration." He then laughed, to perhaps signal that he knew what was what, and hoped that perhaps everyone understood his position here.

TRUMP HAD NO GREATER CHAMPION OF HIS ELECTORAL DISRUP-tion project than Ted Cruz. There was a certain symmetry to this. Four years earlier, after Trump lost to Cruz in the Iowa caucuses, the future president trotted out his usual playbook of insisting he had won and accusing the actual winner (Cruz) of election fraud. This was, even then, entirely predictable for Trump, who was never a huge adherent of that old Republican ethic of "personal responsibility." He had previously complained that he'd "gotten screwed" out of, among other things, an Emmy Award and would later insist he'd have won the popular vote against Hillary, except for the ever-present "voter fraud" and the (nonexistent) "busloads of people from Massachusetts" brought in to vote illegally in New Hampshire. After Obama defeated Romney in 2012, at the height of Trump's birther phase, he immediately jumped on Twitter to helpfully inform everyone about "more reports of voting machines switching Romney votes to Obama. Pay close attention to the machines, don't let your vote be stolen."

"What Donald does, when he loses, is he blames everybody else," Cruz explained in 2016, after he'd allegedly stolen the Iowa caucuses. "It's never Donald's fault."

Cruz wound up being the last Republican standing against Trump in the 2016 primaries. He proved determined in his defiance and appeared to carry an unusually intense grudge against the eventual nominee. Cruz even gave a ballsy address in Cleveland at the Republican National Convention in which he refused to endorse Trump. "Vote your conscience" was the marquee line of the speech, which ended with Cruz being booed offstage and his wife, Heidi, being heckled out of the arena.

I shouldn't overstate the degree to which Cruz was ever a beacon of courage, even during this valiant last stand in Cleveland. His reputation as a towering and self-interested conniver was never not fully justified. Cruz probably just calculated that Trump would lose to Clinton in 2016, the GOP would wash their hands quickly of him, and Cruz would then be well positioned to say he told you so when he ran again in 2020. He even laid out his reasoning explicitly, albeit five years later. "Historically," Cruz said in an interview with *The Truth Gazette*, a conservative news outlet operated by a fifteen-year-old, "the runner-up is almost always the next nominee."

Cruz vowed in 2016 that he would never become a "servile puppy dog" to Trump. By 2020, he had fully transformed himself into a pit bull on behalf of his former rival's cultish coup attempt.

Cruz never looked back. His degree of prostration was breathtaking even by Trump-era Republican standards—just as his shamelessness was striking even by Ted Cruz standards.

"When he turned, he really turned, didn't he?" Senator Mazie Hirono, Democrat of Hawaii, marveled of her colleague. "Into a total suck-up."

LOSING ON ELECTION DAY WAS HARD ENOUGH FOR TRUMP. NO LESS losing to Joe Biden, "the worst presidential candidate in history," as the forty-fifth president had called his successor. Trump could not lose just once, either. He had to keep losing, never got tired of losing, and kept finding fresh and innovative ways to lose and new courtrooms to lose in—more than sixty times after November 3. Trump's helter-skelter efforts kept smashing into ballot math and election law. The final count always held firm: Biden won by more than seven million ballots and seventy-four Electoral College votes.

Each rebuke of Trump's appeals from another exasperated authority brought a new flourish. "Stitched together like Frankenstein's monster," one federal judge in Pennsylvania wrote of Trump's case. The president's "Elite Strike Force" of attorneys, as they called themselves, were not helping matters. His lawyers, led by Rudy Giuliani, filed documents claiming voter fraud in Michigan—and then cited townships in Minnesota. (Rudy was never a precise-detail guy.)

Giuliani, who took over Trump's legal team after nearly every other lawyer either had quit or was frozen out by the client, trekked to Williamsport, Pennsylvania, to argue his first case in federal court in nearly three decades. The rust showed.

He demanded that the judge invalidate nearly seven million votes cast because of what he called "widespread, nationwide voter fraud." Later, after being pressed for evidence, Giuliani pivoted rather dramatically. "This is not a fraud case," he said.

At a news conference at the RNC headquarters, Giuliani then unleashed a spigot of conspiracy theories, wild claims, and made-up charges. As he spoke, a dark liquid—seemingly hair dye diluted by sweat—dribbled down both sides of his face, a strangely mesmerizing sight that conveyed an impression of a ghoulish figure melting motor oil in plain view. This became a meme for the ages.

Trump's more sober advisers had become progressively alarmed by Giuliani's outsized role in this excuse for a legal challenge. Barr described him as "a fucking idiot" who was "drinking too much and was desperate for money." Other than that, he was happy to vouch for him.

Rudy's mental state was seemingly unraveling in full view, right along with his client's. Friends and aides first noticed a change in Trump after he contracted COVID-19. The doctors at Walter Reed pumped him with Canseco levels of steroids. Trump's physical condition improved, but he seemed more paranoid and erratic in the aftermath.

Trump had become "all but manic" in the view of General Mark Milley, the chair of the Joint Chiefs of Staff, wrote Bob Woodward and Robert Costa. The president was "screaming at officials and constructing his own alternate reality about endless election conspiracies."

The final weeks of the 2020 campaign at least gave Trump a focus and kept him out of the White House for long stretches. His staff welcomed the reprieve, but knew it was temporary, and that things would soon get worse again, especially if he lost.

Sure enough, the spiral accelerated after November 3. Trump turned bitterly against even his staunchest caretakers—Barr, Pence, Fox News, the Supreme Court, and some of his longest-suffering staff. "Barely showing up for work," one of his people told me. Trump was spending several hours a day watching TV and rage-tweeting, whether he was in the Oval Office or the residence. (In fairness, this had been largely true before the election, too.)

He would occasionally take a break from this regimen to pursue a favorite pastime, like golf or pardoning felonious Republican congressmen. Or offering clemency to various other criminals who were "nice" to him (Paul Manafort, Roger Stone) or related to him (Jared's dad). But for the most part, it was all furor and irrational demands, all the time.

Longtime allies started avoiding Trump. His most steadfast aides did everything they could to stay away, if they hadn't already quit. He came to rely almost exclusively on a crackpot collection of lawyers, hobbyists, and anyone willing to entertain some way to keep him in office. Mike Lindell, CEO of MyPillow—peddler of lavish bedding products, slippers, and extravagant conspiracy theories—became a top-level adviser, speaking several times a day to the president.

Apparently, the Clintons, the Venezuelans, and those ever-present deep state agents had executed a massive scheme to steal victory away from Trump (while still allowing other, victorious Republicans to keep their jobs). It was a stunningly far-reaching and complicated plot that only counselor MyPillow seemed to have the bandwidth to grasp.

It was safe to assume this was a low-morale period over at the White House. Word circulated that anyone caught looking for a new job would be fired immediately. The First Lady announced the completion of the new White House tennis court pavilion.

MEANWHILE ON CAPITOL HILL, A LARGE MAJORITY OF TRUMP'S elected accessories were redoubling their efforts at hiding. They did everything possible to avoid talking to the media about the election. Any Republican who implied that the campaign was over, or slipped and made some casual reference to "the next administration," was committing a grievous act of disloyalty in Trump's eyes. A few Republican senators were caught on C-SPAN fist-bumping with their colleague the vice president–elect, Kamala Harris, and this was *noted in the building*. Oh, shit! Thankfully, Trump was never much of a C-SPAN viewer.

The dwindling West Wing team parsed even the most anodyne statements from elected Republicans for proof of treasonous intent. Representative Jim Banks, a conservative Republican from Indiana and reliable White House friend, gave an interview to the *Washington Examiner* in which he expressed interest in being a leader of a "post-Trump" GOP. Big mistake. The president's people caught wind, and none became more exercised than Lou Dobbs, the Fox Business host whose infatuation with Trump and general ardor for the man might actually rival Trump's own.

Dobbs began his show with an extended riff against Banks for his blasphemy. This was a problem for Banks, not because Dobbs had a lot of viewers, but because Trump was reliably one of those viewers. Banks knew this. An ambitious Kevin McCarthy loyalist, Banks always made a point of regularly going on Dobbs's show, which would often result in the coveted attaboy phone call from the Audience of One himself. They developed a relationship. Banks was invited to the White House a bunch of times. He found this extremely cool.

So yes, for Banks to be featured in this "post-Trump GOP" story could be a major issue for him, because it stood at extreme cross-purposes to the White House's new mission and—duh—merchandising interests, too. ("Stop the Steal" T-shirts were selling for $30 on Don Jr.'s website.)

After November 3, the Trump GOP's messaging apparatus moved almost immediately from screeching about Hunter Biden to a singular focus on getting the president's stolen tricycle back. Banks resolved to be more careful in the future, and thankfully, Trump was preoccupied with more powerful traitors.

In a session with Capitol Hill reporters, Mitch McConnell uttered a sentence that in more normal times would be received—and quickly forgotten—as just the kind of drab boilerplate the Senate majority leader had been mumbling since the womb.

"I think we all know that after the first of the year there's likely to be a discussion about some additional package of some size next year," McConnell said at a press conference as he discussed prospects for a coronavirus relief bill. At which point he delivered this bombshell: "Depending on what the new administration wants to pursue."

Aha!

McConnell said *"new* administration." Implying there would be an outgoing administration. This is what passed for a jolting revelation in December 2020.

Maybe McConnell did not mean to be so forthcoming. It was, after all, a delicate dance he was engaged in. He feared alienating the significant portion of the party's base that still believed that Trump had won. He especially needed the Republicans who lived in Georgia to remain interested long enough to vote in that state's January 5 Senate runoff, made necessary after the incumbents, Kelly Loeffler and

David Perdue, both failed to surpass a 50 percent vote threshold on November 3.

McConnell was asked a follow-up question to his "new administration" statement, and he quickly retreated to inscrutable form.

"The future will take care of itself," he clarified.

"I MADE THE CARDINAL MISTAKE OF CONGRATULATING JOE BIDEN, and there was hell to pay for me," said Representative Adam Kinzinger, Republican of Illinois. He said he was happy to face the consequences, the inevitable trial by MAGA Twitter. "I didn't care at that point," he said. But much of his caucus still cared deeply and would prefer to avoid the torrents of grief—and possible primary challenges—that came with such a brazen admission of the obvious.

"For all but just a handful of members, if you put them on truth serum, they knew that the election was fully legitimate and that Donald Trump was a joke," Kinzinger said. "The vast majority of people get the joke. I think Kevin McCarthy gets the joke. Lindsey gets the joke. The problem is that the joke isn't even funny anymore."

And the truth serum was not exactly flowing, either, at least when microphones were around.

"When we talk in private, I haven't heard a single congressional Republican allege that the election results were fraudulent—not one," said Senator Ben Sasse, Republican of Nebraska.

Even after the court challenges failed, the local disputes were resolved, and the state electors convened, Republicans always had another new benchmark placed before them. They could never reach a point where they could just declare the race lost and move on. As had happened within forty-eight hours of the polls' closing in every election in recent American history except for 2000.

Just as George W. Bush had prevailed after the U.S. Supreme Court declared him victorious—in one of the most controversial court decisions ever, to decide the closest U.S. election ever—Trump, too, held out hope that his ultimate backstop would be the high court. "My judges," he believed, would step in and save him in the end. He figured because the court leaned right and he had appointed three of the justices himself, they would surely do him the solid of nullifying the election and keeping their favorite president in office. They owed him.

Trump was focused on a case that he called "the Big One," an appeal of Biden's victory filed in an imbecilic lawsuit from the Republican attorney general of Texas. The suit demanded—with extremely dubious reasoning—that Biden's victories be reversed in four battleground states. Not happening, said the Supremes, which sent the president into another tizzy, complaining about how "disloyal" his loser judges had been to him.

The high court's verdict came in at a devastatingly concise 126 words, or exactly the number of Republican House members who had endorsed the Texas lawsuit. Nearly all of these members knew the case had no chance. But again, what's the harm for humoring him, just a little more? Maybe you're giving Trump false hope, but it was still hope. It would at least keep him occupied.

The only rationale for Trump at this point rested with his "a lot of people are having doubts about the election" assertions, doubts sowed and spread entirely by the president and his toadies. Republicans in the House and Senate then cited "deep distrust in our democratic process" as their reason to challenge the certification of Electoral College votes. The whole gambit proceeded in a tight circle.

In addition to all the court and state election decisions, Attorney General Barr said the DOJ had found no proof of meaningful fraud (Barr resigned on December 14), Christopher Krebs, the head of cybersecurity at the Department of Homeland Security, said the claims "either have been unsubstantiated or are technically incoherent" (Trump fired him the same day), and any number of authorities up and down the executive branch said the same.

The legislative branch, however, was another matter. "We've seen in the last two months unprecedented allegations of voter fraud," said Cruz on Fox News. "And that's produced a deep, deep distrust of our democratic process across the country. I think we in Congress have an obligation to do something about that."

Trump turned his focus on persuading Mike Pence to disrupt the once-routine process of counting electoral votes, which was scheduled for January 6—the next Big One.

It was just a question of getting Pence to act "with extreme courage!" as Trump tweeted on the morning of his grand finale. "Do it Mike."

"It's the ultimate irony that a guy who acted like a total sycophantic pussy for four years, Trump wants him to be the Six Million Dollar Man at the end," one of Trump's advisers later observed to Leonnig and Rucker.

"Well, shit, the guy hasn't stood up to anybody for four years and now you want him to stand up illegally, unconstitutionally to the United States Senate and the House of Representatives? Are you nuts?"

In concert with Pence's act of "extreme courage," Trump envisioned a culminating rally, something big and perfect for TV. He would be at the center of it, of course.

"Big protest in D.C. on January 6th," Trump tweeted on December 19. "Be there, will be wild!"

——

THE PRESIDENT'S GROWING OBSESSION WITH JANUARY 6 MADE
it difficult for McConnell to keep his interest on January 5, the date of
the Georgia runoff.

After much cajoling, Trump agreed to travel to the state on a Saturday night in December to do an event in Valdosta for Perdue and Loeffler.
He went only after the senators became willing evangelists for his stolen
election fantasy. Both candidates publicly demanded the resignation
of Georgia's Republican secretary of state, Brad Raffensperger, citing
unspecified "failures" in the vote counting process and setting off the
requisite hail of death threats against Raffensperger and his family.
(Raffensperger became famous after *The Washington Post* posted a
recording of a phone call that he received from Trump pressuring the
secretary to "find votes" for him and turn the Georgia results in his favor.)

Trump's Valdosta rally was the first major event the president participated in after the election. The coronavirus was still on a rampage
coast-to-coast, killing thousands of people every day. It had been the
most lethal week so far in America. Yet the president was long past caring, if he ever cared. He was much more interested in detailing the many
crimes perpetrated against him, the likes of which "no president has
ever seen."

Here was another thing the president *really* did not care about: the
job fortunes of David Perdue and Kelly Loeffler. Specifically, whether
anyone bothered to come out and vote for them again on January 5. Republican campaign operatives were worried that Trump would spend
his rally talking about how rigged the November 3 vote was—not exactly
a big motivator to get people to cast another ballot, and in an election
that Trump wasn't even on the ballot for.

The concern was justified. Trump barely mentioned Perdue and Loeffler in his nearly two-hour speech and spent the bulk of it talking about the only topic that mattered. "We won Georgia!" he said. He won a "great victory everywhere," Trump added. And this great victory was being taken away, not just from Trump, but from all of them.

"If I lost, I'd be a very gracious loser," the president reassured everyone at the rally, held exactly one month after he was decisively defeated and one month prior to the deadly insurrection he incited.

"We're all victims, everybody here," Trump went on. "All of these thousands of people here tonight. They're all victims. Every one of you."

This was as good a summation as any for what the Republican Party had become under Donald Trump.

As it turned out, there were no bigger victims at the rally than David Perdue and Kelly Loeffler. They might have deserved it, but they were victims nonetheless as turnout among demoralized Republicans plummeted in the runoff. Both Perdue and Loeffler had been favored but wound up losing to the Democrats Jon Ossoff and Raphael Warnock.

When aides told Trump on the night of January 5 that Perdue and Loeffler had lost, he predicted (correctly) that he would be blamed for it. But he moved on quickly. It was, after all, the eve of the Big One.

CHAPTER 20

THE BIG ONE

———

January 6, 2021

Eventually, this had to end, right? Someone would decide that enough was enough and step in.

McConnell? McCarthy? Melania? The Interns?

That was how it finished up for Nixon after Watergate. The Republican elders mostly stood behind him *for this little bit of time*. Until they didn't. A trio of the quasi-responsible—Senator Barry Goldwater, House minority leader John Rhodes, and Senate minority leader Hugh Scott—went to the White House and told the spiraling president it was time to leave. And he was soon gone.

The Watergate comparisons go only so far. Trump enjoyed weapons and support systems Nixon could only dream of. Trump had Fox News, with its juggernaut ratings and nightly drumbeat. He had Facebook's colossus of like-minded fans as a conduit for disinformation. He had an amped-up army of supporters that Republican officeholders lived in fear of. The terrified included McConnell, McCarthy, Graham, and pretty much anyone who might have taken up the "Enough is enough" mantle.

Before January 6, they were terrified only politically: the office holders feared Trump because he could end Republican careers just by tapping out a few disparaging words about them to his 88.7 million Twitter followers. It was an unpleasant prospect, to be avoided if possible, but if worse came to worst, it would still be a peaceful transfer into private life.

Now, though, the terror had moved into the realm of physical harm. As the president's rhetoric became more bellicose, his herd followed suit. Reports of death threats to Capitol offices were through the roof. Rallies around the capital were becoming more scary and violent.

"We take this for granted, or we used to, that when you're in a position of public prominence, you want to avoid maybe saying something that will activate that nut out there," Mitt Romney said. "The challenge is that we had a president who was not particularly sensitive to that." Romney always had a knack for understatement.

Everything was building to January 6. Trump was orchestrating it that way, in his classic showman's style of growing suspense and the promise of a crescendo. Few were left at his side who would tell him to stop. Like so much of the Republican Party, the White House had been reduced to its most loyal Trump-worshipping essence.

What was the degenerating president capable of at the bitter end? What could his supporters pull off? That was the eerie cliff-hanger.

Rally goers posted their plans online for January 6—billed as the MAGA July 4, 1776. It would be their moment to "Save America" and "Stop the Steal" and preserve *their* "landslide." They included pictures of the weapons they would bring. Car pools were announced, caravans. "If you are not prepared to use force to defend civilization, then be prepared to accept barbarism," a member of the Red-State Secession group on Facebook posted on the eve of the rally. They urged followers to circulate the home addresses of their "enemies," which included federal judges and members of Congress.

"Be there, will be wild!"

REPRESENTATIVE JIM BANKS'S YOUNG DAUGHTER DIDN'T HAVE school that Wednesday and asked her dad if she could go to work with him; nope, not a good day for that, he said. Kinzinger brought his gun to the office and told his staff to stay home. Romney was harassed on his flight from Salt Lake City to D.C. by a boisterous group of protesters headed to the January 6 festivities. Little appetizer scenes like this spread all over social media.

The dwindling ranks of people whom Trump listened to saw where this could be headed. They shared their concerns, but only to one another and of course privately. "I'm very worried about the next 48 hours," Sean Hannity told Mark Meadows, Trump's chief of staff, in a January 5 text message made public by the House Select Committee on January 6.

The White House was a ghost town. Everyone either had quit or was scared or did not want to be around whatever Trump had planned. That was where the path of humoring had led. All of the "I did my best to help him succeed." All of the "I wanted a seat at the table to stop it from being worse." All of the "I offered my opinion *in private*."

Eventually, the president became more and more isolated and enraged. This was where it all led.

There would be a million snippets and testimonials to emerge from January 6. "It seemed like it couldn't be happening, like we were all in a dream," Representative John Curtis, Republican of Utah, recalled. "You heard banging on the House chamber doors, they were literally right outside," said his fellow Utahan Blake Moore.

"'Hang Mike Pence, Hang Mike Pence.' I'll never forget those chants," Senator Collins said. Her first thought was that the Iranians had followed through on their earlier threat to attack the Capitol. She texted Ivanka ("I had her number. I was horrified"). Graham tried the First Daughter, too ("You need to tell these people to leave"). "We're working on it," Ivanka kept saying.

They tried the beaten-down Meadows. "He's got to condemn this shit ASAP," Don Jr. texted. "I'm working on it," the overwhelmed chief of staff also kept saying. A bunch of people tried McCarthy, who said the same.

They were all "working on it"!

"I tried to get to him four times," Chris Christie said of Trump: "I went 0-4." Trump was off in his little Oval Office dining room, watching the action on TV along with everyone else. He appeared riveted, not at all horrified.

Paul Ryan was sitting at home, watching the situation devolve. He never thought it would come to this. That was what most Republicans said. Ryan figured the president would bitch and moan and maybe make a big show of "fighting" for his supporters for a while. Everyone could feel good and victimized. But eventually Trump would just leave; hopefully, he would know to do this on his own. And everyone could then just get on with their lives. The former Speaker hadn't spoken to Trump since he left Congress, and said he expected never to speak to him again.

Now, as he watched the Capitol being ransacked on TV, Ryan found himself sobbing. He's never been much of a crier, he said, but something snapped in him.

"I spent my whole adult life in that building," Ryan told me later. "And I saw my friends, a lot of cops, some of my old security detail—I'm still friends with a bunch of those guys. It really disturbed me, foundationally." He sat down and wrote a letter to his former protectors, figuring they could use all the love they could get right now.

I couldn't help wondering, as I thought of Ryan sitting there watching and weeping, if he felt any guilt. That maybe *he* was one of the people who protected Trump. What if he had taken a harder line against him when he was Speaker? Or even now, as Ryan sat on the board of the parent company of Fox News, which had contributed so much to the creation, perpetuation, and continual rehabilitation of Trump, and the events that preceded January 6?

Ryan was not inclined to grapple with questions of complicity. "I was absolutely horrified," he would only say of the insurrection, generally.

LIZ CHENEY IS MORE WILLING THAN HER FELLOW REPUBLICANS TO entertain weighty matters of legacy and responsibility and how history will remember these times. "This is about being able to tell your kids that you stood up and did the right thing," she said.

Cheney was in the Republican cloakroom on that Wednesday morning, preparing to give her speech in support of certifying Biden's victory, when her father called.

Dick Cheney had just watched Trump on TV at his rally, vowing to get rid of "the Liz Cheneys of the world." The former vice president became worried that his daughter's floor speech could inflame tensions. Was she sure she wanted to go ahead?

"Absolutely," she told him. "Nothing could be more important."

A few minutes later, Trump's supporters stormed the entrance. House members were told to grab gas masks from under their chairs and leave. Jim Jordan, the pugilistic Trumpist from Ohio, offered Cheney a hand. "Get away from me," she snapped, waving him off.

Cheney had grown disgusted with many of her colleagues over what they were willing to tolerate. She understood the pressures of learning to coexist with Trump as an elected Republican. She even understood humoring him, if only as a short-term path of least resistance in the initial days after the election.

But it had now gone dangerously beyond that. The indulgence Cheney saw from her colleagues for the president outraged her. "I kept saying, 'Guys, this is our constitutional obligation here,'" Cheney told me. "'This is what the Constitution says. This is what the courts have decided.'" She couldn't believe her fellow Republicans were still abiding this into December, then January.

"We've got people we've entrusted with the perpetuation of the Republic who don't know what the rule of law is," she said.

Cheney had spent years working in and studying autocratic regimes of Eastern Europe and the Middle East. She warned her colleagues about the dangers of being cavalier about basic democratic traditions. "We're seeing what can happen," she said. This was the price of submission.

"You fucking did this," Cheney snapped at Jordan as she was being chased out of the chamber. Cheney never gave her speech. Her political life was scrambled. She went from third-ranking Republican in the House, with a decent shot at becoming the GOP's first woman Speaker, to complete pariah inside the party in which her family had been royalty.

January 6 altered many such career trajectories. It left a million what-ifs.

What if Cheney had been mid-speech when the breach occurred? What if Romney had escaped down a different hallway, away from the Capitol police officer Eugene Goodman, who diverted him from the mob? "And I would have met them at the stairs," Romney said of the rioters.

"Oh, they would have been happy to see me," Romney recalled.

"Maybe we'd have had a kumbaya moment. Selfies." He chuckled at his own sarcasm, but was not smiling.

I thought about pressing Romney on this. What if the insurrectionists had gotten to him? What if he, or one of his colleagues, or Mike Pence, had actually been badly hurt or even killed? Romney was not eager to contemplate this further.

His first reaction was anger. As with Cheney, Romney's rage was directed at certain colleagues. "You have caused this!" he exploded at Josh Hawley, Republican of Missouri, who, along with Cruz, had been spearheading the effort to get members to vote against Biden's certification.

"I think we've seen that there are consequences to messing around like this," Romney said of the scene in general. "It was all around us."

CERTAIN ACCOUNTS FROM THE INSURRECTION LINGERED FOR ME. One was from Representative Peter Meijer, a thirty-two-year-old freshman Republican from Michigan who had just been sworn into Congress that week. Late on Wednesday night, Meijer saw one of his new House colleagues on the floor, looking deeply distressed. Meijer asked if he was okay.

No, the shaken Republican said, he was not okay. He confided that he wanted to vote for Biden's certification. And in a normal time with a normal president, of course he would have, probably nearly everyone would have. But he no longer felt he could vote for certification, purely out of concern for his family's safety.

"Remember, this wasn't a hypothetical," Meijer recalled to *The Atlantic*'s Tim Alberta. "You were casting that vote after seeing what some of these people are capable of."

This was a pure case of governing by intimidation, which is the essence of authoritarianism. It occurred during what had always been a pro forma yet sacred rite of democracy. The members' votes were being influenced not by argument or political position, but in response to the threat of physical harm. It's worth spelling this out from time to time, as obvious as it is. Because with few exceptions, Republicans keep ignoring the obvious, in favor of cowering and humoring.

Stories like Meijer's were common from many of the 139 House Republicans who voted against certification. "There have been discussions for some time among House members—those who voted to impeach and those who didn't—about things like 'Where do you buy body armor?'" said one member who asked not to be named discussing personal security (which members are told not to discuss publicly). "So yes, it's a real thing."

A basic freedom of movement that members once took for granted has become complicated. They are now typically met by police in airports, who accompany them from gate to gate. "That is something that is brand-new in this country," the member said. They are endangered simply because they are representatives in Congress and the former president of the United States has made them targets.

"The vast majority of elected Republicans understand how dangerous Trump is," Cheney said. "But they also act as though they're bystanders. And I put McConnell in that category. Where McCarthy has been a full-on embrace, McConnell's has been more like, 'Let's hope he goes away.' And the problem is, just hoping he goes away, that enables him."

Other well-known Republicans up and down the ranks have adopted Trump's ominous strongman rhetoric. On the day before my last interview with Cheney, in January 2022, Gingrich had said on Fox News that if Republicans won a majority in Congress, the members of the January 6 committee could "face a real risk of jail." Cheney chuckled when I mentioned this, but she was clearly not amused. "Newt Gingrich has always been a bomb thrower, there's no question," Cheney said. "But Newt Gingrich was also a professor of history. He knows that that's un-American. I don't know if he just started on a roll in this TV interview and he went too far, but I don't think so."

KEVIN McCARTHY DOES NOT LIKE TALKING ABOUT JANUARY 6. IT was a few months later, and he was sharing a few safe details. He told me he talked to Pence several times that day. He heard gunshots while he was being driven from the Capitol. He said he talked to Trump from the car. What did he say to Trump? I asked.

McCarthy laughed. He became cagey, as if he were under oath. (In fact, he was eating fried chicken for lunch at a restaurant in Davenport, Iowa, not under oath. He'd just attended a campaign event for a member.) "I talked to the president," McCarthy repeated. And?

"I said, 'You have to do something.' He said he'd put something out on Twitter."

Trump did, several hours later. There were reports that the president suggested to McCarthy that the rioters cared about the election more than the minority leader cared. And that McCarthy was a pussy. "He never called me a pussy to my face," McCarthy protested. "What about over the phone?" I nearly replied, but it felt unnecessary.

"It was pretty heated," McCarthy assured me, of his conversation with Trump. But "My Kevin" also remained intent on making excuses for his master. The president did not have a full appreciation for the deteriorating situation inside the Capitol from TV, McCarthy explained. "And I was telling him what was happening." What did he tell him? I asked.

McCarthy laughed. This was going nowhere.

Even less than January 6, McCarthy does not *at all* like talking about Donald Trump. "Why do you keep asking me about Trump?" he said, annoyed. It was as if the former president were sitting on his shoulder, watching for any sign of disloyalty. McCarthy flashed something between a wince and a grimace whenever Trump was mentioned. He looked worried that a ceiling fan was about to drop on his head.

But McCarthy did become quite animated at one point. He was telling his one favorite story from January 6. After the House chamber was evacuated, McCarthy retreated to his Capitol office with a Republican colleague, Bruce Westerman of Arkansas. When it became evident that rioters were breaking into the office, McCarthy's security team insisted that McCarthy leave.

Westerman, though, was somehow left behind in McCarthy's inner work sanctum. For protection, he commandeered a Civil War sword from a display on McCarthy's office wall. Westerman then barricaded himself in McCarthy's private bathroom and waited out the siege while crouched on the commode. McCarthy appears to have shared that story with half of his caucus. "It's a great image," he said.

Indeed it was: another scared Republican, clutching a decorative sword, waiting out a coup in the loo.

KINZINGER WAITED OUT THE DAY IN HIS OFFICE, WITH A THICKEN-ing sense of dread. A retired U.S. Air Force lieutenant colonel who served in Afghanistan, Kinzinger has seen evil and felt danger up close. In 2006, he wrestled and disarmed a knife-wielding man who was trying to stab a woman on a street in Milwaukee.

"I definitely had some PTS on the stabbing thing," Kinzinger told me. "It changes you, definitely." Political violence has worried him for a long time. He was also concerned about where the insanity of the Trump era could lead. "When your engines are constantly on red line, it's going to overheat and it's going to crush and eventually break."

January 6 felt like a breaking point. The Illinois congressman sat alone, watching the president's rally on TV and clutching his gun. "I was prepared to defend against my own party," he said.

"And then Trump says, 'I'm going to go down with you to the Capitol.' I'm like, 'Man, this is bad.'"

Trump's "I'll be there with you" line did not receive much attention amid the horrors of the day. But to me this aside distilled an essential part of Trump and his relationship to his supporters. The dynamic reflected the level of total servitude that Trump had come to expect, the casual lies that everyone involved in the transaction took for granted.

The president was of course not "there with" his supporters at the Capitol. Six minutes after he finished speaking, Trump was headed in the other direction, back home to the most secure facility in Washington, certainly more secure than the Capitol. The one-way nature of Trump's loyalty is so glaring it barely needs mentioning. He might be the single most perfect opposite of a "stand-up guy" ever to haunt our national character. Yet scenarios like January 6 underscore just how extreme this has become and the contempt Trump quite clearly reserves for those most devoted to him.

Pence was the most vivid example of this: he was the most cringey, groveling, and fawning VP in history, who spent four years extolling Trump's "broad-shouldered leadership" and whom Trump nonetheless had no problem leaving to the hanging mobs at the Capitol. When Trump was asked months later by ABC's Jonathan Karl if he had any concerns about Pence's well-being, he brushed off the question. "Well, the people were very angry," he said.

"The people," of course, were arrested in droves. Hundreds of Trump supporters were rounded up across the country in the days following January 6. Time and again, the initial rationale of those arrested was "Trump sent us." They were carrying out the wishes of *their* president. While this has not shown to be an effective legal defense, you can see where Trump's now criminally charged supporters might have gotten this idea.

In the days after January 6, Trump would pardon or commute the sentences of 143 people, the majority of whom were prominent Republicans, celebrities, or people who had some kind of personal or financial connection to the outgoing president: Steve Bannon, who was charged with bilking Trump supporters who thought they were helping fund the border wall; Elliott Broidy, one of Trump's top fundraisers, who pleaded guilty to conspiring to violate foreign lobbying laws; the former Republican congressman Randall "Duke" Cunningham, who was sentenced to eight years for bribery, and was one of the poster children for the Republican "culture of corruption" that Democrats ran against in the 2006 midterms. None of them, from what I could tell, were anywhere near the Capitol on January 6.

"The people Trump despises most love him the most," said the radio legend Howard Stern, who hosted Trump for years on his show. "He'd be disgusted by them. Go to Mar-a-Lago, see if there's any people who look like you. I'm talking to you in the audience."

You hear variations on this theme: Trump expressing contempt for the "bullshit" prayer rituals of his most fervent evangelical followers;

Trump talking about how much he dislikes shaking hands with "these disgusting people," meaning his supporters. I have no desire to plumb Trump's psyche any more than I have. But I suspect the codependency at work here between Trump and his minions runs deeper than the glib "they love him and he hates them" explanations.

That was as plain as the heavy, haunted expression on the president's face as he stood in front of the White House on the night of January 6. Finally, grudgingly, he had agreed to tell his supporters to go home in a brief video message.

Trump sounded oddly moved as he spoke that these "great patriots" could pull off this spectacle just for him. Who imagined that the president would actually tell them, in so many words, to storm the Capitol and that they would? That it had actually come to this and that there would be no one to tell him he couldn't?

His words were designed to calm "my people," if not admonish them, but his voice sounded more like gratitude. "We love you," he said, in the doting tone of a parent tucking a child into bed. "You're very special."

I kept thinking about this "We love you—you're very special" message. For all the effort that's gone into understanding Trump voters, this seemed to go directly to the void many of them have come to feel about their own place in the country.

THERE STILL WERE SEVERAL HOURS LEFT TO RUN ON THIS AWFUL day. The Capitol remained anything but secure. The entire Senate remained locked down, all members bunkered together in a safe room. They could hear the "Hang Mike Pence" chants outside in the hallway. One of the Senate administrators kept shouting out the roll call—one through a hundred—just to make sure everyone was accounted for. When Trump finally came on to deliver his message, the senators gathered around the TV.

Lame, was the consensus.

"It was like a gut punch," Romney said of the president's "you're very special" statement. Biden came on soon afterward. The senators gathered back around the TV. Much better, was the consensus. "When he was finished, we all broke into applause," Romney said.

They reconvened on the floor a few hours later to complete the certification. Everyone looked shell-shocked. Did that really happen? At the very least, this did feel like the end for Trump, at long last. This *had* to be the line that could not be uncrossed.

Even so, after everything, 147 House and Senate Republicans still came back and voted against certifying the election. Trump, according to people who spoke to him, was watching closely. He was eager to see who among "my people" would show courage and be strong. "Who would be loyal?" the president kept asking, according to someone who spoke to him before the vote.

"They aren't loyal, they have Stockholm syndrome," the *Wall Street Journal* columnist Peggy Noonan wrote about Republicans still hanging in. "They've come to identify with the guy who took them hostage and hope the cops don't hurt him . . . They were scared little rabbits who finally knew what they'd unleashed."

The GOP senators Kelly Loeffler, James Lankford of Oklahoma, and Mike Braun of Indiana all had said they would vote against certifying, but then ended up voting in favor. Perhaps, it was hoped, this was a sign that the fever was finally breaking.

When it was his turn, Graham got up and seemed to be speaking for many, even Trump's staunchest allies. He was flush and overcome and everything about him screamed, "I'm done." "Trump and I, we had a hell of a journey," Graham said late Wednesday night. "But today all I can say is count me out. Enough is enough. I tried to be helpful."

It was quite a dramatic and overwrought presentation, even for Lindsey Graham. (Seth Meyers would compare it to "a monologue from the Tennessee Williams play *A Streetcar Named De-Liar.*") But the floor speech also sounded as if it could serve as an epitaph for an era, a Republican courtier's version of "Will you shut up, man?"

Several of Graham's colleagues said as much.

"When Lindsey got up and said, 'I'm through with this,' many of us thought that was it," Collins said. The clip, which was met with some applause, had been played over and over, to illustrate the "good riddance" vibe of the moment.

As always, this moment of moxie would not last. Graham later clarified that when he said "I'm through with this," he meant he was "through" arguing about this particular postelection dispute, not "through" with his bromance with the spiraling president. (To wit, here was Lindsey, via Hannity, exactly one year later: "I'm not going to vote for anybody [for Senate leader] that can't have a working relationship with Trump.")

Graham would also reiterate that he still enjoyed the president's company. He loved golf. And yes, he would continue to try to be helpful.

WHILE MANY VERY POWERFUL PEOPLE WORK THERE, CAPITOL HILL can still feel like a small town. January 6 had many components of a small-town tragedy, similar to how lower Manhattan was in the days after 9/11. Everyone knew someone—elected leaders, employees, and first responders—who was directly affected.

There are certain occurrences you live through that, even decades later, remain truly hard to believe. We're talking "Holy Shit, Man Walks on Fucking Moon"–level events. Did that actually take place? Hijacked planes, the Twin Towers crumbling to dust on live TV—then, fifteen years later, Donald Trump winds up in the White House? And then January 6: The president's supporters actually stormed the *Fucking Capitol?* At the urging of *the president?* Yes, that really happened.

I spent January 6, 2021, in the same place I spent much of the previous year: at home, working remotely, glued to my laptop. A bunch of other *Times* reporters and I were "live chatting" a feed of the events throughout the day. We were in no danger, unlike our Capitol Hill colleagues, whose dispatches kept coming in about the threats they were facing and the horrors they were witnessing. Several friends on the Hill suffered post-traumatic stress complications that lingered for months, some to this day.

There was no way I could sleep after the floor proceedings finally ended on the morning of January 7. I had much psychic company. Senator Collins told me she was afraid to go home—she'd been doxed and her address had been widely circulated and her husband was out of town—so Senator Lisa Murkowski, Republican of Alaska, invited her to spend the night at her place. Murkowski's husband greeted them with two massive glasses of red wine and a roaring fire. They processed the day through what remained of the night.

I scrolled around on Twitter, texted with colleagues, and ate for the first time since breakfast. I watched Trump's speech from the morning's rally. It was quite something to see again, especially in light of what would transpire later. He said all of the usual scary and ominous things, but none more scary than this: "Today is not the end. It's just the beginning."

CHAPTER 21

HAVE A GOOD LIFE

———

The spotlight now shifts to incoming president Joe Biden, who takes the oath of office in front of a festive throng of 25,000 National Guard troops.

—Dave Barry, 2021 Year in Review

January 20, 2021

Once you got past the oddity of a presidential inaugural held at the biggest crime scene in America—with the outgoing president as the main Person of Interest—this would be a fairly routine transfer of power. Under a crystalline sky and a bunting-draped Capitol, the Marine Band welcomed Joe Biden into office in front of the same building that a mob answering the call of his predecessor ransacked two weeks earlier. Interesting synergy here.

Biden's inauguration included no mention of Donald Trump, the newly departed and deplatformed commander in chief who skipped town early in the morning with yet another unpleasant distinction to his name: he was the first president in 152 years to refuse to attend the swearing-in of his successor.

It was probably for the best.

The sense of bipartisan relief was unmistakable. Supreme Court justices greeted former presidents with elbow bumps and waved to masked senators in a pandemic-mandated separation of powers. Amy Klobuchar saluted Lady Gaga. Michelle Obama hugged General Milley. Kamala Harris gave special thanks to Mike Pence, who looked thrilled to have escaped the White House, even if it meant a return to the site of his near hanging. Bernie Sanders wore massive mittens and became a meme. Mitch McConnell looked like the happiest man on the dais. It felt like a new day in Washington, at least for a few days.

If January 6 was Trump's culminating disruption, January 20 was Biden's attempt to restore regular order. He sounded less authoritative than simply reassuring—and reassured. The center had held, at least this time.

"On this hallowed ground where just a few days ago violence sought to shake this Capitol's very foundation," the new president said in his twenty-one-minute address, "we come together as one nation, under God, indivisible, to carry out the peaceful transfer of power as we have for more than two centuries."

Shorter version: "Phew."

Left unsaid was that it took some doing to get here. The two weeks from insurrection to inauguration (bisected by an impeachment) were as disquieting a period as I've ever lived through in D.C. There were immediate comparisons to the post-9/11 days—the checkpoints, tanks, and constant rumors—but this was something entirely different. "There is no forerunner," the historian Michael Beschloss said. "We've never had a situation where you have an inauguration two weeks after a terrorist attack and in the same location."

While the threat to America after 9/11 was from some shadowy external force, the main menace in early 2021 still resided at 1600 Pennsylvania Avenue. Trump remained in full command of the government and military, if not of his senses. He was a seething, desperate, and dangerous leader, as volatile as ever. Who knew what else he was capable of, beyond what he'd just shown?

"Just land this plane" became the key phrase among what remained of the administration, Trump's confidants and shell-shocked Republicans on the Hill. As in, just deliver the country to January 20 without further catastrophe. "Guys, we have a clear path to land the plane in 9 days," Hannity wrote in a January 10 text message to Meadows and Jim Jordan. "He can't mention the election again. Ever."

The "land the plane" types did not care about draining any swamps (blatant mixed metaphor, I realize, but I got a plane to land, too). Trump pardoning his friends and accomplices was certainly wrong and unethical, but at least no one would die. This was now about triage. The Milleys and McConnells were worried about a massive plane crash, on the level of Trump declaring war on China or invading Iran. Pelosi, McConnell, and several House and Senate committee heads were placing wit's-end calls to Milley and other top Pentagon, Justice, and Homeland Security officials.

Graham's "Enough Is Enough" phase lasted nearly a full news cycle, long enough for him to be heckled through Reagan National Airport by a swarm of Trump rally goers skipping town the next morning. But soon he would again be the Senate Republicans' main liaison with the White House, almost immediately back in the fold.

In fairness, while Graham's legacy as a feckless charlatan was safe, his involvement at this point was probably *helpful*. He worked with those who remained at the White House—Meadows, Ivanka, and Jared—to keep Trump from causing further trouble. The idea was to keep Trump occupied. They discussed a series of events that would highlight Trump's all-important *legacy* and *great achievements*. Everyone agreed that it would be important to keep the president feeling good about himself.

Trump made a January 12 trip to the Mexican border in the Rio Grande valley town of Alamo, Texas, the first time he was viewed in public after January 6. There, he boasted of having completed four hundred miles of his coveted border wall, though this included a substantial amount of construction that occurred on parts where previous administrations had built existing structures. (Also, needless to say, Mexico did not pay a pretty peso for any of this.)

They did their best to keep Trump away from the TV and the still-circling outside "advisers" trying to fill his head with last-ditch insanity. Toddler-in-chief terminology was never in greater evidence: Graham, Ivanka, and company would do anything to keep Special Boy's attention—feed him the whole bag of Cheese Puffs, whatever got you to bedtime. Whatever landed the plane.

NO ONE WANTED A REPEAT OF JANUARY 6, LET ALONE SOMETHING worse. One former White House official told me of an evening text-chain/support group he participated in for terrified current and former co-workers, where they were encouraged to express gratitude that another day had passed, and they had all moved twenty-four hours closer to the runway. "The people who were around this madness, even on the periphery, are going to be feeling the trauma of these last weeks for a long time," the official told me. "It was that bad."

Contempt for Trump grew considerably from the traditional right, if not from his own hard-core followers. The *Wall Street Journal* editorial board called for Trump's resignation and said that January 6 "probably finished him as a serious political figure." President George W. Bush, the last pre-Trump Republican president, said he was "appalled by the reckless behavior of some political leaders" and likened it to a banana republic. Trump's former defense secretary, James Mattis, said Trump's disgraceful actions were "enabled by pseudo political leaders whose name will live in infamy as profiles in cowardice." Mattis then predicted that after this "Mr. Trump will deservedly be left a man without a country."

Anti-Trump Republicans spewed hot rage, with distinct notes of schadenfreude. As an admirer of good screeds, I found many of them quite artful. *The Atlantic*'s Caitlin Flanagan described the rioters as "deadbeat dads, YouPorn enthusiasts, slow students, and MMA fans" who had "heard the rebel yell, packed up their Confederate flags and Trump banners, and GPS-ed their way to Washington. . . . They had pulled into the swamp with bellies full of beer and Sausage McMuffins, maybe a little high on Adderall, ready to get it done." Flanagan didn't bother visiting any Rust Belt coffee shops to better *understand these people.*

The I Told You So impulse was strong. "And, while we're at it," Kevin Williamson wrote in *National Review*, "maybe turning your party over to Generalissimo Walter Mitty, his hideous scheming spawn, and the studio audience from *Hee-Haw* was not just absolutely *aces* as a political strategy."

Even among the elected and appointed Republicans who had previously been Trump allies, a growing number sounded ready to move on, and fast. Some were brave enough to even say as much, although they would soon regret it. Nikki Haley, the former UN ambassador, was "looking at" running for president in 2024, and people (close to Haley) were piping up in the press again about her being *seen* as a "future leader of the party." Haley figured it was now safe to trash Trump, so she told *Politico* that the lame-duck president "will not have a future in the Republican Party" and that she was "disgusted" by his conduct on January 6, especially toward Pence.

Haley was next seen trying to grovel her way down to Mar-a-Lago to ensure that she and Donald were "okay." Trump told her not to bother. (Message: Not okay.)

McConnell called Trump's actions "a disgraceful dereliction of duty" and held him "practically and morally responsible for provoking the events of the day." The four-year cabinet secretaries Betsy DeVos (Education) and Elaine Chao (Transportation) quit in protest, as did others. McConnell, who is married to Chao, let it be known that if the Democrats moved to impeach Trump again, he would not be displeased. The likes of Graham and Cruz referred to the rioters as "terrorists," and several members of both parties said that they believed that the break with Trump could really be permanent this time.

In addition to the calamity Trump orchestrated on January 6, Republicans had abundant political reasons to sprint away as fast as possible. It went well beyond the precedent of losing presidential candidates being banished to the sidelines, or one-term presidents rarely being asked back into the fray. (Did anyone want Carter or Bush 41 to run again?)

Trump's always-low approval ratings—now down in the 30s—were the well-earned product of a toxic personality and now fully disastrous final scorecard: he would leave office as the first president in history to be impeached twice, the first since Hoover to preside over his party's loss of the House, Senate, and White House in a single term, the first president in history to leave office with fewer jobs than he entered with, the indirect cause of (conservatively) thousands of coronavirus deaths, countless international embarrassments, and a nation that felt far more divided and deranged than at any time in decades. Trump was easily the sorest loser, most prodigious liar, and most insufferable whiner in presidential history. And no commander in chief had ever departed the White House with as massive a legal and financial burden as Donald Trump would now face.

Other than that, the forty-fifth president was a perfect hybrid of Lincoln and FDR.

In a rational world, it would seem unlikely, or ill-advised, for Republicans to consider the above body of work and then say, *"Yes, more of that please!"* Yet everyone had seen—many times over—the repeating pattern of Trump's never-ending outrages met with the same pattern of never-ending denial and cowardice up and down the Republican ranks.

It happened again and again. Trump did something; the GOP found a way to justify it. He then did something worse; they justified that. And the next thing you know, they're defending a lethal attack on the Capitol and Trump is issuing statements declaring his "Complete support and Endorsement" for the reelection of Hungary's ultraright prime minister, Viktor Orbán, and no one thinks twice about it. Full speed ahead! The routine was so entrenched, it was, even before the tear gas cleared on January 6, difficult to be optimistic that this could end in anything but full capitulation.

"For a brief moment I thought what happened would be a shock to the system, like a defibrillator pulling our country back into rhythm," said Representative Andy Kim, Democrat of New Jersey. The speeches were raw, Kim recalled, and people were dazed and "swimming in the uncertainty of the uncharted moment." But then he felt a change in the room as soon as everything switched back to the Electoral College debate and Republicans trotted out their same Big Lie speeches about voter fraud, "as if the riot never happened." Kim said he started to walk out of the House chamber in disgust. "While the riot damaged our Capitol, I felt the scene that I witnessed would ultimately do more harm." He felt the "selfish silence and purposeful amnesia" set in, and he knew that Republicans would be reverting to their passive precedent in no time.

Sure enough. Trump's rehabilitation would commence on schedule even before he was safely out of the White House. McConnell, after condemning Trump in the strongest possible terms, then declined to schedule a Senate trial immediately after the House impeached Trump again on January 13, this time with ten Republican votes. That ensured that the Senate could not act before Trump left office.

And then, conveniently enough, all but seven Senate Republicans voted against conviction in mid-February, largely on the rationale that he was out of office anyway. It was a nifty two-step, and classic McConnell, who of course did not himself vote to convict in the end. This ensured that Trump would be the leader of the party and de facto standard-bearer going forward. Accordingly, McConnell went on Fox News two weeks later and revealed that he would "absolutely" support Trump if he became the nominee again in 2024.

Around the same time, some Republicans began suggesting that January 6 wasn't *that* bad—or not as bad as Democrats and "their friends in the mainstream media" were saying. Senator Rubio was happy to offer important context, as always. He did a local TV interview in Miami in which the anchor reminded him that in 2016 he'd warned against the potential for Trump-incited violence. Rubio replied that in fact Trump's words were not *always* irresponsible. "If you look over the last four years, the president spoke on an almost daily basis and there weren't daily riots," Rubio explained. "In fact, there's one instance that we now have of this sort of unrest." It's true, the media *did* tend to ignore the instances where no deadly insurrections took place in the wake of the president's speeches from January 20, 2017, through January 5, 2021. Why did everyone have to focus on that one bad day of riots? Why always focus on the negative?

WITH IMPEACHMENT TWO SAFELY ON THE BACK BURNER, THE FOCUS returned to simply making it to January 20. My personal inauguration plan was to check into the Trump Hotel over the weekend and stay through January 21. I figured it would be a fascinating vantage point to experience these chilling final few days. This was not even my idea: my *Times* bosses ordered up a "scene" piece about what it was like at the center of Trump Town during Biden's inaugural. When I mentioned that rooms were going for over $1,000 a night, my editor said fine, do it anyway. (Okay, then!) I called and made the reservations myself, not wanting to go through the *Times* travel office, figuring that might set off alarms. I booked three nights on my personal credit card, Saturday to Tuesday. The woman who took my reservation could not have been nicer and a confirmation email arrived within a few minutes. And then, about an hour or so later, a RESERVATION CANCELED email followed. No explanation. I called the hotel to see what was up, left a message, but never heard back. Too bad. I had a perfect cigar to have sent over to Rudy's table.

As for Trump, it felt downright strange at the end, and so markedly different after they took away his toy drums—or Twitter feed. The quiet of the barricaded capital was accompanied by the psychic silence of not having the next presidential tweet out there, waiting to drop at any second. Yes, everyone was still thinking and talking about Donald Trump, wondering what he still might do. And that, to him, was the ultimate gift of his elevation to the presidency, and of the parallel rise of Twitter. But that was going away, almost entirely, in a few days. And how terrifying that must have been for him. After noon on January 20, what tools of ubiquity could ever measure up like this to Trump's preexisting grandeur and mania? Being in the White House, and on Twitter, was probably as close as it got to a fully realized existence for Donald Trump.

I always imagined, or maybe fantasized about, a world where Trump would no longer be president and was somehow deprived of Twitter. How terrifying would those withdrawal symptoms be to him after a full term of unlimited supply? It was as if Trump knew that if this paradise was ever taken away from him, he would become just another shriveled-up and attention-starved *former guy*, found toasted to death one day on a Mar-a-Lago tanning bed.

No wonder he never seemed to go away for four years. No wonder he clung to the gig so desperately at the end.

Anyway, Trump reportedly wanted to do some big send-off for himself at Andrews, but the event fizzled. He gave a low-key speech from the tarmac in which he managed to wish great success to the next administration without mentioning his successor's name. "We will be back in some form," Trump vowed, which was a bit confusing. (Some *form*? Like, as a bumblebee in the Rose Garden?)

"Have a good life," Trump concluded before boarding Air Force One for the last (?) time. His flight took off without incident, and a presidency in flames was safely brought in for landing.

HELICOPTERS PULSING OVER THE CITY ARE NEVER A REASSURING sign. Neither are black fences, concrete barriers, or the swelling ranks of National Guard troops—twenty-five thousand in total, or five times the number of American forces that were still stationed in Iraq and Afghanistan at that point.

Even without Trump's physical or social media presence, the most striking mark of his legacy in Washington was the weary place he left behind. Remnants of the January 6 assault remained everywhere: broken windows, dislodged signs, and closed-off corridors inside the Capitol. The few who ventured into the area looked as if they were attending a vigil. "It feels a little postapocalyptic, to be honest," said Betsy Brightman, who drove to Washington from Philadelphia over the weekend. She came, she said, "just to see this for myself."

I ran into Senator Romney on Monday afternoon at the Capitol Visitor Center, where he was waiting to receive a coronavirus test so he could attend the inauguration. He said he had spoken to a historian that morning about the urgency of preserving some of the physical damage from January 6 for posterity.

"I don't know if it's broken glass or a broken window or something like that," Romney said. "But it's important that we have artifacts to remember this by. It's important that we not forget so fast."

As usual, Romney's instinct was the exact opposite of his party's, which was already well down the memory hole, pretending January 6 never happened.

CHAPTER 22

THE LIFELINE

A man never stands taller than when he is down on all fours
kissing somebody's ass.

—Rahm Emanuel

January 28, 2021

When the history of How Trump Happened is complete, January
28 will loom large. That was the day Kevin McCarthy, the
House minority leader, made his fateful makeup trip to Mar-a-Lago to
"check in" on his wounded emperor.

There they were, Kevin and Donald, the two old besties, who'd definitely been through a rough patch. In the photo, which shot across social
media, Trump and "My Kevin" were standing together again, side by side
in some sunlit ballroom that looked like a wax museum. They wore the
same dark blue suits and held the same stiff smiles. McCarthy stood with

his stomach sucked in and his chest pressed out and his arms held wide, like the weight-lifting football player he used to be.

McCarthy was a tight end at Bakersfield High School in California, exactly forty years earlier. He still mentioned that a lot. "I wasn't that good," McCarthy conceded. But he was always well liked, one of the guys, and still kept a bunch of photos on his phone of himself with his old friends, which he loves to show off. "You can never have too many friends" was McCarthy's mantra.

Admittedly, his "friendship" with the broken former POTUS needed repair. January 6, especially, presented some challenges. They had at least one conversation on that day, and it was a bumpy one. Trump felt that McCarthy had not been "nice" to him when the minority leader called over to the White House to nudge him about those pesky supporters of his who kept pillaging through the Capitol carrying nooses, clubs, and gallows. Whatever happened to civility?

In the aftermath of January 6, McCarthy was getting killed from all directions. People were, not unreasonably, calling him one of Trump's chief enablers who was partly responsible for allowing things to reach that brutal point. He was being accused (accurately) of promoting Trump's stolen election lies.

But Trump was also enraged at McCarthy for not doing more to help "save" his election from the *real criminals*. And the president's supporters had just trashed McCarthy's office.

"This is the first time I've been depressed in this job," McCarthy confided on January 7 to one of his closest colleagues, Representative Patrick McHenry, Republican of North Carolina. "Patrick, man, I'm down, I'm just really down."

Several Republican members had complained that McCarthy had offered them zero leadership about how to proceed before and during the insurrection. They faulted McCarthy for giving no guidance on the certification vote—was it, you know, physically safe to vote to affirm Joe Biden's victory?

The former congressman Bill Thomas, McCarthy's longtime mentor, boss, and predecessor in the Bakersfield House seat, unloaded on his protégé in a local television interview. Thomas called McCarthy a "hypocrite" and accused him of being an eager trafficker of Trump's lies—which led to January 6—and placing his own political standing ahead of the country's.

Numerous friends and colleagues of McCarthy's urged him to distance himself from Trump immediately. For as dreadful as January 6 was, it was also an obvious off-ramp from Trump. Take the off-ramp, McCarthy was urged. If not now, when? Not everyone was gentle. "I was just getting the crap kicked out of me," McCarthy told me.

McCarthy suggested early that he was open to a motion to censure Trump that would have spared them another impeachment vote. No way, Democrats said. McCarthy had even taken the temperature of his caucus about whether he should call on Trump to resign early, according to my *Times* colleagues Jonathan Martin, Maggie Haberman, and Nicholas Fandos, quoting three Republican officials.

On January 13, McCarthy gave what would be his most forceful public repudiation of Trump. "The president bears responsibility for Wednesday's attack on Congress by mob rioters," McCarthy said in a floor speech. "He should have immediately denounced the mob when he saw what was unfolding." Okay, not bad, maybe a little mild, and definitely nowhere near as forceful as McConnell's, but at least it was something.

Or, in Trump's view, seditious.

He was not happy. "He totally fucked me," Trump complained. He told associates that he would fuck McCarthy back ten times harder. (Actually, the version I heard had Trump using a more sodomizing image.)

McCarthy started feeling sorry for himself. Initially, after the election, he had been praised for leading his caucus to a much better performance than expected. It was supposed to be a bloodbath, especially with Trump at the top of the ticket. But Republicans wound up gaining thirteen House seats and reducing the Democrats' margin to nine by the start of 2021.

"Here I am, we did better than we ever thought in the election," McCarthy said. "I should be riding high. And then the whole thing gets wiped out from under me, not by something I've done. And now I've got to lead through this."

McHenry told him to remain calm and settle down. "Kevin, you're not thinking straight," he told him. McCarthy just had to decide what he wanted to do.

Here's what McCarthy wanted to do or, more to the point, what he wanted to be: the Speaker of the House. It's all he'd aspired to for years.

And he was so close in 2015, after former Speaker John Boehner quit. McCarthy had been the favorite to replace him, until he did an interview with Hannity where he boasted that the Republicans' investigation into the 2012 Benghazi attack had tarnished the then secretary of state, Hillary Clinton, and made her a weaker presidential candidate in 2016. Republicans had previously claimed—dubiously—that all they cared about was getting to the bottom of an attack on an American diplomatic compound in Libya that killed four Americans. McCarthy admitted otherwise to Hannity, which was factual but not something he was supposed to admit out loud, dummy. (This is what is known as a Kinsley gaffe, coined by the journalist Michael Kinsley, referring to when a politician accidentally blurts out the truth.) Recriminations against McCarthy were swift. He bled support from his caucus and wound up dropping out of the Speaker's race.

Now McCarthy was this close to the brass ring, once again. He would do what it took. And that, McCarthy determined, required making it work with the disgraced ex-president newly rehomed in Florida, who despite his many handicaps remained the most popular and motivating figure inside the GOP. Republicans couldn't win back the House in 2022 without Trump's still-loyal base of supporters. And without Trump's blessing, there was no way McCarthy would be elected Speaker.

McCarthy popped into Mar-a-Lago exactly eight days after the former president departed the White House and three weeks and a day after the latter's supporters terrorized the Capitol. The visit did not earn universal praise. McConnell was not happy about it, according to two sources close to the leader. A number of the dwindling ranks of non-Trumpy Republicans in the House and Senate did not approve, either, saying it lent Trump legitimacy at a time when he had been marginalized and they could have easily moved beyond him.

"Voters looking for Republican leaders want to see independence and mettle," said Paul Ryan, McCarthy's once-close friend and predecessor as House GOP leader, in a subsequent speech at the Reagan Library in Simi Valley, California. "They will not be impressed by the sight of yes-men and flatterers flocking to Mar-a-Lago." It was clear whom Ryan was talking about.

When I spoke to McCarthy in early April, his Mar-a-Lago trip was another topic he was in no hurry to discuss—along with January 6 and Trump in general. Why did he go? I asked him. He told me it was important to "keep up a dialogue" with Trump.

He added that he was in Florida anyway, and figured what was the harm in stopping by? McCarthy had offered this "happened to be in the neighborhood" explanation before, and the claim always rang more than a bit ridiculous. I imagined him hastily stopping at an Edible Arrangements store on the way to pick up a gift basket/peace offering for FPOTUS, maybe sprinkle in some pink and red Starbursts as a special surprise.

"Look, I didn't want him to leave the party," McCarthy said of his Mar-a-Lago sojourn. "Mitch had stopped talking to Trump a number of months before. People criticize me for having a relationship with the president. That's my job." He said that we all need to talk to each other more. That would be a good thing, wouldn't it? Even better, becoming Speaker of the House would be a *really* good thing. And he needed to keep Trump happy, so there he was, just in the neighborhood.

McCarthy added that he would happily talk to Biden, too, if the president had any interest (he seemed not to). Dialogue, it's all about dialogue! "We used to do stuff together," McCarthy said of Biden, referring to the period when McCarthy was majority leader and Biden was vice president. "He would have me up to eat breakfast at his residence." McCarthy showed me a photo on his phone of him and the then VP, separated by tall glasses of orange juice and plates of freshly cut melon and blueberries. Just a couple of Irish Catholic backslappers, poor man's Reagan and Tip O'Neill, breaking bread and getting shit done.

McCARTHY'S MAR-A-LAGO FORAY HAD NO BIGGER CRITIC THAN LIZ Cheney. Cheney was beside herself over the visit and told McCarthy as much. Cheney was, at that point, still the chair of the House Republican Conference, the third-ranking GOP position in the chamber, behind McCarthy and the minority whip, Steve Scalise. And while Cheney never had terribly high regard for many of her Republican colleagues, including McCarthy—and always believed Trump was a big-time clown, for sure—she was ambitious and usually aligned with Trump's policy agenda, so she'd also been willing to try to make it work, at least for a while.

But it was now clear that her position at the leadership table was becoming untenable, especially after Election Day. Her scorn for Trump after the insurrection had easily been the harshest among Republican leaders. "The President of the United States summoned this mob, assembled the mob, and lit the flame of this attack," Cheney said in a statement. "There has never been a greater betrayal by a President of the United States of his office and his oath to the Constitution." With that, Cheney announced that she would be voting in favor of Trump's second impeachment, along with nine of her Republican colleagues.

When Cheney saw the photos from Mar-a-Lago, she was stunned. She had no advance word of McCarthy's visit and no idea he was going. Why, she asked him, was he serving as an instrument for Trump's rehabilitation, just eight days after Trump fled Washington in deep disgrace? The visit, she said, propped up Trump at a moment when they all could have moved on. "When we look back, Kevin's trip to Mar-a-Lago will, I think, turn out to be a key moment," Cheney said. It would, she said, go down as one of the most shameful episodes in a period full of shameful episodes.

In addition to his paeans to the importance of "dialogue," McCarthy defended his visit by saying that "the Republican Party is changing, and we all have to adapt." The first part of this statement was undeniable. This is indeed no longer the Republican Party of Dick Cheney, as McCarthy had said explicitly—to Liz Cheney and to others. It was no longer the Republican Party of 2016, which, despite Trump's takeover of it, still had a number of traditional conservative figures like Jeff Flake in the Senate and Paul Ryan in the House and a majority of "institutional Republicans" working to stop Trump's nomination.

It was no longer the Republican Party of 2018, which still counted George H. W. Bush, John McCain, and Bob Dole among the living, and enough supportive Republicans to elect Mitt Romney to the U.S. Senate from Utah and to reelect Adam Kinzinger to the House from Illinois. It was no longer even the Republican Party of late 2020, which still had a solid majority of senators to support Biden's no-brainer certification and enough state election officials unwilling to abide the idiocy of Trump's "stolen election" claims and courageous enough to do their jobs despite repeated threats to their well-being.

Nor was this the GOP of the U.S. Chamber of Commerce and the Koch brothers, whose conservative "leaders" paid close attention to *National Review* and *Wall Street Journal* editorials. This was the party of Donald Trump, not George W. Bush. Fox News, not the *Drudge Report*. Steve Bannon, not William F. Buckley. And as far as McCarthy's caucus was concerned, Marjorie Taylor Greene and not Liz Cheney. McCarthy was now concerned primarily with keeping the MTGs of the world happy, despite knowing full well she was nuts ("batshit crazy," he described her to colleagues). He has to deal with the likes of Matt Gaetz, who when he first came to Congress worshipped Paul Ryan until he realized that Trump was much better for business. McCarthy has made no secret inside the caucus that he thought Gaetz was a "bozo" and a "sleazeball," but as he often said (paraphrasing Hyman Roth in *The Godfather: Part II*), politics is the business he's chosen. And this is the caucus he was given. *"We all have to adapt."*

Cheney had no interest in adapting, at least to that. She wanted to fight, she said. "This is a matter of conscience and history and what is fundamentally right," she said. Her Republican colleagues would prefer she did not speak that way. They often agreed with her, *in private*, but Cheney's voicing her disagreement made them look weak and made it harder for them to keep their heads down. It also made it harder for McCarthy to drop by Mar-a-Lago, make nice with Trump, and restore the pre–January 6 order, such as it ever was.

"The violent assault of the Capitol was a moment to say, 'Whoa,'" Cheney told me. "Clearly, this is fundamentally going down a path that unravels the Republic."

"UNRAVELS" IS A WORD CHENEY USES A LOT. IT SIGNIFIES NOT JUST a set of bad outcomes (for example, losing elections, inciting insurrections) but also a spiral, of things only getting worse. That's what's occurred after January 2021. Far from being a line of demarcation against Trump, January 6 would result in a rehabilitation of the former president that would propel a narrative of denial, lies, and autocratic intolerance of dissent that has become the hallmark of the GOP. It has only accelerated since, as Trump has remained, by far, the most powerful leader, kingmaker, and saboteur in the Republican Party. It goes without saying that he had a great deal of help to get and remain in this position.

An obvious casualty of this unraveling has been Cheney's career. She was, inevitably, removed from her leadership post over her continued criticisms of Trump. She was replaced by Elise Stefanik, a thirty-six-year-old moderate from Albany, New York, whose career trajectory represented its own object lesson for the Trump era. Stefanik was a bright, Harvard-educated protégée of Paul Ryan's and vocal advocate for attracting women to the Republican Party and supporting the rights of LGBTQ Americans. She was a frequent critic of Trump's in 2016, always ready with an arch *"This is not who we are as a country"* whenever he piped up with something racist or misogynist or the usual.

But Stefanik was also a breathtaking opportunist, eager to move up in the ranks, and that would require *adapting.* It became clear during the first impeachment hearings that she seemed to view them as an audition for "rising star" status in the MAGA galaxy. As a member of the House Intelligence Committee, Stefanik was initially viewed as one of the "serious" Republicans on a panel otherwise populated by bomb-throwing dimwits such as Gaetz, Jordan, and Nunes. That dream died quickly, however, as Stefanik fatefully toed Trump's noisy line of defense throughout, engaged in conspicuous spats with Chairman Schiff, and collected huzzahs from the White House and recognition as a "team player."

When it was clear that Cheney was about to be ousted as the conference chair, Stefanik made her move, despite having been a vocal admirer of Cheney's and having previously nominated her twice for that same job.

After her election, Stefanik said she was "honored and humbled" to assume the position. She thanked Trump fulsomely and hailed him as "a critical part of our Republican team" and still "the leader that voters look to." And with that, Stefanik became a fully sanctioned Trump Girl, and the GOP was MAGAfied even further beyond recognition.

"I think you can basically tell a lot of the story of the GOP over the last several years by looking at two women, Liz Cheney and Elise Stefanik," Adam Schiff said. Cheney, he said, had proven herself to be a person of great courage and character. Stefanik was the other extreme. "She basically just put up her hand and said, 'Do you need someone to tell a Big Lie? Sure, I'll tell any lie you want me to tell, just give me that position.'" Tragically, Schiff added, there are only two Liz Cheney types in the caucus—the other being Kinzinger. "There are two hundred Elise Stefaniks in the caucus. And you can't even blame it on being uninformed, in the case of Stefanik. It's just pure ambition, and nothing else matters. She just wanted the job."

McCARTHY, OF COURSE, CAN RELATE. HE WANTS THE JOB. BECOMING Speaker is his singular project and only focus: to raise the money, keep the MTGs somewhere close to the rails and Trump in the vicinity of them, and make it to the end of the line—the Speaker's office. Once McCarthy wins, nothing else matters: he will have made it.

The plan could certainly work. Republicans have a better than average shot of winning the House in 2022, at which point McCarthy will have a better than average shot at becoming Speaker. "Sure, Kevin could definitely be Speaker," Kinzinger said. "And if he is, he's going to be miserable and feckless and led around by the nose, but he can definitely be Speaker. When you don't believe that your actions have historic ramifications, you can do that."

McCarthy has no patience for talk of "historic ramifications." Nor does he use words like "unraveling," because it requires attention to where things might be headed. Like Trump, his focus is purely on what's in front of him, eliminating barriers along the way, and whatever gets him the win.

Politics should be fun, McCarthy said. He likes to attend Super Bowls and Hollywood award shows and is enamored, clearly, of the wild-ride aspects of his job. He invited me to join him in April on a trip home to Bakersfield. We went to dinner, exchanged Washington gossip, and bantered about sports, politics, and whatnot. He was a perfectly pleasant bro. McCarthy would periodically brandish phone photos of himself posing with celebrities, including Trump, Pope Francis, Arnold Schwarzenegger, and Kobe Bryant.

And I would periodically make things uncomfortable by asking McCarthy about things he'd rather not discuss.

Did he think Trump would run for president in 2024?

McCarthy flashed a look, not a nice one. He accused me again of asking him only about Trump. "I think he'll talk about it," McCarthy said of Trump, finally. "I don't think he'll make his decision until later." He then showed me a picture of himself from high school in the early 1980s, with majestically feathered hair.

Did he want Trump to run? I asked.

He flashed me a dirtier look. "I think it's a long way away," McCarthy said. "There's a lot that can happen between now and then."

CHAPTER 23

THE UNRAVELING

———

June–December 2021

Senator Rick Scott, Republican of Florida, made his own ring-kissing pilgrimage to Mecca in the spring. Not to be outdone by Kevin McCarthy—are you serious, *Kevin McCarthy?*—Scott brought with him to Mar-a-Lago a special prize that he created just for his favorite President-in-Exile: He brought a trophy!

And not just any trophy. It was the first-ever "Champion for Freedom" trophy, which was conceived by Scott just for this extremely special occasion. Scott, the head of the National Republican Senatorial Committee, had been a bit nervous that Trump might still be sore at certain GOP senators for not being nicer to their favorite president on January 6. (Why didn't they vote against Biden's certification? Why didn't they blame *Biden* for the riots? Why didn't they praise Trump more in general? What riots?)

So, to smooth things over, Scott had come to present Trump with something to recognize him for being a "proven champion for all Americans" and also to thank him for his incredible hard work and dedication.

It was kind of a lame trophy, to be honest—a puny silver bowl, roughly the size of the participation trophy my daughter got for her *incredible hard work and dedication* on the fifth-grade soccer team (great job, Franny!). But Trump, who cupped the memento with two hands and held it out for the cameras like a hot fudge sundae, was beaming at the recognition.

Did Obama ever win a Champion for Freedom trophy? We think not!

"We are grateful for his service to our country," Scott said of the Big Winner in a statement. "And we are honored to present President Trump with the NRSC's first Champion for Freedom award."

The recipient appeared quite touched.

I mention Senator Scott's endeavor at Mar-a-Lago here not because this book needs another example of Republicans debasing themselves before the neediest man in America. I mention it as a sad marker of how the GOP would be proceeding *after* the traumatic final days of Trump's traumatic presidency. Same as it ever was. Meet the new boss, same as the old boss.

Recall that after Trump's election loss, and the deadly riots and the *nasty* impeachment that followed, a number of soul-searching Republicans were beginning to dare to (perhaps, perchance, possibly) suggest, "Okay, maybe we need to have a little discussion about how we should move on from this total fiasco." By spring, though, it was clear that that discussion would not be occurring, and everyone knew exactly where the GOP would be heading, again.

I was reminded of a 2019 *New Yorker* profile of Secretary of State Mike Pompeo, by Susan Glasser, in which she quoted a former American ambassador describing Pompeo as "like a heat-seeking missile for Trump's ass." This image stuck with me (unfortunately) and also remained a pertinent descriptor for much of the Republican Party long after said ass had been relocated to Florida. Senator Scott would merely be the latest in a bombardment of heat-seeking missiles launched from Washington directly at the wide-targeted presidential posterior in Palm Beach.

IT SOUNDED REALLY BAD, THE MORE WE LEARNED ABOUT THOSE final days. Over the first months of the so-called post-Trump era, new details began to dribble out about how far Trump was willing to go. Namely, about how hell-bent the president really was to overturn his defeat and actually remain in office. He really seemed to believe he could do this.

Many of these *troubling new revelations* focused on Pence, Trump's ever-loyal deputy whose dogged acquiescence over four years had given him a certain folk hero status within the MAGA fellowship. One Trump supporter in Sioux Center, Iowa, even compared Pence ("a wonderful gentleman") to "the very supportive, submissive wife to Trump" who was willing to do "the hard work, and the husband gets the glory." This had essentially become the Pence brand. And you can see where this might get a tad, uh, emasculating for a lesser man.

Yet Pence did have certain lines he would not cross. To paraphrase Meat Loaf, he would do anything for love, but he would not do *that*—*that* in this case not attempting to overturn the democratic will of an entire nation. Seemed kind of dirty, you know? Trump, of course, was having none of this. His pressure on Pence leading up to January 6 was relentless. Trump then brought out the big artillery and dropped the utmost threat down upon Pence's bowed head. He warned Pence that if he did not refuse to certify the Electoral College results, he could face the ultimate consequence (pausing to let tension build here). "I don't want to be your friend anymore, if you don't do this."

And yet Pence refused. Wow. What a dishonest, disgusting loser Mike Pence turned out to be.

As more came to light about what Trump was willing and trying to do, and how close the country truly came to the precipice, Republicans seemed to become only more and more determined to forget, ignore, and cover up on behalf of the former president while simultaneously trying to rehabilitate him. The twin Big Lies—(1) that the 2020 election was stolen from Trump and (2) that the January 6 insurrection was (a) the Democrats' fault, (b) the work of antifa, (c) "a normal tourist visit" (per the GOP representative Andrew Clyde), (d) "legitimate political discourse" (per the RNC), or (e) the work of "great fighters and beautiful patriots" (per Trump)—became the thematic frame through which the continued unraveling of the GOP would take place going forward.

IF EVERYTHING REALLY UNRAVELED ON JANUARY 6, THE CONTINUED unraveling had proceeded apace since then. It only got worse. It only *gets* worse. Biden, as advertised, restored a certain degree of normalcy and calmed things down. He screwed up a bunch of things, royally in some cases, but they have usually been within the normal contours of presidents royally screwing shit up (botching a withdrawal of troops from Afghanistan, bungling legislation, probably getting clobbered in the midterms). At least Biden doesn't tweet in the middle of the night or lie about hurricanes or muse about extorting Greenland from Denmark or tout the wonders of bleach as a COVID treatment. He does not dump on authentic war heroes or civil rights icons after their deaths. He does not wish ill upon half the country. That's all a win, as far as I'm concerned.

What's clear, though, is that even while relatively dormant, Trump remains the dominant figure of our political divide and at the orange-hot center of our culture wars.

He still looms, like the pandemic, just as Trumpism perpetuates, like a virus. It mutates, from its Alpha version (ensconced in Florida) to its variants (DeSantis, also in Florida). It metastasizes down to the small cells of American civic life. At least 163 Republicans who signed on to Trump's 2020 election fraud fantasies are now running for offices that will have influence over future elections, *The Washington Post* reported. At least five people who are now running for House seats were present at the Capitol on January 6. Roughly six in ten Republicans said the 2020 election was not legitimate, and almost four in ten said they believed that political violence is justifiable in some cases.

"After a while, it stops being about just Trump the man," Kinzinger said. "I worry that we now have a kind of learned Trumpism in our society. Trump himself could keel over tomorrow, but it's not going to change the narrative of the party."

As far as Kinzinger was concerned, that party was gone. At least the one he grew up in—the one of respect, restraint, and actual conservatism as defined by fiscal discipline, traditional values, and the greater cause of freedom he fought for in Afghanistan. That party has been replaced by the permission structure of Trumpism, one that allows for, even encourages, crassness in the name of "authenticity," freedom in the name of "I make my own rules" and "I do my own research," and straight-up encouragement of political violence in the name of "being strong" and "fighting for our great country."

Trumpism becomes more of a style and an ethic. It is not tethered to a particular set of ideas so much as an expansive code of denial and openness to lies. It jumps easily from misinformation about the 2020 election to "newfound appreciation" for, say, Confederate statues (must protect *our history*) or adherence to garbage science about the alleged dangers of coronavirus vaccines (counties that voted for Trump have consistently shown higher rates of COVID mortality than ones that favored Biden). Learned Trumpism is about always being ready to tackle another massive crisis we had no idea we've been living through: so many scourges and threats to our critical race theory–addled children; antifa marauding through our neighborhoods; terrible crimes hidden on Hunter's laptop and in Hillary's emails. It's a scary world, all that woke contamination everywhere. Sarah Sanders's husband was even kicked out of his fantasy football league! "Not because he worked for President Trump," the former White House press secretary complained, "but because I did."

Likewise, the thuggish impulses of stolen election enthusiasts now convey seamlessly to casual threats hurled at any dissenters, over any number of issues, not just Trump related. Fred Upton, a veteran congressman from Michigan and one of the thirteen Republicans who voted in favor of Biden's $1.2 trillion infrastructure bill, described the flood of abuse he received for supporting the legislation. Marjorie Taylor Greene promptly railed in a tweet against "those 13 Republican traitors," and the barn doors were flung open from there.

"I hope you die. I hope everybody in your fucking family dies," one caller to Congressman Upton's office said in a voice mail, which the congressman then played for CNN's Anderson Cooper. The caller did not address Mr. Upton by his customary honorific ("Congressman"), opting instead to address him as "a fucking piece-of-shit traitor." Upton, who was first elected to Congress in 1986, announced in April 2022 that he would not seek reelection.

THE INITIAL FEARS THAT AFTER TRUMP'S DEPARTURE REPUBLICANS would not only move to forget the lessons and tragedies of the ordeal but actually double down on their embrace of Trump and Trumpism proved to be 100 percent correct. They cleared every possible marker of dereliction as the months of 2021 ticked off.

McCarthy almost immediately backed away from his "the president bears responsibility" faux pas of January 13. McConnell worked to ensure that a bill that would create a bipartisan commission to investigate January 6—a measure supported by thirty-five Republicans—would be snuffed out by filibuster in the Senate. (Cheney and Kinzinger later joined seven Democrats on the House Select Committee to Investigate the January 6th Attack on the United States Capitol.)

Graham said he hoped Trump would run for president again in 2024 and described the former president (correctly) as "the most popular Republican in the country by a lot." Graham added (probably also correctly) that "if you try to drive him out of the Republican Party, half the people will leave."

With a few exceptions, most of the ten House Republicans who voted to impeach Trump the second time never repeated their earlier rebukes of the former president and for the most part have lain low. Some of the higher-profile Republican impeachers (Kinzinger, Upton, Anthony Gonzalez of Ohio, and John Katko of New York) announced their retirements from Congress.

And Cheney, who not only stood by her condemnations of Trump but kept repeating them, was ousted from her House leadership position in May. This would signal quite the downward career detour for one of the most stalwart and conservative Republicans in the House—who voted with Trump 93 percent of the time during his term and whose father was both a certifiable Republican icon in his day and Darth Vader to Democrats everywhere. Liz Cheney had now become, easily, the single biggest undesirable inside the GOP.

YOU CAN LEARN MUCH ABOUT A PARTY BY LISTENING TO ITS DISsenters and watching how they are treated. In the latter category, Cheney's life had become a constant state of siege and abuse. She had endured threats, censures, and continued demands for her resignation from the same party that had overwhelmingly supported her in November 2020, giving her a 44 percent margin of victory in a state where Trump received 70 percent of the vote (his largest margin in the country).

Wyoming, the least populated state in the United States, contains no shortage of buildings and landmarks bearing the name of its de facto royal family. Yet the state's at-large congresswoman was forced to spend $58,000 on personal security during the first quarter of 2021, according to documents filed with the Federal Election Commission. She would also receive special protection from the Capitol Police, an unusual measure taken for a House member no longer in leadership.

I talked to this besieged vintage of Liz in June 2021, at a "secure undisclosed location" in Wyoming. She was on a congressional recess, which she spent mostly in the state yet rarely being seen in public. The appearances she did make—a visit to the Chamber of Commerce in Casper, a hospital opening (with her father) in Star Valley—were barely publicized beforehand, in large part for security concerns.

Getting inside the Dick Cheney Federal Building, which houses Liz's district office in downtown Casper, was like trying to enter a prison: names and IDs were required, armed guards, metal detectors, wands, and ear-pieced agents lining darkened hallways.

By the middle of 2021, the unraveling of the GOP was continuing apace and was perfectly reflected in the news climate that accompanied my visit with Cheney. To wit, that day's headlines underscored the forces that are arrayed against Cheney in her uphill battle against the juggernaut MAGA wing of her party: Trump had been putting out "statements" from Mar-a-Lago all morning—the usual flurry of media criticism ("Crazy Joe Scarborough and his blood-curdling, psycho wife"), stolen election lies, and promotion of a new Ipsos/Reuters poll in which over half of Republicans (53 percent) said they believed Trump was in fact still "the true president" of the United States. In an ABC/Ipsos survey taken six months later, 71 percent of Republicans said they believed Trump's claims that he was the rightful winner in 2020.

Also on this sunny June day, Cheney's freshman colleague, the honorable gentlewoman from Georgia, Representative Marjorie Taylor Greene, went out and likened the House's mask mandates to the yellow stars Jews were forced to wear during the Holocaust.

"I am aware of what I'm up against, yes," Cheney said drily.

Just as Cheney's father was always attuned to doomsday scenarios and existential threats he perceived from America's enemies (the Soviet Union during the cold war, al-Qaeda and Saddam Hussein after September 11), Liz had come to view the current circumstances with Trump in the same apocalyptic vein. The difference was that today's threat resided inside her own party.

Unlike some colleagues who have backed off their initial critiques of Trump, Cheney has never wavered, and her sense of mission post–January 6 has remained resolute. "I will do everything in my power to make sure Donald Trump never gets near the Oval Office again," Cheney said. That, along with surfacing the details of the insurrection, has become the cause of her professional life. It might well cost Cheney her career, at least in Congress. A Trump-backed primary challenger, Harriet Hageman, appears to have an extremely strong shot at defeating her. It has cost Cheney her safety, dozens of friendships, and any chance of becoming Speaker of the House, a goal that her father had encouraged her toward for years.

What's more, many of Cheney's longtime supporters say she has betrayed not only them but a basic code of the citizen solipsism that, in their view, should define leadership in the Trump era. Their main critique of Cheney is that she is not doing what *they* want her to do, which is to support *their* president. "She speaks about her conscience, but you weren't elected to do what you think is right, you were elected to do what the people want you to do," explained Sam Eliopoulos, a Cheyenne Republican who was running for a state house seat. "She didn't do what the people want her to do. At the end of the day, that's it."

Cheney mostly just shrugs and keeps pleading her case, which can feel a bit quixotic. "This is just bigger than all of that," Cheney said. "When you're in a moment like this—and we've never been here before, never have had a president doing what Donald Trump is doing—the obligation to speak out is absolutely clear."

THE WONDER OF THIS WAS THAT MANY REPUBLICANS AGREE WITH Cheney, quite a few of them members of her caucus. They say as much, tell her what a great job she is doing, how heroic she's been. But they only ever tell her this privately, always privately—just between you and me, please don't repeat this, off the record, okay?

Just as they tell Cheney that they really wanted to vote for Biden's certification (because why wouldn't they?). And they probably would have voted for Trump's impeachment, too, at least the second time around, if only it had been a secret ballot. But, well, of course, that's not how it works, so. Their voices tend to trail off from there.

Colleagues approach Cheney, people she's been friendly with for years, a colleague who might have just trashed her into a microphone or voted to bounce her as the House Republican Conference chair. They look at her, as if they were really worried about her well-being—especially certain male colleagues. They look her in the eye, all faux caring and protective, maybe touch her arm. And they'll ask, "Are you okay? You hanging in there?" Cheney tends not to appreciate these gestures of concern.

"You get some 'good jobs' from members, but even more from the Republican staffers," Kinzinger said. "They'll come up to you—they might work for [Paul] Gosar, they might work for Jim Jordan—they'll just say 'thank you.' And I feel bad for them, because they can never say this too loud because they need the job."

I mentioned that apparently many elected Republicans really seem to need the job, too. Otherwise, why would they put themselves through this? They like the power and they want to stay, obviously, and in order to do so, they rarely turn to their best selves, follow their better angels.

Still, there's something about the dirty devotion that Trump has fostered that transcends the psychology of power and belief systems. It goes well beyond the fear of losing a job and a parking space. "We're not really talking about common sense or even politics anymore in my party," said Alan Simpson, the longtime Republican senator from Wyoming. Now ninety, Simpson said he is beside himself at what he calls "the tragedy of what has occurred" at the hands of "this vicious animal who has poisoned our democracy."

Simpson, who left the Senate in 1997, said he voted for Trump (the aforementioned "vicious animal") in 2016 but not in 2020 and never would again. He commiserates about how bad things have gotten with his old Republican friends, including one of his oldest and closest, Dick Cheney. "This is not a Republican Party anymore," Simpson said. "It's a cult."

These parallels to cults come up frequently with regard to MAGA World, usually among disdainful Trump opponents. Representative Jamie Raskin, a Democrat of Maryland and a member of the Select Committee on January 6, said he has read books about cults in an effort to better understand his colleagues across the aisle.

Usually, these cult references carry some undertone of jocularity, or certainly exaggeration. But the more germane point is that rigid and irrational belief systems tend to thrive in the presence of group affirmation and absence of critical dissent. When too many inside resisters stop fighting and float away, the sect that remains becomes only purer, stronger, and self-reinforcing.

My mind sometimes jumps to one of the more hilarious Trump gaffes—few even remember it—from six months or so after the coronavirus spread to the U.S. in 2020. This was back when Trump was dazzling everyone daily with his scientific genius ("maybe I have a natural ability") and generously sharing his ideas to a grateful and reassured nation. The coronavirus, Trump insisted in an ABC News Town Hall in Pennsylvania, would "disappear" even without a vaccine. He laid out his reasoning. "You'll develop, you'll develop herd, like a herd mentality," Trump explained. "It's going to be herd-developed, and that's going to happen," Trump said. "That will all happen."

Presumably, Trump meant to say "herd immunity," not "herd mentality," but in a sense the latter is more applicable to Trump's ongoing mastery over this onetime party of rugged individualists. He is not much for seeing the humanity of the herd, the actual people and stories and lives inside that make up the herd. But the fact of the herd still fascinates Trump, to peer into its collective soul and see it reflected back up at him with such passionate allegiance. And to be able to wield it as such a dangerous weapon, what a touching gift that is.

THERE WAS ONE PARTICULAR OVAL OFFICE ACCOUNT FROM JANU-ary 6 courtesy of Stephanie Grisham, the former White House press secretary who later returned to her original position working for Melania Trump. Grisham, who, like so many veterans of Trump World, was complicit in all manner of wretched lies and wrongdoing on Trump's behalf, knew it all too well as it was happening, says she was miserable the entire time, and then wrote a book about it, nonetheless provided an instructive vantage point on the experience, especially on Insurrection Day.

She described what it was like to actually watch Trump as he sat there, taking this all in. "He was in the dining room, gleefully watching on his TV, as he often did," Grisham said.

"Look at all those people fighting for me," Trump kept saying as he watched, according to Grisham. He kept pressing rewind—as he does—to savor the action, again and again.

There have been several accounts from those who were around Trump on January 6, all confirming that he indeed spent hours trans-fixed by the screen. No one has offered any inkling that he was at all troubled by anything he saw, let alone that he might have felt any remorse about it. People have focused, rightly, on the idea that Trump seemed to do absolutely nothing to stop it and just sat there seemingly indifferent to the very real danger at hand, to Mike Pence on down.

But I appreciated Grisham's descriptions about what exactly it looked like to see Trump so affected, so stirred, as he sat and watched. That his "special people" would all be so willing to demonstrate their highest measure of love for him, on this historic day, and that they would be willing to go down "fighting for me," whatever the steep cost to their own lives.

Trump was, it sounds like, in genuine awe of his followers as they did their work, whether they wore suits and congressional pins, home-made body armor, or a Viking hat. This was, to his mind, the truest and purest expression of Trumpism. What a beautiful love language it was, this burning show of force, servitude, and capitulation.

As far as Trump was concerned, this was the country at its very best, something that everyone who supported him—every Republican, certainly—should be aspiring to.

This, from the disgraced president's warped view of the action, was what it looked like to see America, finally, for this brief moment, becoming great again.

THE HOUSE OF SUBMISSION: STILL OPEN

―――――

March 2022

I made a few last visits to the Trump Hotel in early 2022, for full-circle's sake. In an upset, the gilded ghost town continued to operate under the Trump name, though it wouldn't for much longer. The family unloaded the asset to a Miami investment firm in late 2021 for $375 million, or well over $100 million more than the Trump Organization paid for it.

The transaction illustrated another proud D.C. tradition that its owner perfectly embodied: failing upward. What better monument than this shunned and largely deserted property whose sale still turned a massive profit for its multibankrupted owner? And what better exemplar than a multidisgraced former president who somehow remained the overwhelming favorite to be renominated by his party in 2024?

Trump's outgoing vow to return to Washington *in some form* loomed over the capital like a black-orange funnel cloud. He was never much for giving closure, anyway (if he had been, he'd have conceded the last election by now). As for the hotel, the plan was for it to be rebranded as a Waldorf Astoria in due course. The trophy-gold Trump signage remained glaringly in evidence for now, in keeping with the outgoing proprietor's penchant for hanging around in the loudest possible way. But the family's main for-profit manor had moved south to Mar-a-Lago, with swarms of Republican office holders, House and Senate candidates, and favor seekers of all stripes bowing their way through the Palace in Exile to prove devotion.

I would still stop by 1100 Pennsylvania from time to time, even after Trump left office. The lounge area remained a palatial curiosity to the occasional MAGA tourist visiting D.C. It wasn't the same, though. When you pay $35 for, say, a cheese board appetizer, you expect a little something extra with your order, perchance to gratify a president. Without that, it's just overpriced cheese: *fromage sans hommage.*

The shrimp cocktail even vanished from the snack menu, another sign of the apocalypse. And another one: Madison Cawthorn, Lauren Boebert, and Marjorie Taylor Greene had all been spotted here in recent weeks. (I was sorry to miss them, but would miss the shrimp more.) They were what passed for big-ticket celebrity sightings here in 2022, a far cry from the glory days of Rudy getting photographed outside after the Mnuchin wedding, cigar in mouth and red wine staining his unbuttoned tuxedo shirt.

Before I checked out for good, I wanted to make a final visit to the hotel to meet Zach Everson, an enterprising hospitality journalist who in 2018 launched the essential *1100 Pennsylvania* newsletter, tracking the various comings, goings, and preenings at the hotel. Everson was a tremendous resource for me and for any Washington reporter attempting to capture the Trump-era swamp in all of its decadent contours. He staked out this House of Submission far more than I could ever stomach, and when he couldn't be here himself, Zach scoured Twitter and Instagram for updated sightings. What, you think I witnessed Marco Rubio's wife eating a fruit salad at the BLT myself?

It was Everson who tallied that twenty-nine out of the thirty-eight Trump cabinet members had been spotted at the Trump Hotel, some multiple times, including eight alone at a going-away bash for Sarah Huckabee Sanders; and it was Everson who noticed that within a day of Trump's infamous "Be there, will be wild!" tweet about his January 6 rally, the cheapest room at the Trump Hotel immediately jumped from $476 to $1,999. "Donald Trump didn't just inspire the Jan. 6 riot," Everson wrote. "He seems to have made money off it."

I wanted to buy Everson a steak lunch at the Trump Hotel, which seemed a fitting thank-you. Alas, he informed me that he had been banned from the place a few months earlier, for reasons never explained. A security guard intercepted him one night outside the men's room and told him to leave and never return.

Instead, Everson and I grabbed lunch across the street at the much cheaper Elephant & Castle. He sounded almost nostalgic. "It seemed as if every thread from the Trump years worked its way through the hotel at some point," Everson said. Indeed, there were multiple meetings there related to both impeachments: Rudy did a lot of his Ukraine scheming here in 2019 and some of the alleged planners of January 6 stayed and socialized here. Organizers of the white supremacist rally in Charlottesville convened here, as did desperate pardon seekers and access peddlers, shady foreign leaders and lobbyists and pretty much every major Republican and grasping grifter eager to impress the president. No one had his nose pressed harder against the glass of this aquarium tank than Zach Everson. I told him I'd buy him a proper steak after the Waldorf took over.

SINCE I DID NOT VENTURE INSIDE THE HOTEL WITH ZACH, TECHNI-cally my last visit occurred the evening before, at nearly the exact hour that Russia was launching its invasion of Ukraine. It was one of those horrifically riveting news nights when a shock-and-awe war begins— flashes and explosions on TV and the sick mystery of what destruction might be concealed by the smoky darkness. You remember where you were on these nights, and where you watched. I was at the Trump Hotel, looking up once more at the soundless bar TVs.

Trump was on Fox, praising Putin again, apparently (I learned this later, given the lack of volume). In the previous forty-eight hours, Trump had also hailed the Russian strongman as "savvy" and "a genius," even as lines of demarcation between the righteous and evil causes had been drawn more clearly in the Russia-Ukraine conflict than in any the free world has seen in years. Putin managed to turn himself into an irredeemable global pariah in a matter of days. The Ukrainian resistance, led by President Volodymyr Zelensky, provided a near-unanimous rallying point and inspiration.

Even Trump finally came around to praising Zelensky, but he could never bring himself to criticize Putin. He kept going on about how "strong" and "smart" the Russian autocrat was, especially compared with how "weak and dumb" Biden was. He continued to trash NATO alliances while maintaining that "the rigged election" of 2020 was what had caused this whole horrifying situation. It was, as ever, bizarre and appallingly in character for Trump. The elder-statesman, Habitat for Humanity phase of his ex-presidency had not yet commenced.

Meanwhile, the same Republican leaders who had spent five years cowering before Trump were now hailing the bravery of "our Ukrainian brothers and sisters" and "our good friend Ukrainian president Volodymyr Zelensky." They did not care as much that Putin had tried to influence the 2016 U.S. election in Trump's favor, or that Trump got himself impeached over trying to strong-arm Zelensky into helping him in 2020. Nor would they say anything that critical of Trump's continued praise of Putin now.

The official RNC Twitter account—following Trump's lead—also heaped derision upon Biden and said not a word about Putin in the days after the invasion. Not surprisingly, surveys of Republican voters continued to show higher regard for Putin than for Biden. Trump gave a speech at the Conservative Political Action Conference (CPAC) in Orlando a few days into the invasion in which he encouraged the audience to keep their focus on "our most dangerous threat" to freedom and peace, the "radical Democrats who hate our country because they make us weak."

Trump then returned to the core grievance of his crusade: the stolen election. The lost landslide, how it ruined everything. "We are a laughingstock," the former president of the United States said. "We are a laughingstock."

Like Trump, Vladimir Putin takes what people let him take. He will do what he can get away with. The Russian president has now placed himself in league with some of history's genocidal monsters, the likes of Hitler, Pol Pot, Osama Bin Laden, and a select group of others. He is isolated from every country and leader in the free world, with a few conspicuous exceptions that include the ex-president of the United States. Trump sounded as if he watched "genius" Putin's slaughter of Ukraine with the same relish as he did his supporters' ransacking of American democracy on January 6.

We know how far Trump would go in his first term—catastrophically far, even in the narrow pursuit of staying in office. We can also assume he'd have gone much further if the likes of Pence, Barr, and a few state and local Republican election officials had not performed their bare minimum duty at the bitter end. We already know who Trump is, and that he still appears infatuated with the Russian president.

But we also know, thanks to the example of Ukraine, what true sacrifice, valor, and patriotism look like. The country has provided a stirring reminder: a brave president who truly is "fighting right there with you" alongside his people, and in pursuit of a great and vital cause.

We see the same reminder in the everyday defiance being shown and blood being spilled by terrorized Ukrainians of all ages. This is courage and character to an astonishing degree, and such a perverse contrast to Donald Trump and the acolytes who have sustained him. Unlike so many feckless Republicans now slapping on "Stand with Ukraine" buttons in Washington, these patriots would never collaborate with their occupiers as these alleged "leaders" had.

THERE WAS A SPATE OF "ANALYSIS" PIECES IN EARLY 2022 SUGGESTing that perhaps Trump's six-year lock on the GOP might be weakening a bit. "Trump alternative" candidates, such as Florida governor Ron DeSantis, had been showing decent strength in way-too-early polling for 2024. Fairly high numbers of Republicans in focus groups were saying they wouldn't mind a fresh face, and some RINO squishes were even daring to suggest the party should stop trying to overturn 2020.

Even the zealously acquiescent Pence gave a speech in February saying Trump had been "wrong" to expect him to intercede in the counting of electoral votes on January 6—which the media treated as a major act of rebellion and Trump treated as another act of blasphemy from his former VP.

Personally, I wasn't buying the "Trump's hold on the GOP is weakening" proposition. Maybe it was a little, but it was hard to envision any Republican beating him if he ran in 2024, which Trump was sounding more and more certain of. "We did it twice and we'll do it again," Trump vowed at CPAC, where a life-sized cutout of his head superimposed over Rambo's body was displayed and a five-volume collection of his tweets was on sale.

Copycat Trumps were popping up all over Fox, running in state and local races and becoming more and more wanton and belligerent about America's "woke enemies." Several of these Trump knock-offs across the country are bound to prevail in the midterms. Even if they are not authentic dumbasses in real life like Cawthorn and Boebert, the rich and Ivy-bred likes of J. D. Vance (in Ohio) and Dr. Oz (in Pennsylvania) learn to adapt quickly enough. The next wave of GOP members will almost certainly resemble the less responsible, more outrageous likes of Greene and Gaetz more than Republicans such as Senators Richard Burr of North Carolina, Richard Shelby of Alabama, and Rob Portman of Ohio, all of whom are retiring. In other words, it's hard to foresee that the next GOP majority in Congress will usher in a sober period of reflection, pragmatism, and comity.

The fringe has become the standard. As MSNBC's Brian Williams said in signing off from his final show in December 2021, "The darkness on the edge of town has spread to the main roads and highways and neighborhoods." This was certainly true within the GOP, though Williams framed it in terms of its poisoning effect on our broader national enterprise. "Grown men and women, who swore an oath to our Constitution—elected by their constituents, possessing the kinds of college degrees I could only dream of—have decided to join the mob and become something they are not," Williams said. "They've decided to burn it all down with us inside."

Trump remains, overwhelmingly, the master arsonist of this enduring "burn it all down" worldview and approach. But the main reason Trump will remain in control of the GOP is that the same dynamic that has kept him atop the GOP heap for this long—Republicans quaking before him, humoring him, and fetishizing him—has remained unchanged.

Yes, we know "who Donald Trump is" at this point, and what he's capable of. Just as significant, maybe more so going forward, is that we know who Kevin McCarthy, Lindsey Graham, and Ron DeSantis are. That would be McCarthy, the probable speaker in a Republican House majority; Graham, an even more "relevant" broker in a Republican Senate majority; and DeSantis, who unquestionably took a populism class or two at Yale (or maybe Harvard Law) and appears well positioned for a big role in the next GOP reality smackdown.

For now, though, they've all demonstrated the most vital survival skill for any Republican to possess: reverence before the incumbent trauma monger, who is looking to renew for another season. They will bow down to Trump for as long as is needed, adhere to the same orthodoxy that's gotten them this far.

There have been a few breaks from the Trump-worshipping ranks of late, but usually in keeping with the patterns that prevailed during Trump's presidency. People loyal to Trump in public speak "candidly" about him, but only under the cover of anonymity in the press, or under oath before a judge or Congress (unless they could avoid it). Or, even better, if they can get a book deal, speaking "candidly" about Trump could serve a rehabilitative purpose for them, as well as a remunerative one.

William Barr, the former attorney general, who did more to protect Trump and advance his interests than any other cabinet member, came out with his own memoir in March. Predictably, Barr slammed Trump, who, he wrote, "surrounded himself with sycophants, including many whack [*sic*] jobs from outside the government." Yep, sounds about right. "People are worthwhile to Trump only as a means to his ends—as utensils," Barr concluded. (Also checks out.) "Trump cared only about one thing," the former AG wrote. "Country and principle took second place." (Ditto.)

The book was full of these Captain Obvious critiques. Barr even served up the very fresh take that his former boss was an "incorrigible" narcissist. I gleaned this just from the excerpts and news stories, by the way. No chance I'm reading this book, though I'm sure the parts about Barr's childhood and early legal career are awesome.

Trump, for his part, said he won't be reading Barr's book, either. "I would imagine that if the book is anything like him, it will be long, slow, and very boring," Trump wrote in a letter to NBC's Lester Holt that was obtained by Axios. I think I'm with the (non)reader in Palm Beach on this one.

I AM WRITING THESE FINAL PAGES IN EARLY MARCH, NOW ABOUT two weeks after the Ukraine invasion and a week after Biden's State of the Union address. The speech got decent reviews and was mostly forgotten a day later. A bunch of Republicans, such as Freedom Fighter Marco Rubio, skipped the address rather than take the required COVID test to enter the House chamber. Boebert and Greene heckled Biden and played their roles to the hilt, as did Leader McCarthy, who did nothing. Bill Barr was spotted dining across town at the Palm.

It is always difficult to press Send on a book that will publish a few months later, especially in such a volatile news environment. Who knows how many times the world can turn upside down again in the interim? How will Ukraine resolve and COVID mutate? What will Putin do with the nuclear arsenal that he just placed on high alert? (Bit of a wild card there, admittedly.)

Assuming we all survive, my main interest in this saga remains the accomplices who make Trump possible. His story does not so much move in circles as it does in spirals. The longer it goes on, the worse it gets. Trump only becomes more determined when his next big goal comes into view. It is getting closer.

We are now on a collision course with a decisive next chapter: Trump and 2024. The GOP did not stop him in 2016 and have barely reckoned with him in the six years since, despite everything.

Trump was correct in his original assessment of so many Republican "leaders." They have proven to be weak, conniving, and two-faced cowards. They fear Trump as much as they despise him. They fear his (and their own) voters as much as they have contempt for them.

It would be silly at this point to expect any of these profiles in courage to place themselves between Trump and whatever his next campaign looks like, let alone if it leads to his next presidency. Their answers and brush-offs to questions about what they would do if Trump ran again in 2024 have already been revealing enough.

In promoting his memoir, Barr has been inevitably asked about 2024. Specifically, he is asked whether he would still support Trump, whom he spent a portion of his over-six-hundred-page memoir trashing as utterly unhinged, delusional, and possessing "neither the temperament nor persuasive powers" to be president. You can guess how this ended. "I believe that the greatest threat to the country is the progressive agenda being pushed by the Democratic Party," Barr said on NBC's *Today* show. "It's inconceivable to me that I wouldn't vote for the Republican nominee."

Brad Raffensperger, the Georgia secretary of state, whom Trump called on January 2, 2021, and leaned on to "find votes" for him after the election—and whose refusal to go along subjected his family to unrelenting abuse and threats—spent about three minutes not answering the same question in a cringey MSNBC interview from November 2021.

"That is so far out in the future I haven't even thought about that," Raffensperger said. When pressed by host Mehdi Hasan, the secretary of state refused to rule out voting for Trump again in '24, as he had in '20. Raffensperger did say, however, that he thought Republicans would definitely have a "robust debate" in 2024 and then settle on a nominee who would "stand on character and have the moral compass to lead this nation." Good to know!

"I'm not answering hypothetical questions," Chris Christie told me in December in response to the question of whether he would vote for Trump again.

You hear that a lot, the same calculated avoidance. In fairness, Christie has taken up a progressively vocal critique of Trump since the latter left office. He, too, wrote a book, *Republican Rescue,* in which he harshly criticized Trump's conduct after the election. The former New Jersey governor has evidently been positioning himself of late as a truthtelling alternative to Trump for '24. But when we last spoke, in December 2021, Christie did not want to get too far ahead of himself. He was keeping his options open.

I asked Christie whether Trump's behavior in the last months of his term (and since) should disqualify him from serving as president again. Again, Christie said, no hypotheticals. "I want to talk about what Donald Trump is doing now," he said. "Whatever he does in the future, whether he can change his stripes and become somebody who's productive . . . that's his choice. But I'm not going to sit here and predict what he'll do."

A former Republican congressman told me recently that the party's only real plan for dealing with Trump in 2024 involved a darkly divine intervention. "We're just waiting for him to die," he said. That was it, that was the plan. He was 100 percent serious.

But soon enough, 2024 won't be a long way off. Trump will likely still be alive. His running again will no longer be hypothetical. The crowds will return to the arenas and to the next Trump Hotel, or wherever the lights go on next. So will the original owner, primed for a return engagement as the Republican standard-bearer—because what could possibly go wrong?

And who's going to stop him?

ACKNOWLEDGMENTS

———

Enough about servitude. On to gratitude.

As a getter of the joke, I know full well this is the second most important part of the book—the first being the index, which I'm including this time (you're welcome, Lanny). Free idea: Someone should write an entire book of acknowledgments followed by an index and perhaps some photos. I'm certain it would kill in D.C. And I expect to be acknowledged.

Undying thanks to Dean Baquet, A. G. Sulzberger, Meredith Kopit Levien, and everybody at *The New York Times*. You run the most vital newspaper in the world, and it only gets more so. It was nothing but a pleasure and an honor to be bylined there for sixteen years.

The best part about the *Times* has been the people I've gone to work with—at least when "going to work" was still a thing. Jake Silverstein and Elisabeth Bumiller were superstar bosses and leaders of my twin incubators, the *Times Magazine* and *Times* Washington bureau. Thank you both for being cool, wise, and, most of all, kind.

Vast appreciation for my collaborators in the various *NYT* clubhouses: At the *Magazine*, Charlie Homans, Mike Benoist, Dean Robinson, Ilena Silverman, *Bob* Draper, Jason Zengerle, Jonathan Mahler, and Gail Bichler. In D.C., Bill Hamilton, Rebecca Corbett, Dick Stevenson, Julie Davis, Mikayla Bouchard, Tahirah Burley, Maureen Dowd, Mark Mazzetti, Carl Hulse, Annie Karni, Katie Rogers, Peter Baker, Michael Shear, Jonathan Martin, Zolan Kanno-Youngs, Alan Rappeport, David Leonhardt, Nick Fandos, Lara Jakes, Helene Cooper, David Brooks, Mike Schmidt, Doug Mills, Clif Meadows, and Jeff Burgess. At points in between and all over: Jim Rutenberg, Mark Landler, Maggie Haberman, Adam Nagourney, DAMatt Flegenheimer, Rachel Dry, Pat Healy, Compadre Ken Belson, David Segal, Kate Zernike, Michael Barbaro, Sarah Lyall, Carolyn Ryan, Matt Purdy, and torch carrier Lori Leibovich.

I will never forget the great Robert Pear, Fred Hiatt, Robin Toner, David Carr, and Janet Elder.

Thank you to Jeffrey Goldberg, Adrienne LaFrance, and my new colleagues at *The Atlantic* for letting me join the Beatles. Appreciation, too, for the generous start date, which allowed me to finish this (somewhat) on time. This next safari will unquestionably be a blast.

I always hated the conceit that Donald Trump was some great gift to Washington journalism—the idea being that because he made *so much news* and was *so entertaining*, we must surely be having so much fun, right? Uh, nah. In fact, on many days, it's been quite exhausting and depressing to be among the Enemies of the People. And trying to write about Whatever This Is can sometimes feel like pushing peas around a plate.

Yet the Trump era has also bred a bonanza of great journalism, in all flavors—beat reporting, investigative, opinion, longform, and yes, even tweets. I've had the privilege of knowing, learning from, or just consuming the fruits of some of the best. They include, off the top of my head: David Fahrenthold, Charlie Sykes, Tim Miller, Jonathan Chait, Shawn McCreesh, Phil Rucker, Carol Leonnig, Ashley Parker, Dan Balz,

Swanathan and Mike Allen at *Axios,* James Bennet, Jake Sherman, Olivia Nuzzi, Caitlin Flanagan, Jen Senior, Anne Applebaum, Franklin Foer, Tim Alberta, George Packer, Ruby Cramer, John Harris, Susan Glasser, Paul Farhi, Sarah Ellison, Margaret Sullivan, Julia Ioffe, Jack Shafer, and Jack's former editor. Special bonus mention to the aforementioned Sykes for coining the best synonym for Trump's sycophants: "the brigade of dutiful turd-polishers."

Thank you for the laughs, coffee, Bertucci's, Santarpio's, cucumbers, tomatoes, and sunshine: Paul, Train, and all the Farhim; Mike Barnicle, Nem Hackett, Josh King, good ol' Maggie Jones, Ned Zeman, Matt Brune, Jim Boyd, Zippy Zeitlin, Mark Salter, Dafna Linzer, Nicolle Wallace, Walter Shapiro, Jeff Zeleny, Jonathan Lemire, Joe Scarborough (and Bobby Dalbec), Beth Myers, Jon Kelly, Hugo Lindgren, Mark McKinnon, David Axelrod, Alex Wagner, Katy Tur, Tom Brokaw, Sally Quinn, Bill Smee, Wendy Jacobson, David Plotz, and Hanna Rosin.

Thank you, also, to my (hopefully) unindicted co-conspirators. Also known as sources. This book is the product of more than 250 interviews conducted over six or so years, some overlapping with assignments for the *NYT,* where small portions of this book may have originated in some form. All praise to the *Times* for its support and indulgence on this. Every direct quotation that appears here was derived from author interviews, unless indicated otherwise in the context or in the endnotes. All errors of fact and oversight are my own. Unless I end up blaming somebody else.

But definitely *not* Sonia Schlesinger. Sonia has been an absolute godsend of a researcher/fact-checker/troubleshooter/all-around marvel down the stretch. And will be a godsend to whoever is lucky enough to get her next. I could not have asked for a better fellow traveler and neighbor.

ACKNOWLEDGMENTS

Wow, has it really been ten years now with Elyse Cheney, Super Agent to the stars, divas, and neurotics? She's simply the best at what she does and the full package—dealmaker, editor, ultra-friend, and literary shrink, who even laughs at my very unfunny shit. You outdo yourself every time. As always, thanks to the Super Team at the Cheney Agency: Claire Gillespie, Isabel Kaplan, Isabel Mendia, and Beniamino Ambrosio.

Talk about best in the biz: The great Scott Moyers at Penguin Press made this book possible from the start and better at every turn. He also made it fun. Boundless appreciation for your wisdom, humor, and overall menschiness and brilliance. Next time we stick to sports.

Big-time thanks to associate editor Mia Council, for keeping things on the rails and for being the fundamental force of this project. Stellar work, also, by Ingrid Sterner (copy editor), Andrew Rae (did the killer cover illustration), Daniel Lagin (designed the interior), Darren Haggar (did the jacket), Daniel Novack (did the lawyering), Sarah Hutson, Liz Calamari, Matt Boyd, and my people at Penguin. You are all extremely good at your jobs.

Ever-thanks, in book perpetuity, to the incomparable David Rosenthal, for being the right voice in my head at all the key times, but especially at the start. Blue Rider forever (missing you, Aileen Boyle).

So much love to my originator family in their various units, especially my mother, Joan Leibovich, and sister, Lori Leibovich. You are at my side and in my heart, always. Eternal abrazo fuerte, too, to my father, Miguel Leibovich, and dear brother, Phil Leibovich. We had joy, we had fun, and we went candlepin bowling.

Shout-outs to bonus parents Ted Sutton, Betty Grossman, and Jack Kolbrener; bonus sibs Michael Kolbrener and Resistor Larry Kanter ("Book edits are lame! Rock music rules!"). Big hugs to bonus youths Carlos, Clara, Theo, Avi, and Charlie.

Sad but true, but I've spent more home-office time these last two years with my feline muses, Eloise and Iris Kolbrener. Sadder but true: I just acknowledged cats! Definitely time to wrap.

Finally, and most important, this book is dedicated to my favorite germ-circle of Leibobreners, who are, simply, everything to me. I endlessly adore my daughters—Nell, Eliza, and Franny—and remain in awe of who you are and the women you're becoming. Speaking of awe: Meri Kolbrener is the Essential One who makes it all possible. Love, love, love, and I could not be luckier.

NOTES

PROLOGUE: LAST CALL AT THE TRUMP HOTEL

2 **"There is a comfort level"**: Julie Bykowicz, "Trump Hotel Is RNC Annex, Abuzz with Republican Players," *Wall Street Journal*, Aug. 26, 2020, www.wsj.com/articles/trump-hotel-is-rnc-annex-abuzz-with-republican-players-11598473116.

4 **"Well, okay, from my point of view"**: Mark Leibovich, "How Lindsey Graham Went from Trump Skeptic to Trump Sidekick," *New York Times Magazine*, Feb. 25, 2019, www.nytimes.com/2019/02/25/magazine/lindsey-graham-what-happened-trump.html.

6 **"I believe this election was fixed"**: Linda Chavez, "The 'Intellectual' Right's Assault on Democracy," *Bulwark*, Dec. 10, 2020, www.thebulwark.com/the-intellectual-rights-assault-on-democracy/.

7 **"serious mental decline"**: Bob Woodward and Robert Costa, *Peril* (New York: Simon & Schuster, 2021), xiv.

8 **"I would just say"**: Tara Palmeri, "'Tis the Season of Year-End Lists," *Politico Playbook*, Dec. 24, 2021, https://www.politico.com/newsletters/playbook/2021/12/24/tis-the-season-of-year-end-lists-495550.

8 **He would savor one last favorite:** Josh Dawsey, Ashley Parker, and Philip Rucker, "'Have a Good Life': Trump Leaves for Florida in Low-Key Farewell," *Washington Post*, Jan. 20, 2021, www.washingtonpost.com/politics/trump-farewell-florida/2021/01/20/c6ca8a82-5b50-11eb-a976-bad6431e03e2_story.html.

9 **"We've got this perverse"**: David Brooks, "When the World Is Led by a Child," *New York Times*, May 15, 2017, https://www.nytimes.com/2017/05/15/opinion/trump-classified-data.html.

10 **"The essence of obedience"**: Stanley Milgram, *Obedience to Authority* (New York: Harper Perennial Modern Thought, 2019), xiv.

10 **"The cliché says that power"**: Robert Caro, *The Years of Lyndon Johnson: The Passage of Power* (New York: Vintage, 2013), xiv.

12 **French fries, shrimp cocktail:** Jessica Sidman, "Trump Hotel Employees Reveal What It Was Really Like Catering to the Right Wing Elite," *Washingtonian*, Feb. 19, 2021, www.washingtonian.com/2021/02/19/trump-hotel-employees-tell-all-what-it-was -really-like-serving-right-wing-elite/.

14 **McCarthy was once flying:** Josh Dawsey and Robert Costa, "Kevin McCarthy Relishes Role as Trump's Fixer, Friend, and Candy Man," *Washington Post*, Jan. 15, 2018, www .washingtonpost.com/politics/kevin-mccarthy-relishes-role-as-trumps-fixer-friend -and-candy-man/2018/01/15/a2696b4e-f709-11e7-b34a-b85626af34ef_story.html.

14 *The Truman Show*: Dan Zak, "Rep. Matt Gaetz Wants You to Know Who He Is, and His Plan Is Working," *Washington Post*, Feb. 20, 2018, www.washingtonpost.com/lifestyle /style/rep-matt-gaetz-wants-you-to-know-who-he-is-and-his-plan-is-working/2018 /02/20/2dfce71e-126a-11e8-8ea1-c1d91fcec3fe_story.html.

CHAPTER 1: THE PROBLEM

19 **"If you killed Ted Cruz"**: Lindsey Graham, speech, 72nd Annual Congressional Dinner at the Washington Press Club, Washington, D.C., Feb. 26, 2016.

22 **"If your standard-bearer"**: Erick Erickson, speech, RedState Gathering, Atlanta, Aug. 8, 2015.

24 **"gave a stamp of credibility"**: Tim Miller, "The Biggest Bully Is a Half Decade Late," *Bulwark*, Nov. 11, 2021, www.thebulwark.com/the-biggest-bully-is-a-half-decade -late/.

CHAPTER 2: THE JOKE

30 **"Donald Trump is everything"**: Andrea Gonzales, "South Carolina Gov. Nikki Haley Doesn't Understand Why Chris Christie Endorsed Donald Trump," with video of *This Week*, ABC, Feb. 28, 2016, https://abcnews.go.com/Politics/south-carolina-gov-nikki -haley-understand-chris-christie/story?id=37242074.

31 **"He gets it"**: Philip Rucker, Dan Balz, and Robert Costa, "Trump Is Playing 'a Part' and Can Transform for Victory, Campaign Chief Tells GOP Leaders," *Washington Post*, April 21, 2016, www.washingtonpost.com/news/post-politics/wp/2016/04/21/trump-is -playing-a-part-and-can-transform-for-victory-campaign-chief-tells-gop-leaders/.

33 **"If you say nice things"**: Maegan Vazquez, "Graham: You Could Be the Pope and Trump Would Still Fire Back," CNN, Jan. 18, 2018, www.cnn.com/2018/01/18/politics/graham -trump-pope-cnntv/index.html.

36 **"they should leave"**: Patrick Healy, Jonathan Martin, and Maggie Haberman, "With Donald Trump in Charge, Republicans Have a Day of Reckoning," *New York Times*, May 4, 2016, www.nytimes.com/2016/05/05/us/politics/trump-gop.html?smid=tw -share.

36 **"We can no longer trust"**: Cliff Sims, *Team of Vipers: My 500 Extraordinary Days in the Trump White House* (New York: Thomas Dunne Books, 2019), 34.

37 **"No, that's incense"**: Mark Leibovich, "Will Trump Swallow the G.O.P. Whole?," *New*

York Times Magazine, June 21, 2016, www.nytimes.com/2016/06/26/magazine/will
-trump-swallow-the-gop-whole.html.

CHAPTER 3: UNITY—OR ELSE!

41 **"not knowing much"**: Patrick Healy, Jonathan Martin, and Maggie Haberman, "With
Donald Trump in Charge, Republicans Have a Day of Reckoning," *New York Times,*
May 4, 2016, www.nytimes.com/2016/05/05/us/politics/trump-gop.html?smid=tw
-share.

41 **"a guy with no knowledge"**: Healy, Martin, and Haberman, "With Donald Trump in
Charge."

43 **"Don't worry, Malcolm"**: Malcolm Turnbull, "Former Australian PM Malcolm Turnbull
on Donald Trump: 'You Don't Suck Up to Bullies,'" *Guardian,* April 19, 2020, www
.theguardian.com/australia-news/2020/apr/20/malcolm-turnbull-on-donald-trump
-you-dont-suck-up-to-bullies.

45 **"I think you'd have riots"**: Trump to Chris Cuomo, CNN, March 15, 2016, www.cnn
.com/videos/tv/2016/03/16/trump-brokered-convention-intv-cuomo-newday.cnn.

46 **"Seeing this just breaks your heart"**: Alex Isenstadt, "Furious GOP Donors Stew over
Trump," *Politico,* June 11, 2016, www.politico.com/story/2016/06/gop-donors-donald
-trump-224218.

47 **"Republicans have gone from being"**: Tom Nichols, "Worse Than Treason," *Atlantic,*
Jan. 24, 2021, www.theatlantic.com/ideas/archive/2021/01/what-republicans-are-doing
-worse-treason/617538/.

CHAPTER 5: APOCALYPSE 45

61 **"emblematic of the disdain"**: Charles Murray, interview with Sam Harris, *Waking
Up* (podcast), April 23, 2017, posted as "Charles Murray and Sam Harris on the New
American Upper Class," YouTube, https://www.youtube.com/watch?v=08m6YNv
pLaw&t=30s.

61 **"When I get to Washington"**: Cliff Sims, *Team of Vipers: My 500 Extraordinary Days
in the Trump White House* (New York: Thomas Dunne Books, 2019), xvii.

66 **"mentally retarded"**: Bob Woodward, *Fear: Trump in the White House* (New York:
Simon & Schuster, 2018), 216.

CHAPTER 6: THE PUNCH LINE

70 **"There are doctors who help"**: Ben Terris, "What Happens When You Tie Your Career
to Donald Trump? Ask Sean Spicer in a Few Months," *Washington Post,* Aug. 17, 2016,
www.washingtonpost.com/lifestyle/style/what-happens-when-you-tie-your-career
-to-donald-trump-ask-sean-spicer-in-a-few-months/2016/08/16/c492be3a-5f4f-11e6
-8e45-477372e89d78_story.html.

71 **"You're really big"**: Howard Kurtz, *Media Madness: Donald Trump, the Press, and the
War over the Truth* (Washington, DC: Regnery, 2018), 54.

71 **"The point was to demonstrate"**: Anne Applebaum, "History Will Judge the Complicit,"

Atlantic, July/Aug. 2020, www.theatlantic.com/magazine/archive/2020/07/trumps
-collaborators/612250/.

74 **"Sean can't even complete":** Philip Rucker and Carol Leonnig, *A Very Stable Genius: Donald J. Trump's Testing of America* (New York: Penguin Press, 2020), 33.

CHAPTER 7: BONFIRE OF THE GENUFLECTORS

82 **"When you put a snake":** Bob Woodward, *Fear: Trump in the White House* (New York: Simon & Schuster, 2018), 237.

85 **Karen was so certain:** Jonathan Mahler and Dirk Johnson, "Mike Pence's Journey: Catholic Democrat to Evangelical Republican," *New York Times,* July 20, 2016, https://www.nytimes.com/2016/07/21/us/politics/mike-pence-religion.html.

85 **When he did pop the question:** Ashley Parker, "Karen Pence Is the Vice President's 'Prayer Warrior,' Gut Check and Shield," *Washington Post,* March 28, 2017, https://www.washingtonpost.com/politics/karen-pence-is-the-vice-presidents-prayer-warrior-gut-check-and-shield/2017/03/28/3d7a26ce-0a01-11e7-8884-96e6a6713f4b_story.html.

87 **Bolton's memoir lays out:** John Bolton, *The Room Where It Happened: A White House Memoir* (New York: Simon & Schuster, 2020).

88 **calling Trump an "idiot":** Woodward, *Fear,* 286.

88 **calling him a "dope":** Michael Wolff, *Fire and Fury: Inside the Trump White House* (New York: Henry Holt, 2018), 304.

88 **calling him "dumb as shit":** Wolff, *Fire and Fury,* 304.

CHAPTER 8: SNOWFLAKE CITY

92 **customer yelling "fascist":** Nikki Schwab, "Protester Yells 'Fascist' at Stephen Miller Dining in Mexican Restaurant," *New York Post,* June 20, 2018, nypost.com/2018/06/20/protester-yells-fascist-at-stephen-miller-dining-in-mexican-restaurant/.

92 **Nielsen, the top enforcer:** Metro DC DSA, Facebook livestream, June 19, 2018, www.facebook.com/MetroDCDSA/posts/803611493171511.

92 **"How can you enjoy":** Helen Rosner, "The Absurdity of Trump Officials Eating at Mexican Restaurants During an Immigration Crisis," *New Yorker,* June 22, 2018, www.newyorker.com/culture/annals-of-gastronomy/the-unsurprising-absurdity-of-kirstjen-nielsen-and-stephen-miller-eating-mexican-food-during-a-border-crisis.

92 **teacher who posted:** Kristin Mink, Facebook livestream, July 2, 2018, www.facebook.com/kristin.mink/videos/10108378335754806/.

93 **WANTED posters bearing Miller's likeness:** Paul Schwartzman and Josh Dawsey, "From Kellyanne Conway to Stephen Miller, Trump's Advisers Face Taunts from Hecklers Around D.C.," *Washington Post,* July 9, 2018, www.washingtonpost.com/local/dc-politics/viciousness-trump-aides-endure-public-fury-toward-presidents-policies/2018/07/09/23d3b9a2-8051-11e8-b0ef-fffcabeff946_story.html.

96 **"I spent two years going":** David A. Fahrenthold, Josh Dawsey, and Jonathan O'Connell, "'It Was Like a Breeding Ground': Trump Hotel's Mix of GOP Insiders and Hangers-On Helped Give Rise to Impeachment Episodes," *Washington Post,* Feb. 28, 2020, www

.washingtonpost.com/politics/it-was-like-a-breeding-ground-trump-hotels-mix
-of-gop-insiders-and-hangers-on-helped-give-rise-to-impeachment-episodes/2020
/01/16/2e4cdf3a-3888-11ea-bb7b-265f4554af6d_story.html.

96 **"It's an absolutely stunning hotel":** Matea Gold and Jonathan O'Connell, "Trump's
Washington Hotel Is Hub of Inaugural Action—and Potential Conflicts," *Washington
Post,* Jan. 19, 2017, www.washingtonpost.com/politics/trumps-washington-hotel-is-hub
-of-inaugural-action—and-potential-conflicts/2017/01/19/df4f20a0-de85-11e6-918c
-99ede3c8cafa_story.html.

96 **"Go buy Ivanka's stuff":** Kellyanne Conway, *Fox & Friends,* Fox News, Feb. 9, 2017,
insider.foxnews.com/2017/02/09/kellyanne-conway-ivanka-trump-retailers-go-buy
-her-stuff.

97 **authoritative "Hi, Dad":** Philip Rucker and Carol Leonnig, *A Very Stable Genius: Donald J. Trump's Testing of America* (New York: Penguin Press, 2020), 92.

CHAPTER 9: THE CARETAKER'S DILEMMA

100 **"It boomerangs":** Mark Leibovich, "This Is the Way Paul Ryan's Speakership Ends,"
New York Times Magazine, Aug. 7, 2018, www.nytimes.com/2018/08/07/magazine/paul
-ryan-speakership-end-trump.html.

CHAPTER 10: FUNERAL PORN

115 **"We talked about how our international":** Jonathan Martin, "At His Ranch, John Mc-
Cain Shares Memories and Regrets with Friends," *New York Times,* May 5, 2018, www
.nytimes.com/2018/05/05/us/politics/john-mccain-arizona.html.

115 **"This will all be over someday":** Mark Salter, *The Luckiest Man: Life with John McCain*
(New York: Simon & Schuster, 2020), 24.

116 **"It was almost as if":** Davis in a pre-funeral interview with CNN, Sept. 1, 2018, covered
in *Atlantic,* www.theatlantic.com/politics/archive/2018/09/we-have-come-to-mourn
-american-greatness/569194/.

116 **"I'm sure he would rather play golf":** Salter, *Luckiest Man,* 535.

CHAPTER 11: STINKBALL

125 **"I don't like what he says":** Steven T. Dennis, "Trump Ally Lindsey Graham Is Also the
Democrats' Go-To Guy," Bloomberg, June 7, 2019, www.bloomberg.com/news/articles
/2019-06-07/trump-ally-lindsey-graham-is-also-the-democrats-go-to-guy.

126 **called Trump's reactions:** Lindsey Graham, *This Morning,* CBS, Aug. 30, 2018, www
.cbsnews.com/video/lindsey-graham-trump-response-to-mccain-death-disturbing/.

128 **"God bless you":** Bob Woodward, *Fear: Trump in the White House* (New York: Simon
& Schuster, 2018), 316.

129 **"They were inseparable":** Mark Leibovich, "How Lindsey Graham Went from Trump
Skeptic to Trump Sidekick," *New York Times Magazine,* Feb. 25, 2019, www.nytimes.com
/2019/02/25/magazine/lindsey-graham-what-happened-trump.html.

131 **"Graham is essentially":** Steve Schmidt, Twitter thread @SteveSchmidtSES, Nov. 22, 2019, twitter.com/steveschmidtses/status/1198003125552111616?lang=en.

132 **"Don't believe anything":** Lloyd Grove, "Lindsey Graham, a Twang of Moderation," *Washington Post,* Oct. 7, 1998, www.washingtonpost.com/wp-srv/politics/special /clinton/stories/graham100798.htm.

132 **"I know it's really gonna upset":** Robert Draper, "Lindsey Graham, This Year's Maverick," *New York Times Magazine,* July 1, 2010, www.nytimes.com/2010/07/04/magazine /04graham-t.html.

134 **One party activist:** Molly Ball, "How Lindsey Graham Stomped the Tea Party," *Atlantic,* June 10, 2014, www.theatlantic.com/politics/archive/2014/06/how-lindsey-graham -stomped-the-tea-party/372521/.

CHAPTER 12: BRISTLING, EXPLODING IN RAGE, AND INCREASINGLY ISOLATED

141 **"Trump has retreated":** Eli Stokols, "Must Reads: Trump, Stung by Midterms and Nervous about Mueller, Retreats from Traditional Presidential Duties," *Los Angeles Times,* Nov. 13, 2018, https://www.latimes.com/politics/la-na-pol-trump-absent-20181113 -story.html.

147 **"Trumpism is not the philosophy":** Kevin D. Williamson, "Trumpism Expanded the GOP Tent: Don't Expect Republicans to Abandon It Now," *Washington Post,* Nov. 9, 2020, https://www.washingtonpost.com/outlook/2020/11/09/trump-trumpism-gop -republicans-election-outreach/.

148 **"He was not an ideologue":** Adam Schiff to Charlie Sykes, "Adam Schiff: The GOP Has Created a Monster," *The Bulwark Podcast,* Nov. 18, 2021, bulwarkpodcast.thebulwark .com/p/adam-schiff-the-gop-has-created-a.

148 **"It ended up bonding him":** Schiff to Sykes.

149 **"It happens one day at a time":** Schiff to Sykes.

149 **"Since then, 115 (48%)":** Dave Wasserman (@Redistrict), Twitter, July 1, 2020, 10:27 a.m., twitter.com/redistrict/status/1278334401244549120?lang=en.

150 **Bush had no use for Trump:** Mark K. Updegrove, *The Last Republicans: Inside the Extraordinary Relationship Between George H. W. Bush and George W. Bush* (New York: HarperCollins, 2017), 397–98.

CHAPTER 13: CONTAGION

161 **"She's going to get us":** Philip Rucker and Carol Leonnig, *A Very Stable Genius: Donald J. Trump's Testing of America* (New York: Penguin Press, 2020), 27.

164 **given roughly $10,000:** Ephrat Livni and David Yanofski, "William Barr's Donations to Senate Republicans Spiked Just Before They Confirmed Him as Attorney General," *Quartz,* July 18, 2019, qz.com/1667918/barrs-donations-to-senate-republicans-spiked -before-confirmation/.

167 **"My legacy doesn't matter":** Bob Woodward and Robert Costa, *Peril* (New York: Simon & Schuster, 2021), 153.

CHAPTER 14: THE FIFTH AVENUE CROWD

169 **"I don't care":** Graham to Maria Bartiromo, *Sunday Morning Futures,* Fox News, July 14, 2019, www.foxnews.com/transcript/sen-lindsey-graham-ice-raids-are-focused-on -those-who-already-had-their-day-in-court.

175 **"absorbed Trump's couch-potato mentality":** David Frum (@davidfrum), Twitter, Nov. 14, 2021, 8:05 a.m., twitter.com/davidfrum/status/1 459870076442714125.

175 **"There's not a functional brain":** Tim Alberta, *American Carnage: On the Front Lines of the Republican Civil War and the Rise of President Trump* (New York: HarperCollins, 2019), 93.

CHAPTER 15: TROUBLEMAKER

186 **Seventy-two percent of Republicans:** Josh Clinton and Carrie Roush, "Poll: Persistent Partisan Divide over 'Birther' Question," NBC, Aug. 10, 2016, www.nbcnews.com /politics/2016-election/poll-persistent-partisan-divide-over-birther-question-n627446.

187 **That tracks almost identically:** Brittany Shepherd, "Majority of Americans Think Jan. 6 Attack Threatened Democracy: Poll," ABC, Jan. 2, 2022, abcnews.go.com/Politics /majority-americans-jan-attack-threatened-democracy-poll/story?id=81990555.

189 **"I had an instinct":** Mark Leibovich, "Romney, Defying the Party He Once Personified, Votes to Convict Trump," *New York Times Magazine,* Feb. 5, 2020, www.nytimes.com /2020/02/05/us/politics/romney-trump-impeachment.html.

CHAPTER 16: HELL, IN REVIEW

192 **"more aspirational on my part":** Collins to Martha MacCallum, Fox News, Feb. 5, 2020, www.foxnews.com/media/susan-collins-on-trump-ukraine-call-the-president-should -simply-not-do-it-again.

195 **"We didn't really intend":** Mark Dee, "Joe Biden Pitches Vision to Blaine County," *Idaho Mountain Express,* Aug. 7, 2019, www.mtexpress.com/news/blaine_county/joe -biden-pitches-vision-to-blaine-county/article_c4b68760-b885-11e9-8d42-ebee907fc0bf .html.

198 **"A bit bizarre":** Peter Nicholas and Ed Yong, "Fauci: 'Bizarre' White House Behavior Only Hurts the President," *Atlantic,* July 15, 2020, www.theatlantic.com/politics/archive /2020/07/trump-fauci-coronavirus-pandemic-oppo/614224/.

198 **"We're going to lose":** Carol Leonnig and Philip Rucker, *I Alone Can Fix It: Donald J. Trump's Catastrophic Final Year* (New York: Penguin Press, 2021), 114.

CHAPTER 17: CARACAS-ON-THE-POTOMAC

203 **Collins said she found:** Susan Collins, remarks to reporters at the U.S. Capitol, Washington, D.C., June 2, 2020, reported in *Bangor Daily News,* bangordailynews.com/2020 /06/02/politics/susan-collins-calls-trump-church-photo-op-unsympathetic-and -insensitive/.

207 **"We have the Hatch Act":** Michael McFaul (@McFaul), Twitter, Aug. 28, 2020, 1:08 p.m., twitter.com/mcfaul/status/1299393440959012864.

CHAPTER 18: "WILL YOU SHUT UP, MAN?"

209 **The party did not bother:** Matthew Continetti, "Is Trump Really All That Holds the G.O.P. Together?," *New York Times,* Dec. 22, 2020, www.nytimes.com/2020/12/22 /opinion/trump-republican-party.html.

211 **"He's a symptom":** Jeffrey Goldberg, "Why Obama Fears for Our Democracy," *Atlantic,* Nov. 16, 2020, www.theatlantic.com/ideas/archive/2020/11/why-obama-fears-for -our-democracy/617087/.

213 **"Go write this down":** Jonathan V. Last, "Mike Pence Is the Future. God Help Us," *Bulwark,* Oct. 8, 2020, thetriad.thebulwark.com/p/mike-pence-is-the-future-god-help.

213 **"losers" and "suckers":** Jeffrey Goldberg, "Trump: Americans Who Died in War Are 'Losers' and 'Suckers,'" *Atlantic,* Sept. 3, 2020, www.theatlantic.com/politics/archive /2020/09/trump-americans-who-died-at-war-are-losers-and-suckers/615997/.

216 **"That day alone, 983 Americans died":** Clare Malone, "How Trump Changed America," *FiveThirtyEight,* Nov. 7, 2020, fivethirtyeight.com/features/how-trump-changed -america/.

216 **$717.30 for meals:** Zach Everson, "Trump Administration Appointed a Donor to the Eric Trump Foundation to a $160,000/Year Position in the Small Business Administration," *1100 Pennsylvania,* Dec. 14, 2020, www.1100pennsylvania.com/.

217 **"He is no doubt":** Remarks at Mar-a-Lago, Dec. 1, 2021. Video via Greg Bluestein, Twitter, https://twitter.com/bluestein/status/1466467440217542661.

219 **"Help me":** Graham to Hannity, Fox News, Sept. 24, 2020, covered in *Washington Post,* www.washingtonpost.com/lifestyle/media/lindsey-graham-help-me-money -contributions-fox/2020/09/25/ea2d6d14-ff57-11ea-8d05-9beaaa91c71f_story.html.

221 **Radio news was filled:** Mark Leibovich, "Washington, on Edge About the Election, Boards Itself Up," *New York Times Magazine,* Nov. 2, 2020, www.nytimes.com/2020 /11/02/us/politics/washington-dc-boarded-up-election.html.

CHAPTER 19: "WHAT IS THE DOWNSIDE FOR HUMORING HIM?"

223 **"Is there anybody":** Bob Woodward and Robert Costa, *Peril* (New York: Simon & Schuster, 2021), xxii.

224 **"one of the most dangerous":** Chris Christie, *Republican Rescue: Saving the Party from Truth Deniers, Conspiracy Theorists, and the Dangerous Policies of Joe Biden* (New York: Threshold, 2021), 114.

225 **"agressive [*sic*] strategy":** Jake Tapper and Jamie Gangel, "CNN Exclusive: Jan. 6 Investigators Believe Nov. 4 Text Pushing 'Strategy' to Undermine Election Came from Rick Perry," CNN, Dec. 17, 2021, www.cnn.com/2021/12/17/politics/rick-perry-jan-6 -text-mark-meadows-nov-4/index.html.

Note: The text was included in nine thousand pages of documents turned over to the congressional Select Committee on January 6; CNN confirmed that the phone number associated with the text messages belonged to Perry.

226 **"They existed to cast blame":** Benjy Sarlin, "Republicans Warned This Day Would Come. Then They Forgot," NBC, Jan. 7, 2021, www.nbcnews.com/politics/donald-trump /republicans-warned-day-would-come-then-they-forgot-n1253394.

227 **"busloads of people":** Eli Stokols, "Trump Brings Up Vote Fraud Again, This Time in Meeting with Senators," *Politico,* Feb. 10, 2017, www.politico.com/story/2017/02/trump -voter-fraud-senators-meeting-234909.

227 **"the runner-up is almost always":** Brilyn Hollyhand, *The Truth Gazette* (@Truth _Gazette), Twitter, Dec. 22, 2021, 9:38 a.m., twitter.com/Truth_Gazette/status/147366 4240959565824?s=20.

228 **"When he turned, he really":** Mike DeBonis, "Ted Cruz Once Called Trump 'Utterly Amoral' and a 'Sniveling Coward.' Then He Worked to Save His Presidency," *Washington Post,* Feb. 15, 2020, www.washingtonpost.com/powerpost/ted-cruz-once-called -trump-utterly-amoral-and-a-sniveling-coward-then-he-worked-to-save-his-presidency /2020/02/15/db635480-4e70-11ea-bf44-f5043eb3918a_story.html.

229 **"a fucking idiot":** Woodward and Costa, *Peril,* 180.

229 **"all but manic":** Woodward and Costa, *Peril,* xiv.

232 **"Stop the Steal" T-shirts:** Will Steakin (@wsteaks), Twitter, Jan. 5, 2021, 6:22 p.m., twitter.com/wsteaks/status/1346598062093971469.

233 **"When we talk in private":** Ben Sasse, Facebook, Dec. 30, 2020. The post appears to have since been taken down, but a screenshot was posted here: twitter.com/ionward11 /status/1344633833375850497. The link to the original Facebook post is here: www .facebook.com/SenatorSasse/posts/what-happens-on-january-6th-in-november -160-million-americans-voted-on-december-/3517705981660655/.

235 **"It's the ultimate irony":** Carol Leonnig and Philip Rucker, *I Alone Can Fix It: Donald J. Trump's Catastrophic Final Year* (New York: Penguin Press, 2021), 439.

CHAPTER 20: THE BIG ONE

240 **"If you are not prepared":** Dan Barry and Sheera Frenkel, "'Be There. Will Be Wild!': Trump All but Circled the Date," *New York Times,* Jan. 6, 2021, www.nytimes.com/2021 /01/06/us/politics/capitol-mob-trump-supporters.html.

241 **"It seemed like it couldn't be":** Staff, "Utah Delegation Publicly Remarks on Jan. 6 Anniversary," *Ogden Standard-Examiner,* Jan. 6, 2022, www.standard.net/news/gov ernment/2022/jan/06/curtis-romney-lee-publicly-remark-on-jan-6-anniversary/.

241 **"You heard banging on the House":** Dan Bammes and Eliza Craig, "Senator Romney, Representative Moore Remember Chaos and Fear During the Attack on Jan. 6," KSL News Radio, Jan. 6, 2022, kslnewsradio.com/1962176/senator-romney-representative -moore-remember-chaos-and-fear-during-the-attack-on-jan-6/.

242 **"You need to tell":** Bob Woodward and Robert Costa, *Peril* (New York: Simon & Schuster, 2021), 478.

242 **"He's got to condemn":** Nicholas Wu and Kyle Cheney, "'He's Got to Condemn This . . . ': Panel Releases Urgent Jan. 6 Texts from Donald Trump Jr., Lawmakers, and Fox Hosts," *Politico,* Dec. 13, 2021, www.politico.com/news/2021/12/13/hes-got-to -condemn-this-shit-panel-releases-urgent-jan-6-texts-from-trump-jr-lawmakers -524188.

242 **"I tried to get to him"**: Chris Christie, *Republican Rescue: Saving the Party from Truth Deniers, Conspiracy Theorists, and the Dangerous Policies of Joe Biden* (New York: Threshold, 2021), 122.

244 **"You fucking did this"**: Carol Leonnig and Philip Rucker, *I Alone Can Fix It: Donald J. Trump's Catastrophic Final Year* (New York: Penguin Press, 2021), 505.

245 **"You have caused this!"**: Michael Kranish, "Grievance, Rebellion, and Burnt Bridges: Tracing Josh Hawley's Path to the Insurrection," *Washington Post,* May 11, 2021, www.washingtonpost.com/nation/2021/05/11/senator-josh-hawley/.

249 **"I definitely had some PTS"**: Mark Leibovich, "This Town Melts Down," *New York Times Magazine,* July 11, 2017, www.nytimes.com/2017/07/11/magazine/washington-dc-politics-trump-this-town-melts-down.html.

249 **"I was prepared to defend"**: S. E. Cupp, "Tucker Carlson Is a 'Manipulative Son of a Bitch'—and Other Thoughts from Adam Kinzinger," *Rolling Stone,* Nov. 8, 2021, www.rollingstone.com/politics/politics-features/adam-kinzinger-tucker-carlson-january6-trump-insurrection-1254648/.

249 **Six minutes after he finished**: Maggie Haberman and Jonathan Martin, "After the Speech: What Trump Did As the Capitol Was Attacked," *New York Times*, Feb. 13, 2021, https://www.nytimes.com/2021/02/13/us/politics/trump-capitol-riot.html.

250 **"The people Trump despises most"**: Howard Stern on *The Howard Stern Show,* May 12, 2020, www.nydailynews.com/snyde/ny-howard-stern-trump-hates-supporters-20200512-k3z6fmgqgbbtxjsyocj46mtvse-story.html.

250 **"bullshit" prayer rituals**: Michael Cohen, *Disloyal: A Memoir: The True Story of the Former Personal Attorney to President Donald J. Trump* (New York: Skyhorse, 2020).

251 **"these disgusting people"**: Mark Leibovich, "Trump Has Called His Supporters 'Disgusting.' Do They Care?," *New York Times,* Oct. 10, 2020, www.nytimes.com/2020/10/10/sunday-review/trump-supporters.html.

252 **"They aren't loyal"**: Peggy Noonan, "The Jan. 6 Committee Carries History's Weight," *Wall Street Journal,* July 29, 2021, www.wsj.com/articles/jan-6-house-select-committee-capitol-hill-riot-trump-11627594907.

254 **"Holy Shit, Man Walks"**: *Onion* (@TheOnion), "Front Page from July 21, 1969," Twitter, Aug. 25, 2012, 7:34 p.m., twitter.com/theonion/status/239506104181219328?lang=en.

CHAPTER 21: HAVE A GOOD LIFE

257 **"Guys, we have a clear path"**: Sean Hannity to Mark Meadows and Jim Jordan, text message, Jan. 10, 2021, via Margaret Sullivan, "The Ridiculous Hypocrisy of Sean Hannity Hiding behind 'Freedom of the Press,'" *Washington Post*, Jan. 5, 2022, https://www.washingtonpost.com/media/2022/01/05/sullivan-hannity/.

260 **Haley was next seen**: Chris Cillizza, "Nikki Haley Learns There's No Halfway with Trump," *Point*, CNN, February 18, 2021, https://www.cnn.com/2021/02/18/politics/nikki-haley-donald-trump-mar-a-lago/.

261 **"For a brief moment"**: Andy Kim (@AndyKimNJ), Twitter, Jan. 6, 2022, 8:36 a.m., twitter.com/AndyKimNJ/status/1479084339279372288.

262 **Accordingly, McConnell went on Fox**: Matt Steib, "McConnell Would Absolutely Sup-

port Trump as 2024 Nominee," *New York,* Feb. 25, 2021, nymag.com/intelligencer/2021 /02/mcconnell-would-absolutely-back-trump-if-he-were-nominee.html.

CHAPTER 22: THE LIFELINE

269 **McCarthy had even taken:** Jonathan Martin, Maggie Haberman, and Nicholas Fandos, "McConnell Privately Backs Impeachment as House Moves to Charge Trump," *New York Times,* Feb. 12, 2021, www.nytimes.com/2021/01/12/us/politics/mcconnell-backs -trump-impeachment.html.

CHAPTER 23: THE UNRAVELING

281 **"the very supportive, submissive wife":** Elizabeth Dias, "Christianity Will Have Power," *New York Times,* Aug. 9, 2020, www.nytimes.com/2020/08/09/us/evangelicals -trump-christianity.html.

283 **At least 163 Republicans:** Ashley Parker, Amy Gardner, and Josh Dawsey, "How Republicans Became the Party of Trump's Election Lie After Jan. 6," *Washington Post,* Jan. 5, 2022, www.washingtonpost.com/politics/republicans-jan-6-election-lie/2022 /01/05/82f4cad4-6cb6-11ec-974b-d1c6de8b26b0_story.html.

283 **Roughly six in ten:** Dan Balz, Scott Clement, and Emily Guskin, "Republicans and Democrats Divided over Jan. 6 Insurrection and Trump's Culpability, Post-UMD Poll Finds," *Washington Post,* Jan. 1, 2022, www.washingtonpost.com/politics/2022/01/01 /post-poll-january-6/.

284 **"Not because he worked for President Trump":** Elisabeth Egan, "Takeaways from Sarah Huckabee Sanders's Book: Kim Jong-un, Parenting, Trump," *New York Times,* Sept. 2, 2020, https://www.nytimes.com/2020/09/02/books/sarah-huckabee-sanders -book.html.

284 **"I hope you die":** Upton, interview with Cooper, *AC360,* Nov. 9, 2021, news.yahoo.com /gop-lawmaker-says-hes-receiving-033633322.html.

285 **run for president again:** Mark Moore, "Sen. Graham Says He Hopes Trump Runs for President Again in 2024," *New York Post,* Sept. 26, 2021, nypost.com/2021/09/26/sen -graham-says-he-hopes-trump-runs-for-president-in-2024/.

285 **"if you try to drive him":** Graham, interview with Martha McCallum, Fox News, May 11, 2021, www.mediaite.com/tv/lindsey-graham-if-you-try-to-drive-trump-out-of-the -gop-half-the-people-will-leave/.

286 **forced to spend $50,000.** Mark Leibovich, "Liz Cheney's Unlikely Journey from G.O.P. Royalty to Republican Outcast," *New York Times,* June 20, 2021, www.nytimes.com /2021/06/20/us/politics/liz-cheney-republican-party-trump.html.

287 **71 percent of Republicans:** Brittany Shepherd, "Majority of Americans Think Jan. 6 Attack Threatened Democracy: Poll," ABC, Jan. 2, 2022, abcnews.go.com/Politics /majority-americans-jan-attack-threatened-democracy-poll/story?id=81990555.

288 **"She speaks about her conscience":** Reid J. Epstein, "Where's Liz Cheney? The Wyoming Republican's Exile from Wyoming Republicans," *New York Times,* Feb. 9, 2022, https:// www.nytimes.com/2022/02/09/us/politics/liz-cheney-wyoming-republicans.html.

290 **books about cults:** Peter Baker, "A Year Later, Jan. 6 Becomes Just Another Wedge in a Divided Nation," *New York Times,* Jan. 6, 2022, www.nytimes.com/2022/01/06/us /politics/jan-6-capitol-riot-aftermath.html.

291 **"He was in the dining room":** Grisham, interview on *New Day,* CNN, Jan. 6, 2022, www.youtube.com/watch?v=I10AGZAcpYc.

EPILOGUE: THE HOUSE OF SUBMISSION: STILL OPEN

293 **rebranded as a Waldorf Astoria:** Craig Karmin, "Trumps Selling Prized Washington, D.C., Hotel for $375 Million," *Wall Street Journal,* Nov. 14, 2021, https://www.wsj.com /articles/trumps-selling-prized-washington-d-c-hotel-for-375-million-11636923944.

295 **"Donald Trump didn't just inspire":** Zach Everson, "How Trump's D.C. Hotel Cashed In on the Jan. 6 Riot," *Forbes,* Nov. 3, 2021, https://www.forbes.com/sites/zacheverson /2021/11/03/heres-what-was-going-on-at-trumps-dc-hotel-around-jan-6/?sh=76474f 851a4d.

299 **"We did it twice":** Franklin Foer, "The New Republican Battle Cry," *Atlantic,* March 3, 2022, https://www.theatlantic.com/ideas/archive/2022/03/cpac-showed-what-new-gop -cares-about/623883/.

301 **"I would imagine":** Mike Allen, "Scoop: Trump Trashes Barr in Rant to Lester Holt," March 7, 2002, https://www.axios.com/trump-bill-barr-book-e017627f-a26d-4c16-8a72 -fcdf66bf019d.html.

302 **"I believe that the greatest threat":** Scott Stump, "Former Attorney General William Barr Says He'd Still Vote for Trump in 2024," *Today,* March 7, 2022, https://www.today .com/news/politics/attorney-general-william-barr-still-vote-trump-2024-rcna18946.

INDEX